Max Scheler

1874–1928

Max Scheler

MAX SCHELER

1874–1928

An Intellectual Portrait

by

JOHN RAPHAEL STAUDE

THE FREE PRESS, NEW YORK

COLLIER-MACMILLAN LIMITED, LONDON

Library of Congress Catalog Card Number: 67–19239.

10 9 8 7 6 5 4 3 2 1

ISBN 978-1-9821-3496-9

For Laurie and Madole

Preface

MAX SCHELER was one of the leading philosophers of twentieth-century Germany. His interests were wide, and his works ranged across a number of areas: ethics, religion, politics, pedagogy, psychology, sociology, and anthropology. Today, both here and abroad, Scheler is probably best known for his creative application of the phenomenological approach to sociology and social psychology in his books *Ressentiment* and *The Nature of Sympathy*, for his philosophy of religion, and for his attempt to establish phenomenologically an objective hierarchy of nonrelative values and an ethics based thereon.[1] His important pioneering contributions to the sociology of knowledge and to philosophical anthropology are generally acknowledged, though less well known than his phenomenological writings in the United States.

[1] The most complete introduction to Max Scheler's philosophy is Maurice Dupuy's *La Philosophie de Max Scheler: son évolution et son unité*, 2 vols. (Paris, 1959). Werner Stark also provides an excellent summary of Scheler's contributions to philosophy and sociology in his introduction to *The Nature of Sympathy*, tr. Peter Heath (London, 1958). Other commentaries on Scheler's philosophy are listed in the Bibliography.

The purpose of this study is to explain the development of Scheler's social and political ideas. His many other interests will be discussed only to the extent that a knowledge of them contributes to the understanding of his social and political thought. The main social problem which concerned Scheler throughout his life (1874–1928) was the lack of inspired leadership and of inspiring ideals that could heal the ideological, social, and cultural divisions of the German Empire and the unstable Republic that succeeded it. Instead of working for political or social changes to alleviate the pressures in the Empire and perhaps mollify the liberals and socialists who demanded parliamentary reforms, Scheler supported the ruling elite with metaphysical rhetoric. The primary law of society, Scheler said, was that a few were destined to lead, and the majority must always follow and obey. Scheler's political and social function was that of the ideologist. He provided a rationale for the political power drives and the economic and social interests of a certain social group, the ruling elite.

Scheler changed his political allegiances several times, riding the wave of enthusiasm for every group that rose and fell in the turmoil of the last years of Wilhelmian Germany and the early days of the Weimar Republic. Behind his changing allegiances lay a common concern, however: a quest for unity and community in a pluralistic society. Prior to World War I, Scheler looked to the German Youth Movement for leadership and inspiring ideals. During the war he idealized the discipline and cooperation of the Prussian army as a model for German society. Once he became disillusioned with German militarism, Scheler turned to what he called the "community building powers" of the Roman Catholic Church. Conveniently, his conversion to Catholicism in 1916 coincided with the rise of German Catholicism in the Reichstag under Matthias Erzberger and Georg von Hertling, who became Germany's first Catholic Chancellor in 1917. After the war, Scheler flirted briefly with the Socialists, but after their political chances waned, he concentrated once more on the Catholics, until events in his marital life caused him to break with the Church.

Throughout his life, Scheler was an elitist. Whereas until 1922 he had sought to exploit the leadership capacities and community building powers in already existing groups, in his last years, having become disillusioned with the incessant party rivalries in Weimar Germany, Scheler placed his hopes on the emergence of a new type of man from the chaos. This new type might come from the army, the youth movement, the Socialists, or even the Catholics. His origins did not matter, for he would learn to transcend them by means of the sociology of knowledge which Scheler inaugurated in the mid-twenties. Relieved of the myopia induced by his former party perspective, Scheler's new man would be able to grasp reality objectively and to shape the ignorant masses to his purposes, providing them with leadership and a sense of community out of his superior wisdom.

No biography of Max Scheler has yet been written. This lack is unfortunate, because the fluctuations in Scheler's views often resulted as much from changes in the conditions of his personal life as from the historical circumstances he confronted. Ludwig Curtius, who knew Scheler well, recalled in his memoirs that:

Scheler was the one German philosopher in whom personality and theory were deeply intertwined. His infinitely sensitive depth of feeling and his rich and painfully vulnerable nature registered all the various currents of our time like a tuning fork, and he responded to them out of the confusion of his own personality and of his synthesizing, expansive mind. He took part in all the impurities of our time as well, and his need for salvation and his endless search for God along ever new paths sprang from the guilty entanglements of his erotic life.[2]

The materials for a full-scale biography of Scheler — his letters and personal papers — were lost by his widow during World War II. Fortunately, however, Scheler's second wife (he was married three times), Maerit Furtwaengler, saved many of the letters she received from him; she has made them available to us and has written an account of her life with Max Scheler for us as well. From this information and from interviews with numerous men and women who knew Scheler professionally or

[2] Quoted with the permission of the Deutsche Verlags-Anstalt from Ludwig Curtius, *Deutsche und antike Welt* (Stuttgart, 1950), p. 375.

personally, we have constructed a biographical narrative that is intended to indicate the psychological background of Scheler's intellectual development. Although some direct quotations from Max Scheler's unpublished letters would have enhanced this book, we have chosen not to include them out of deference to those members of his family who are still alive. Unless otherwise indicated, italicized words in all quotations in this book were italicized in the original source.

What gives the ultimate unity to Scheler's extensive and diverse writings is the stamp of his personality. People who knew him personally, and even those who only heard him lecture, testify to the same fact: his writings were but a pale shadow of his *presence*. Scheler was one of those rare men possessed not only of intellectual brilliance, but also of extreme sensitivity to nuances of emotion. His highly refined sensibility enabled him to weave a spell over his audiences which blinded them to the contradictions and illogicalities of his arguments.

On the lecture platform, Scheler was a skilled artist. Whereas Socrates spoke of himself as a *gadfly* and a *midwife*, Scheler liked to think of himself as a *puppeteer*. One of his old students explained the metaphor:

His philosophical equipment — the world and his head — he had always with him, as a strolling player has his little theatre. The vagrant mummer needs no preparation, no atmosphere, none of the appurtenances of the big theatre, nor did Scheler require any special setting; given an ear, he became creative and set his ideas dancing. He might be seated with a companion, his head cocked to one side, watching on the unfolded stage of his mind the drama of the world. He looked aslant at his puppets' play, which was his own, always with half an eye for the listener — or better, the spectator. Again and again, by an interjected *Wie?* or *Nicht wahr?* He assured himself of his companion's attention and of the effect of his play. It was truly magic; in an instant he could transform his surroundings and fill the room with his ideas; he made present the things of which he spoke and visible what is often called "abstract." What he called forth from the realm of the

3 Ernst Kamnitzer, "Erinnerung an Max Scheler," (unpublished memoir), quoted by John M. Oesterreicher in *Walls Are Crumbling* (New York, 1953), p. 139.

spirit came, and now and then there gleamed in his eye an unchastened joy that he was so obeyed.[3]

The "half an eye for the spectator" was Scheler's good eye. A stygmatic defect of his right eye gave the impression that it was focused on the infinite.

Although Scheler's spoken word was reinforced by the magic of his personality, his writing style was often clumsy and opaque, verifying his own judgment: "The word I have, but not the sentence."[4] His intuition opened what he called "the sluice gates of the spirit" so that he was often flooded with ideas. He wrote them down as best he could, on whatever paper happened to be at hand — the inside of a book, the back of a menu, a napkin, or an envelope — but he seldom worked over his raw material, shaping it, deleting, clarifying, as a careful writer must do. His art was that of the performer; when the performance was over, he was either tired or bored. Instead of recollecting himself — a practice common to "seers" and "mystics" which Scheler wistfully admired but was unable to emulate — he would plunge into a café in search of a new audience and new inspiration. In fact, the night club or cabaret was for Scheler what the wilderness was for monks and hermits of earlier epochs: the place for flashes of insight. The chameleon-like transformations of his thought never took place in solitude. He needed the inspiration of an audience.

This is not to say that Scheler did not write a great deal — his collected works came to thirteen volumes — but simply that he did not write carefully. The immense fecundity of his mind persuaded him to disdain intellectual toil. Typically, he preferred whatever was natural, organically grown, or spontaneous, to anything that had been worked over (*er-arbeitet*). As a result, his writings abound with ideas of every imaginable variety, from the most profound to the most banal.

In seeking to discover some unity in this amorphous mass of often contradictory material, I have centered my study on Scheler's constant quest for community. His concern with unity and community, which appeared in every phase of his intellectual

4 *Ibid.*

development, provided me with a focal point in which the influence of his personal life could be directly related to that of his historical environment. Scheler's personal desire to belong to a unified group and to heal the political, sociological, and ideological divisions of his country stemmed, in part, from the divided nature of his own personality and of his family background. His personal life reflected and reinforced the disunity and disorder of the society in which he lived.

Scheler's writings and speeches found a wide audience among diverse groups in German society because he articulated their common longing for unity and community. He is historically significant because his thought and character reflected and expressed some of the crucial problems of the twentieth century. Because he was so much a product of his time, his philosophy, his sociology, and his criticism of mass culture provide us with a composite picture of some of the key political, social, and cultural developments of his age.

University of California, Riverside

J. R. S.

Acknowledgments

To begin with, I wish to acknowledge my profound gratitude and respect for my friend and mentor, Carl Schorske. His unrelenting demand for excellence, coupled with a personal concern to allow his students to develop according to their own propensities inspired me throughout my graduate career at Berkeley where this work was born.

This study would have been impossible without the help of Scheler's widows, friends, relatives, and numerous other men and women in Germany who assisted me. I would particularly like to express my gratitude to Maerit Furtwaengler for her willingness to submit to my endless interrogations and her generosity in making Scheler's letters available to me. I would also like to acknowledge my gratitude to Maria Scheler, who, though reluctant to disclose any information about Scheler's life, eventually granted me access to several of his unpublished manuscripts. Of the many men who helped me at various points in this study I want to thank, in particular, Theodor Adorno, Arnold Bergsträsser, Goetz Briefs, Martin Buber, Werner Conze, Victor von Gebsattl, Kurt Goldstein, Romano Guardini, Dietrich von Hildebrand, Paul Honigsheim, Hans Kohn, Kurt Lenk, Friedrich Lilge, Leo Löwenthal, Heinrich Lutz, Gabriel Marcel, Jean de Menasce, Helmuth Plessner, Erich Rothacker, Gottfried Salomon-Delatour, Theodor Schieder, Georg von Schreiber, Herbert Spiegelberg, Eduard Spranger, Erich Voegelin, and Leopold von

Acknowledgments

xiv

Wiese. Of the ladies who revealed the intimacies of Scheler's personal life to me, I would like to mention Tony Förster, Claire Goll, Luisa Koppel, Ingetrud Pape, Bernardine Sugg-Bellini, and Corina Sombart.

Without the financial support of my parents and later of the Duke University Research Council, the complete revision of this work which began as a dissertation at the University of California in Berkeley, would have been impossible. I wish to thank Professors Lewis Coser, Klemens von Klemperer, Erich Kollmann, Martin Malia, Edward Tiryakian, Hayden White, and Sheldon Wolin for having read through various drafts of this manuscript, helping me to discover some order in the chaos of Scheler's life and thought. To Wilfried Hartmann I am grateful for bibliographical assistance. Finally, I wish to thank my wife who helped me with the clerical drudgery of proofreading and bibliography, but above all, by listening. To her, and to my mother, this book is dedicated.

For permission to quote from copyright materials, my thanks are due to the following:

American Sociological Association — for the passages quoted from Howard Becker's "Befuddled Germany, A Glimpse of Max Scheler," published in the *American Sociological Review*, VIII, April, 1943, pages 207–211, copyright © 1943 by the American Sociological Association.

Beacon Press — for passages quoted from Max Scheler, *Man's Place in Nature*, translated by Hans Meyerhoff. Reprinted by permission of the Beacon Press, copyright © 1961 by the Beacon Press; originally published in German under the title of *Die Stellung des Menschen im Kosmos*, copyright 1928 by A. Francke, A. G., Berne; and for passages quoted from Max Scheler, *Philosophical Perspectives*, translated by Oscar Haac. Reprinted by permission of the Beacon Press, copyright © 1958 by the Beacon Press.

Deutsche Verlags–Anstalt GmbH — for passages quoted from Ludwig Curtius, *Deutsche und Antike Welt*, copyright © 1950 by the Deutsche Verlags–Anstalt GmbH. Reprinted by permission of the publishers.

The Devin-Adair Company — for passages quoted from John M. Oesterreicher, *Walls Are Crumbling*, published 1952 by the Devin-Adair Company, copyright 1952 by John M. Oesterreicher. Reprinted by permission of the author and the publishers.

Francke Verlag — for passages quoted from Max Scheler, *Vom Umsturz der Werte*, copyright © 1955 by Francke Verlag; and for passages quoted from Max Scheler, *Die Wissensformen und die Gesellschaft*, copyright © 1960 by Francke Verlag. Reprinted by permission of the publishers.

The Free Press — for passages quoted from Max Scheler, *Ressentiment,* translated by William W. Holdheim, copyright © 1961 by The Free Press, A Corporation. Reprinted by permission of the publishers.

Harper and Row, Publishers — for passages quoted from Count Hermann Keyserling, *The World in the Making,* translated by Maurice Samuel, copyright © 1927 by Harper and Row, Publishers, Incorporated. Reprinted by permission of the publishers.

Routledge and Kegan Paul Ltd. — for passages quoted from Max Scheler, *The Nature of Sympathy,* translated by Peter Heath, copyright © 1954 by Routledge and Kegan Paul Ltd. Reprinted by permission of the publishers.

Student Christian Movement Press — for passages quoted from Max Scheler, *On the Eternal in Man,* translated by Bernard Noble, copyright © 1960 by SCM Press, Ltd. Reprinted by permission of the publishers.

Contents

Man must again learn to grasp the great, invisible, mutual *solidarity of all beings* in total life, of all spirits in the eternal spirit, and simultaneously, the *solidarity* of the world process with the *evolution of its first cause* and the solidarity of this cause with the world process. Man must accept this relatedness of the world, not only as a theory, but also live it and practice and activate it externally and internally. God's essence is no more "lord" of the world than man is "lord and king" of creation, but both are, above all, companions of each other's fate, enduring, overcoming, some day perhaps victorious.

— MAX SCHELER

Max Scheler

1874–1928

1

The Making of a Moralist

MAX SCHELER'S life and thought were by no means conventional. Born of a Protestant father and a Jewish mother, Scheler adopted the religion of neither. At fourteen he repudiated his family background and became a Roman Catholic. Although his intellectual abilities were far above average, he failed to utilize them until he entered the University of Munich. There, while most other students of his age participated in the usual dueling and drinking, Scheler seems to have repudiated these activities because of a single-minded passion for knowledge. A love affair with a married woman soon disrupted his intellectual regimen, however, and eventually drove him from his newly acquired religious convictions. After a futile attempt to escape the woman, who had divorced her husband and was urging Scheler to save her honor, Scheler married Amelie von Dewitz.[1]

[1] My information about Scheler's early life is drawn from interviews with Maerit Furtwaengler, his second wife, Claire Goll, his cousin, and Dietrich von Hildebrand, his close friend.

Although Scheler was unable to control his unruly erotic drive, his Catholic training had convinced him that there are ethical norms that are eternally valid and bind every human being who is aware of them. The contradiction between theory and practice in his own life made Scheler sensitive to the conflict between modern secular morality and traditional Christian ethics in social and economic practice as well as in sexual behavior. Following the practice of German students who frequently pursue their studies consecutively at several universities Scheler wandered from Munich to Berlin and thence to Jena before finding a suitable mentor in Rudolph Eucken. Under his direction Scheler became imbued with the idea of explaining the causes of modern immorality and agnosticism. Why Scheler chose the career of philosophy and how he came to believe that the philosopher's primary task is to act as a critic of the social and cultural tendencies of his age are the questions that this chapter will attempt to answer.

1

A T T H E time of Max Scheler's birth (August 22, 1874), his parents had only recently moved to Munich from a country estate near Erfurt where his father had worked as an administrator of farmlands for the Duke of Saxe-Coburg. Gottfried Scheler deeply regretted leaving his country home. Memories of his country estate were one of the few things that brightened his somber visage after he moved to Munich. He had married a proud, temperamental Jewess,[2] Sophie Fürther, who had been

2 There is very little information available regarding Scheler's Jewish family background. Even today, because of the anti-Semitism in recent German history, people who knew Scheler are reluctant to speak of his Jewish origins. Martin Buber, who became acquainted with Scheler in Berlin in 1912, indicated to me that by that time Scheler had become thoroughly assimilated into German Catholic culture and did not consider himself a Jew. Father Oesterreicher suggests that "for the sake of marriage," Scheler's Gentile father "adopted Judaism." See *Walls Are Crumbling*, p. 141. Both of Scheler's widows, Maerit Furtwaengler and Maria

born and bred in Munich. She had long ago given up any pretense of satisfaction with the provincial life her husband's career required. Worn down by her constant nagging and complaining, Gottfried finally acceded to the wishes of his obstinate wife, sold his estate, resigned his position, and moved to Munich.

Sophie had insisted that they live near her wealthy brother, Hermann, so Gottfried purchased a small house near Hermann's on the Kanalstrasse. According to family legends, Uncle Hermann was very rich, very orthodox, and very stingy. As a boy young Max used to have to go to the synagogue on Saturdays with his mother and Uncle Hermann and afterward partake of a ritual meal at his uncle's house. Sophie seems never to have tired of making derogatory comparisons between the style of life her retired husband could provide and the opulence of her unmarried brother. Max later spoke of the oppressing mood of resentment his mother carried with her wherever she went.[3]

Max's father was hardly more cheerful. It seems that he sought no further employment in Munich but simply pined his years away, dreaming of his beloved country life and submitting helplessly to the taunts and complaints of his discontented wife. Before he died, Gottfried sired one other child, Mathilda, a dark-haired girl whom he loved dearly. The girl was docile and submissive like her father, and was miserably treated by Sophie who adored little Max and favored him at the expense of his sister. Gottfried watched Sophie spoil Max, but did nothing except sulk in sorrowful silence. Crushed by unhappiness and boredom, the poor man lost any will to live. He died before Max entered high school.

With her husband gone, Sophie was forced more than ever to rely on the support of her brother. She moved into Her-

Scheler, vehemently deny this, however. It is really not very important whether or not Gottfried Scheler retained his Protestant faith; even if he did, it played no role in Scheler's upbringing, and Max Scheler was a Jew until he converted to Catholicism as an adolescent.

3 Oral testimony of Maerit Furtwaengler. Compare Claire Goll's account of the Fürther family in her autobiographical novel, *Der gestohlene Himmel* (Munich, 1962), p. 126 ff.

mann's house where she rented a single room for herself and her two adolescent children. Max appears to have felt a strong aversion to Uncle Hermann as well as a resentment for the way his mother had browbeaten his father and persecuted his sister.

He found an escape from this sordid milieu when he entered high school. There the Catholic chaplain introduced him to a conception of love and brotherhood that probably seemed the perfect antithesis of his hateful family environment.[4] Coupled with the subtle arguments of the priest was another influence, perhaps even more telling in Scheler's eventual conversion. In the month of May, in many a church and square in Munich, the Catholic population of the city turned out in throngs for candlelight processions, litanies, and choral devotions to the Virgin Mary. At night several of the young servant girls who worked for Uncle Hermann secretly took Scheler to observe the festivities.[5] The fragrance of the incense and the baroque splendor of the candlelight celebrations mingled with Scheler's affection for the young girls. The spirit of community he saw in these religious festivities probably did as much as anything that the priest said to lead him out of Judaism into Catholicism. The main attraction of Catholicism for the young Scheler seems to have been the sense of community and brotherhood it evoked within his heart.

The fact that Max Scheler had been badly spoiled by his mother and that he experienced no strong paternal authority at home probably accounts for his lack of self-discipline later in life. In high school, he did so poorly that he had to be sent to a private tutoring school, Professor Römer's Institute, which was known as a haven for lazy rich boys who had failed in the public schools. The program of the German humanistic *Gymnasium* consisted largely of Greek and Latin language and literature, modern languages, mathematics, and science. Scheler had no gift for languages and did below average work in mathematics. He was fond of the natural sciences, par-

4 Oesterreicher, *op. cit.*, p. 141.
5 *Ibid.*

ticularly biology, however, and decided to prepare for a medical career at the university. His Uncle Hermann and his mother were furious at him for his betrayal of Judaism and his poor marks in school.

Sophie's other brother, Ernst, took an interest in young Max, however, financing his tutoring and encouraging him to make something of himself.[6] Ernst Fürther had long ago abandoned orthodox Jewry for the modernized version popular among Jews who were eager to become assimilated into German Gentile culture. He was primarily a German, he felt, and only secondarily a Jew: "*Deutscher Staatsbürger jüdischen Glaubens*" as the phrase went. He well understood young Max's desire to escape the family culture and fostered his rebellious spirit by introducing him to the writings of Nietzsche.[7] Perhaps it was he who encouraged Scheler to study medicine. At any rate, had it not been for his guidance and help, Scheler probably would never have finished high school and entered the university.

2

MAX SCHELER'S university career was erratic. He enrolled in the medical faculty at the University of Munich in 1893, transferred to Berlin the following year to study philosophy and sociology, and finally completed his university studies in philosophy at Jena, where he received his Ph.D. in 1897. To wander from university to university and from subject to subject was not uncommon among German students in the

[6] Oral testimony of Claire Goll. See also her description of Professor Römer's Institute in *Der gestohlene Himmel*, p. 127. She recalls that after Scheler made good at the University of Jena, Ernst Fürther, her grandfather, boasted to the family that his faith in young Max had been vindicated.

[7] Nietzsche exerted such a profound influence on the young Scheler that he was later to be known as "the Catholic Nietzsche." See Ernst Troeltsch, *Der Historismus und seine Probleme* (Tübingen, 1922), p. 609.

nineteenth century, but the causes for Scheler's intellectual migrations were somewhat out of the ordinary.

The summer after his graduation from high school, Scheler met a mysterious dark-eyed woman, Amelie von Dewitz, while he was vacationing at Bruneck in the Austrian Tyrol. According to Dietrich von Hildebrand, who became acquainted with Scheler in Munich in 1907, at a time when the latter was trying to separate from his wife, Scheler afterward said that he felt that this woman was his "destiny" from the moment he laid eyes on her. Von Hildebrand recalled that when Scheler first saw her he was filled with foreboding and said to his companion: "There are women who should wear a skull and crossbones round their necks like bottles containing poison."[8] Scheler was fascinated with Amelie von Dewitz, and she became his mistress despite the fact that she was married, had a small child, and was eight years older than her youthful lover.

A recently converted Catholic, Scheler may well have felt ashamed of his liaison with this married woman. He later told von Hildebrand that he sincerely tried to extricate himself from her clutches but was unable to resist the claims of her flesh. This is not surprising; throughout his life whenever he had to choose between his devotion to a transcendent God and the warm body of a woman, with pangs of conscience but unable to do otherwise, he chose the woman.

Scheler's first year at the University of Munich was fraught with turmoil. He enrolled in the medical faculty but seldom attended classes, as the confusion and guilt induced by his personal life left him little time and energy for academic work. The division between mind and instinct that now became apparent in Scheler weighed upon him for the rest of his life. Scheler, in his first year of college, appeared to his young friend Theodor Lessing as a "demoniacal genius who stormed from the heights to the depths of life seeking salvation through debauchery."[9] Lessing pitied his friend, seeing him as a "tragic

---

8 Oral testimony of Dietrich von Hildebrand.

figure driven through life by a frenzied eros which turned his every thought into its own denial and his every love into naked lust."[10]

This picture of a man unable to take hold of himself, of a soul tormented by raging passions pulling him hither and yon, is corroborated by the testimony of almost everyone who knew Scheler in his later years.[11] Whereas people admired his intellectual brilliance, they became horrified as they watched his face contort with determined lust. Some have said of him that he used to sharpen his teeth in order to be able to bite better when making love.[12] No doubt this is an exaggeration, but his ostentatious absorption with sex marked him as a representative of the underside of *fin de siècle* European culture. Even his greatest defenders, Peter Wust and Dietrich von Hildebrand, recalled that Scheler was a Dostoevskian type of philosopher who had to plunge through every kind of experience, never satisfied, forever seeking the novel and unique, forever driven on a restless quest.[13] Lessing's comment on the result of Scheler's frantic debauchery was less generous: "His path led upwards into nothingness, strewn with emptied bottles

9 Theodor Lessing, *Einmal und nie Wieder, Lebenserinnerungen* (Leipzig, 1936), p. 273.

10 *Ibid.*

11 Dietrich von Hildebrand described the extraordinary dualism of Scheler's nature as a "combination of extreme spirituality coupled with a complete lack of control over his sexual drives," in "Max Scheler als Persönlichkeit," *Hochland*, XXVI (October, 1928), p. 80. Erich Rothacker, the historian, who studied with Scheler in Munich in 1908–1909 recalled Scheler's demoniacal tendencies in his *Heitere Erinnerungen* (Frankfurt am Main, 1963), p. 29. See also Heinrich Lutzler's "Zu Max Schelers Persönlichkeit," *Hochland*, XXVI (September, 1928), pp. 413–418.

12 Von Hildebrand informed us that people told wild stories about Scheler's orgies, but that these legends were not true. Many of them grew up during 1910, when Scheler was fired from his position as a professor of ethics at the University of Munich. He was dismissed because of his personal immorality.

13 Peter Wust, unpublished letters to Frau Tony Förster, letter of March 3, 1930. See also von Hildebrand, "Max Schelers Philosophie und Persönlichkeit," in *Die Menschheit am Scheideweg, Gesammelte Abhandlungen und Vorträge*, ed. Karla Mertens (Regensburg, 1954), p. 587 ff.

and crushed cigarettes, like a corpse surrounded by pools of blood."[14]

Unfortunately, we have almost no information about Scheler's political and social views during his early university career. From Lessing's account, however, one gathers that Scheler held a conservative, religious view of politics. Whereas Lessing was a radical democrat, Scheler opposed any form of popular sovereignty, considering it not only against the eternal laws of God, but naïvely sentimental and bourgeois. The two young men met frequently at their philosophical club, and they saw a good deal of each other as Lessing's home was practically across the street from Uncle Hermann's. Lessing recalled that once, while walking home from a lecture on medicine, he and Scheler began to talk over a problem that disturbed them. They both felt it an injustice that the medical professors used helpless paupers who came to the university clinic for free medical attention as guinea pigs. Scheler's solution to the problem differed from Lessing's, however. Lessing thought that a democratic government in Bavaria could reform such abuses, but Scheler was thoroughly dedicated to the traditions of throne and altar. He insisted that moral reforms must precede any institutional reforms.[15] This conversation indicates Scheler's developing concern with ethics during the period when the problem of his own ethics forced its way into the center of his intellectual life. It is significant that even as a young student he viewed politics and society from a moral and religious stance, for he continued to approach them from this viewpoint when he reached maturity.

By the end of the year, Scheler had abandoned his intent to study medicine and had decided to concentrate on philosophy. Furthermore, he decided to transfer from Munich to Berlin. His relationship with Frau von Dewitz seems to have been the primary motivation for his move.[16] She lived in Berlin and Scheler became involved with her again soon after his ar-

---

[14] Lessing, *op. cit.*, p. 275.
[15] *Ibid.*
[16] Testimony of Dietrich von Hildebrand.

rival there. By the end of the year she had divorced her husband, from whom she had been estranged for some time. Soon after this, Scheler married his mistress in a civil ceremony. The marriage, though unhappy, lasted fifteen years — much longer than either of his subsequent marriages — and produced one child, Wolfgang Scheler, born in 1900. Max also adopted Amelie's little girl, oddly called Hans.[17] Max Scheler had never led a normal student life, but now that he had acquired a wife and child, his life diverged all the more from that followed by his fellow students.

Aside from the stimulating lectures of Wilhelm Dilthey and Georg Simmel in philosophy and sociology, Scheler could hardly have found the intellectual life of the great university to his liking. Since the death of Hegel, speculative philosophy in Berlin had become almost nonexistent. By the last decade of the century, academic philosophers had either become entrenched in the narrow monistic positivism preached in Berlin by Emil Du Bois-Reymond, and elsewhere by Ernst Haeckel and Ernst Mach, or had retreated into epistemological agnosticism, logic-chopping, or purely historical studies. The mechanistic categories of science were regarded as self-evident and unshakable. Among students, the hatred of metaphysics took the form of contempt for philosophy in general. The neo-Kantianism of the Marburg and South German schools had hardly reached Berlin.[18]

Although we do not know Scheler's reaction to the university, we can readily imagine his disgust and horror as he awoke to the ills of modern industrial civilization. Munich, where Scheler had grown up, was a lively cultural center, but

[17] Hans is still alive and lives in Munich, but because of age and illness her recollections of her stepfather are dim.

[18] For an account of the status of philosophy at the University of Berlin in the 1890's see Wilhelm Stern, "Autobiographical Sketch," in *The History of Psychology in Autobiography,* ed. Charles Murchison (Worcester, Mass, 1930), Vol. I., p. 256. On the intellectual and social milieu of Berlin at this time, see Paul Honigsheim's essay, "The Time and the Thought of the Young Georg Simmel," in *Georg Simmel: A Collection of Essays with Translations and a Bibliography,* ed. Kurt Wolff (Columbus, Ohio, 1959), p. 169 ff.

10

it had resisted industrialization. In fact, until World War I it retained close ties with the countryside around it. Berlin, on the other hand, was fiercely industrial. As he walked the streets of the poorer sections of the city, he probably saw for the first time the filthy and squalid living conditions of the working class that hardly existed in rural Bavaria. Here no charitable church intervened to alleviate the suffering. Modern society in the raw appeared to have broken loose from its Christian roots. The wealthy industrialist seemed to exploit the helpless worker mercilessly. If Scheler went to the theatre to see the plays of Ibsen and Hauptmann, he saw the corruptions of bourgeois life exposed and condemned. Whatever the reasons, by the end of the year Scheler had become deeply concerned with the ills of modern society.[19]

The next semester he moved to Jena, where he finished his studies in philosophy. By studying philosophy, and particularly ethics, Scheler probably hoped to put some order in his personal life. He had abandoned the church, and now philosophy was to serve as his guide. Scheler's choice of Jena may have been prompted by the fact that he wished to study with the famous philosopher, Rudolf Eucken, who was teaching there. Regardless of what he knew of Eucken beforehand, once he arrived in Jena, Scheler became Eucken's pupil and protégé. Because Scheler spent the next ten years of his life there, a brief summary of the intellectual and cultural traditions of Jena will be helpful as background for an account of Scheler's intellectual development during this period.

3

WHEN MAX SCHELER and his wife arrived in Jena in 1895, the small university town was still living in the afterglow of the Goethean world. Untouched by the rapid development of

---

[19] Information on Scheler's year of study in Berlin is scanty. Maerit Furtwaengler indicated that Scheler later considered his experience there as crucial in awakening him to social problems.

industry that had transformed much of northern Germany in the third quarter of the nineteenth century, Jena had made few concessions to modernization beyond allowing a short railway line to be installed connecting it to Weimar, the capital of the duchy. A number of famous scholars had been brought to the university by the energetic rector, Hofrat Seebeck, who, through his family, had direct personal ties to the classical period when Jena and Weimar formed the cultural center of Germany.[20]

In the course of the nineteenth century, relations between Jena and Weimar had become less intimate. Grand Duke Karl Alexander (1818–1901) occasionally summoned a small group of professors from Jena to visit him in Weimar to discuss questions of the day. By the 1880's, however, the court found that it could get on without the services of the learned men of Jena. At the same time, the professors had begun to take increasingly more interest in the general life of the new Reich than in the affairs of the small Duchy of Saxe-Weimar. But memories of Goethe, Schiller, Fichte, and Hegel remained in the hearts of the citizens of the little university town where the Schelers established their new home. The great poet, temporarily forgotten in much of Germany before the Goethe revival in the nineties, was the main theme of conversation at many a gathering, especially when his grandson, or someone who had known Goethe personally was present. By the last decade of the century, Jena attracted but a sparse seven hundred students. Because many of them came from distant parts of Germany, and some even from abroad, the atmosphere was relatively cosmopolitan for a provincial university town.[21]

When Scheler entered the University of Jena in 1895, there were two full professors of philosophy under whom he could have written his dissertation: Ernst Haeckel, a materialist, and

[20] On the classical period of Jena and Weimar, see W. H. Bruford, *Culture and Society in Classical Weimar 1776–1806* (Cambridge, England, 1962).

[21] This description of Jena, its university and its cultural heritage comes from Rudolf Eucken's *Lebenserinnerungen, ein Stück deutschen Lebens* (Leipzig, 1921).

12 Rudolf Eucken, an idealist. Considering Scheler's religious and ethical interests, it should come as no surprise to the reader that Scheler chose to work with the idealist. Although Eucken had made little impact on the academic world at large, he seems to have been just the right teacher for Scheler at this time. The Jena philosopher considered his mission to be that of "detaching the imperishable kernel from the contemporary shell of religion and presenting it in as original a form as possible."[22] Eucken's religious philosophy appears to have been tailor-made for the needs of a young man who was seeking from philosophy an alternative to the guidance he had been unable to follow in religion. Perhaps Scheler hoped that the eternal core of religion would not be as morally demanding as were its historical incarnations.

Eucken's influence on Scheler was lasting in three areas: philosophical anthropology, metaphysics, and ethics. The question of "Man's Place in Nature," posed by Eucken in several of his works, occupied Scheler intermittently throughout his life.[23] Eucken's insistence on the autonomy of spirit (*Geist*) over life became a cardinal doctrine of Scheler's metaphysics. Finally, Eucken's conviction that a philosopher's primary responsibility was to act as a moral and religious critic of the ethics and the society of his time was adopted by Scheler as part of his own self image.

In his most popular book, *The Problem of Human Life, As Viewed by the Great Thinkers from Plato to the Present Time,* Eucken surveyed the history of man's changing conceptions of himself and his place in nature as expressed in the works of the great philosophers.[24] He attempted to demonstrate that each philosopher's view of life was a product of his own per-

[22] *Ibid.*, p. 174.
[23] In one of his last books, *Man's Place in Nature,* Max Scheler indicated that the main questions that had occupied him throughout his philosophical career were: "What is the nature of man?" and "What is his place in the cosmic order of things?"
[24] Rudolf Eucken, *The Problem of Human Life As Viewed by the Great Thinkers from Plato to the Present Time,* tr. Williston S. Hough and W. R. Boyce Gibson (2nd ed., New York, 1924).

sonal experience (*Erlebnis*) which itself was conditioned by the prevailing ideas and social patterns of his age. Eucken spoke of the modern era as one in which man had lost any sense of his special position in the universe and of his role in the development of spirit in the world. Out of his desire to control and manipulate nature, man had developed an impersonal, aggressive attitude toward it, and had thereby lost any feeling of kinship with it and joy in it. Work had replaced contemplation as the primary form of relating to nature. Science had replaced philosophy and religion as the guiding discipline of modern man, with the result that human life, as the crossroads in the great chain of being, had gradually ceased to have any meaning.[25]

Eucken repudiated positivism, but he did not reject science as such. The trouble with the modern world, he felt, was that science had taken over or driven out all other forms of thought. Eucken did not contest the limitations of nature and the laws of nature that science had discovered. He did insist on the autonomy and freedom of spirit, however.[26] In his most technical philosophical work, *The Struggle to Give Spiritual Meaning to Life*,[27] Eucken attempted to situate man's endless striving after spirit in the spheres of science, art, religion, and the state in a metaphysical matrix. Life was flux, Eucken admitted, but there was a higher transcendental realm of pure being, of ideals and values, that remained unchanged through time. It was man's task to spiritualize life by giving a philosophical meaning to human existence. The ultimate source of philosophical thought was not only the philosopher's personal experience and his historical environment, but also the realm of eternal ideas and values that were refracted through his personal and historical milieu. Psychology, sociology, and history all shaped the evolution of the human spirit, which Eucken spoke of as

[25] *Ibid.*, p. ix.
[26] *Ibid.*, p. xxiv.
[27] Rudolf Eucken, *Der Kampf um einen geistigen Lebensinhalt* (Leipzig, 1896).

the incarnation of absolute spirit itself.[28] This watered-down idealism that paid lip service to the advances of the natural and social sciences in the late nineteenth century provided Scheler with a metaphysical framework for his later studies of the evolution of culture. Although he abandoned it in part during his middle years, he returned to this idealistic metaphysics in the end, after his final rupture with the Catholic Church.

The most important part of Eucken's influence, however, was the example he represented to Scheler of a philosopher *engagé*. Dedicated to the moral uplift of his time, Eucken ventured out to the big cities of Germany, Europe, and even America, eventually earning himself a Nobel Peace Prize for his attempts to provide a common spiritual platform for modern civilization throughout the world.[29] Scheler's own temperament and personal life might have inclined him to be preoccupied with his own problems. His experiences in Berlin had shocked him into recognition of the social problems of the wider world. Eucken provided him with the inspiration and the example to apply his philosophical training to an analysis of contemporary social problems. After writing two works concerned with problems of philosophical method, *The Relationship Between Logic and Ethics*[30] (1897) and *The Transcendental and the Psychological Method*[31] (1899), Scheler published his first article on the social question, "Work and Ethics,"[32] in 1899. Before proceed-

28 *Ibid.*, p.10.
29 In his *Lebenserinnerungen*, p. 195, Eucken explained that he felt the need to criticize the insincerity of contemporary life that professed spirituality but was wholly taken up with material things because "nothing but a rediscovery of the spiritual content of life" all over the world could save modern civilization from self destruction.
30 *Beiträge zur Feststellung der Beziehungen zwischen den logischen und ethischen Prinzipien* (Dissertation, Jena, 1897, pub. 1899).
31 *Die transzendentale und die psychologische Methode, Eine grundsätzliche Erörterung zur philosophischen Methodik* (Jena, 1899, pub. 1900). This work, written under Rudolf Eucken, earned him an assistant professorship at the University of Jena.
32 "Arbeit und Ethik," *Zeitschrift für Philosophie und philosophische Kritik*, CXIC/2, 1899. This essay was reprinted in *Leibe und Erkenntnis*, a collection of some of Scheler's essays (Munich, 1955). I have used this latter edition.

ing to Scheler's critique of bourgeois society, however, a summary of the conclusions of his methodological writings will be helpful as these early works indicate his conception of philosophy and its normative role in human life.

4

THE THESIS of Scheler's doctoral dissertation on the relationship between logic and ethics was that logic and ethics were coordinate but strictly autonomous disciplines. Neither could be reduced to the other, Scheler said, because the true and the good, the subjects investigated by logic and ethics respectively, were so different from each other that even their perception depended on different faculties of the human mind.[33] Truth was a quality of judgments. Goodness was a quality of things, or more precisely, it was the *value* inherent in a thing. Scheler insisted that values could not be apprehended by the intellect. Instead, he posited a separate faculty in man for the perception of values. He called this nonrational faculty *value feeling* (*das Wertgefühl*), and he claimed that it was "rooted in the human heart."[34]

Scheler's belief in the cognitive power of emotion and his hostility to rationalism is significant, for it indicates his tendency to subordinate reason to emotion and after he returned to the Church, to faith.[35] Scheler drew inspiration from the writings of Saint Augustine, Pascal, Malebranche, and more directly from the nineteenth century German philosopher, Herman Lotze, who in his *Microcosmos* (1874), suggested that "in its feeling for the value of things and their relation, our reason possesses as genuine a revelation as, in the principles of logical investigation, it has an indispensable instrument of experi-

33 *Beiträge,* p. 2.
34 *Ibid.,* p. 80.
35 Compare Scheler's later work, *On the Eternal in Man,* tr. Bernard Noble (London, 1960), p. 128 ff.

ence."[36] Scheler's anti-rationalism was probably a product of several factors: his earlier religious training, his resentment and fear of secular liberalism's attack on religion in the nineteenth century, and the conflict between reason and emotion in his own life.

If the theory of emotional cognition of values was the most important point in Scheler's dissertation, a vigorous attack on positivism and psychologism was its main theme. Scheler called for a full-scale "value-critique of consciousness."[37] that would show up the inadequacy of positivism in the normative sciences. Scheler's attack on positivism was far from original; he was simply giving expression to the general mood of the decade of the nineties when the humane sciences (*Geisteswissenschaften*) were liberating themselves from the foolishness of trying to compete, in methods and results, with the natural sciences.[38] Scheler took up the cry that philosophy should be freed from the tyranny of positivism. He believed that the primary task of the day was to eliminate Newtonian mechanistic thinking from psychology and metaphysics, where it was not only irrelevant but really destructive. Philosophy was as objective as science, but its objectivity was of a different kind:

We must abandon the prejudice of thinking that objectivity must be the same for everything. The law of gravity existed long before Newton discovered it. Values have this kind of objectivity: they are independent of all individual opinions and desires. In this way values can be considered no less objective than physical objects.[39]

Science, Scheler said, was too closely tied to changes in man's physical environment for it to be useful to philosophy. If philosophy based its principles on the constantly changing hypotheses and conclusions of science, its own conclusions

36 Hermann Lotze, *Microcosmos* tr. Elizabeth Hamilton and E. Constance Jones, (Edinburgh, 1885), I, p. 245.

37 *Beiträge*, p. 4.

38 On the revolt against positivism in the nineties, see S. Stuart Hughes, *Consciousness and Society, The Reorientation of European Social Thought 1890–1930* (New York, 1958), chapter two.

39 *Beiträge*, p. 83.

would also become obsolete. Philosophy's task was to liberate itself from the bonds of scientific method and to rediscover the primary role of intuition and emotion in the growth of philosophic insight.[40]

Echoing the words of his master, Rudolf Eucken, Scheler complained that in modern times, through the development of science, men had gradually lost their sense of participation in a cosmic drama in which they had a special role.[41] Instead of perceiving reality with his full being, with his heart and spirit as well as with his senses and reason, modern man had rejected all those dimensions of experience that were not amenable to rational analysis. The role of religion and philosophy in giving meaning to life had gradually been usurped by positive science. Scheler admitted that in order for the natural sciences to develop in the seventeenth century, it had been necessary for scientists to abandon all concern with purpose and teleology.[42] He objected to the conclusion drawn by nineteenth-century positivists, however, that religion and philosophy were obsolete. Scheler firmly insisted that the insights of religion and philosophy were both eternally valid and eternally necessary to man. They were truths of a different order than those of positive science, but no less relevant for providing answers to the fundamental questions of man's place in the universe and his relationship to deity.[43]

Scheler's second work, *The Transcendental and the Psychological Method* (1899), which earned him an instructorship at the University of Jena, also betrayed the strong influence of Rudolf Eucken. In this work, Scheler took up and elaborated a distinction made by Eucken between the psychic and the spiritual life of man.[44] Whereas the lower levels of animate

[40] *Ibid.*, p. 140. [41] *Ibid.*, p. 21 ff.
[42] *Ibid.*, p. 42. [43] *Ibid.*, p. 111.
[44] See Eucken's *The Meaning and Value of Life*, tr. Lucy Judge Gibson and W. R. Boyce Gibson (London, 1916) and his *Life's Basis and Life's Ideal, The Fundamentals of a New Philosophy of Life*, tr. Alban G. Widgery (2nd ed. London, 1912) for a full account of his dualistic metaphysics in which man stands at the crossroads between life and spirit and has the mission of lifting life up to the realm of spirit, or as Eucken called it, spiritualizing life.

18 and psychic life were said to be wholly determined by instinctual drives, Eucken and Scheler insisted that man's spiritual life was free of psychic determinism.[45] Eucken's distinction was designed to liberate metaphysics from psychology. To understand man's spiritual activities, i.e., cognition and volition, a transcendental, or as Eucken called it, "noological" method had to be employed.[46] The transcendental method required the recognition of the autonomy of spirit over psyche and was oriented toward the discovery of the laws of thought rather than the reduction of man's mental activities to the laws of psychophysical determinism.

Scheler did little more than repeat Eucken's ideas in his own analysis of the transcendental method. Like his master, he was concerned with establishing the autonomy of spirit and protecting it from the attacks of such monistic materialists as Ernst Haeckel, Eucken's opposite at the University of Jena.

5

B Y 1 8 9 9 Max Scheler had both his dissertation and habilitation behind him, and was teaching ethics and the history of philosophy at the University of Jena. The philosophy faculty was small, and Scheler had few students because the majority of those who studied philosophy followed the lectures of the full professors, Eucken, the idealist, and Ernst Haeckel, the materialist whose book, *The Riddle of the Universe*,[47] became the bible of popular positivism in Germany. Interesting people visited the little university town, however, particularly to take part in the lively activities of Rudolf Steiner and his mystical circle. Between the idealism of his teacher, the positivism of his

---

45 Scheler, *Die transzendentale und die psychologische Methode*, p. 2. Compare Eucken, *Life's Basis*, p. 113.

46 Scheler, *Die transzendentale und die psychologische Methode*, p. 8. Compare Eucken, *Life's Basis, op. cit.,* p. 243.

47 Ernst Haeckel, *The Riddle of the Universe*, tr. Joseph McCabe (New York, 1900).

opponent, and the mysticism of the lunatic fringe Scheler gradually discovered his own voice.

Scheler considered the turning point in his intellectual development to be his meeting with the young Göttingen philosopher, Edmund Husserl; this occurred at a party given by Hans Vaihinger in Halle in 1901. Scheler had become increasingly dissatisfied with the neo-Kantian approach of his master, and for this reason had decided to withdraw from the printer a work on logic that was imbued with Eucken's ideas. The break with Kantian constructivism, as Scheler called his master's approach, was over the role of intuition in knowledge. Scheler had come to the conviction that "what was given to our intuition was originally much richer in content than what could be accounted for by sensuous elements, by their derivatives, and by logical patterns of unification."[48] When he expressed this opinion to Husserl, and remarked that this insight seemed to him a new and fruitful principle for the development of theoretical philosophy, Husserl pointed out that in a new book on logic he had worked out an analogous enlargement of the concept of intuition.[49]

This first conversation with Husserl made a lasting impression on the young Scheler. Husserl had helped him to clarify several points that had been troubling him. For one thing, Scheler was grateful to Husserl for having exposed the psychological relativism implied in Eucken's approach. Scheler had already become somewhat uneasy about the strong strain of German idealism in Eucken's transcendental metaphysics and had begun to wonder whether the transcendental method was really adequate for the comprehension of the immediate data of consciousness.

Husserl introduced Scheler to a conception of philosophical intuition that suited his temperament much better than the transcendental method of his Jena master. Husserl insisted that

48 Max Scheler, "Die deutsche Philosophie der Gegenwart," in *Deutsches Leben der Gegenwart,* ed. Philipp Witkop (Berlin, 1922), p. 197. In this essay Scheler acknowledged his debt to Edmund Husserl.

49 This work was Edmund Husserl's *Logische Untersuchungen* (2 vols., Halle, 1901).

the philosopher must absolve himself of all preconceived knowledge. In exploring the manifold levels of human consciousness, he must follow nothing but the evidence of internal intuition alone. Thus, to Husserl, philosophy presupposed a radical *askesis*. The objective of philosophy was not to *explain*, but to *see* — to understand and reflect upon the totality of experience that was given in direct and immediate intuition. Scheler later came to differ with Husserl on many points, but throughout his life he held to two of Husserl's basic ideas: (1) philosophy required a type of intellectual catharsis, and (2) true philosophical knowledge came through intuition.[50]

Having been introduced to a new respect for philosophical intuition by Husserl, Scheler now turned to the works of the French philosopher, Henri Bergson, who had worked out a critique of positivism and an analogous theory of intuition in his *Essai sur les données immediates de la conscience* (1889) and *Matière et mémoire* (1896).[51] Bergson approached reality with a delightfully naïve sense of wonder at its infinite variety and uniqueness. He was fascinated with multiple levels of reality which he believed that he saw before him. Scientific knowledge, he felt, was based on the will to dominate and control nature, and this will to power prevented the scientist from penetrating to the mysterious depths of life which Bergson believed could only be perceived through an act of sympathetic intuition. Life, in all its pulsating variety, could never be totally grasped by the finite human intellect, Bergson said.

It follows that an absolute can be reached only by *intuition*, while all the rest has to do with *analysis*. We call intuition here the *sympathy* by which one is transported into the interior of an object in order to coincide with what there is unique and consequently inexpressible in it.[52]

---

50 For a detailed account of Husserl's ideas and Scheler's attitude toward them, see Herbert Spiegelberg, *The Phenomenological Movement, A Historical Introduction* (2 vols., The Hague, 1960) I, p. 228 ff. See also Oesterreicher, *op. cit.*, pp. 49–99.

51 On Bergson's idea of intuition, see Hughes, *Consciousness and Society*, pp. 113–118.

52 Henri Bergson, "Introduction to Metaphysics," in *The Creative Mind*, tr. Mabelle Adison (New York, 1946), p. 161. My italics.

These words delighted Scheler. He had found in Bergson a truly kindred spirit.[53] Several years later, when he wrote down his own mature conception of the philosophical point of view, he used Bergson's description of philosophical intuition as his model.[54]

During the next few years, Scheler clarified his ideas on the nature of philosophy and the areas of philosophic study to which he would devote his life. Gradually, he discovered where his own gifts lay. He agreed with Bergson that intellectualization alienated man from Being. The hard cold stare of the impersonal intellect, motivated by the will to power, could grasp only the external contours of being. To discover the inscape of things — to use Hopkins' lovely phrase — Scheler became convinced that the philosopher must purify himself of whatever selfish designs he might harbor in his heart. With Plato, Scheler discovered that philosophy begins in *wonder*.

In an essay published in 1913, entitled "The Search for a Philosophy of Life," Scheler described his new conception of philosophy which he called phenomenology.

This new attitude might first of all be characterized vaguely enough from the emotional point of view as a *surrender* of self to the intuitional content of things, as a movement of profound trust in the unshakableness of all that is simply *given,* as a courageous letting-oneself-go in intuition and in the loving movement toward the world in its capacity for being intuited. This philosophy faces the world with the outstretched gesture of the open hand and the wide-eyed gaze of wonder. This is not the squinting, critical gaze that Descartes — beginning with the universal doubt — casts upon things, nor the eye of Kant, from which comes a spiritual beam so alien as, in its dominating fashion, it penetrates the world of things. The man who philosophizes with the new attitude has neither the anxiety characteristic of modern calculation and the modern desire to verify things, nor the proud sovereignty of the "thinking reed" which in Descartes and Kant is the original source — the emotional *a priori* —

53 According to Moritz Geiger who later knew Scheler in Munich, before he left Jena, Scheler induced the publisher Eugen Diedrichs to bring out a German translation of several of Bergson's works. Moritz Geiger, "Zu Max Schelers Tode," *Vossische Zeitung*, June 1, 1928.

54 "Vorbilder und Führer," *Schriften aus dem Nachlass,* ed. Maria Scheler (2nd ed., Bern, 1960), p. 174 ff.

of all their theories. Instead, the stream of being flows in on him, and seeps down to his spiritual roots, as a self-evident benevolent element, simply that, apart from all content.[55]

This surrender to being is characterized by *love*, a willingness to be dominated rather than to dominate, to bathe in the richness of being rather than to impoverish being by seeking to control it for the sake of one's own subjective assurance.

It is not the will to dominate, to "organize," to determine unequivocally and to fix, which animates each thought, but rather a movement of sympathy, of not begrudging being, of welcoming an increase in the fullness with which, for a gaze of contemplative recognition, the content of the world is constantly disengaging itself from the invasion of human understanding, excelling as it does the limits of mere concepts.[56]

Thus, Scheler's phenomenology not only represented a repudiation of scientific rationalism; it was intended to counteract modern man's tendency to filter his experience through abstract conceptual structures. In this sense, it required what Scheler called "a continuous *de-symbolization* of the world,"[57] forcing man to return to the immediacy of his experience prior to its symbolization and conceptualization. As Scheler conceived it, phenomenology was not so much a method — in the sense of a set of mental operations — as a special attitude (*Einstellung*) or *way of viewing* (*Schauverfahren*) whereby the viewer could enter directly into an immediate, intuitive relationship with things. Scheler's phenomenology would consider "whatever is self-given in the immediacy of experience," no matter what this might be.[58] In short, for Scheler, phenomenology represented

55 "Versuche einer Philosophie des Lebens," *Die Weissen Blätter I*, 3 (November, 1913); reprinted in *Vom Umsturz der Werte*, (4th ed., Bern, 1955), p. 325. Significantly, this passage occurs in the context of Scheler's discussion of Bergson's thought.

56 *Ibid.*, p. 325.

57 *Schriften aus dem Nachlass, I: Zur Ethik und Erkenntnislehre*, ed. Maria Scheler (2nd ed., Bern, 1957), p. 380.

58 As Scheler's meaning is somewhat obscure, following is the German text: "Das erste, was daher eine auf Phänomenologie gegründete Philosophie als Grundcharakter besitzen muss, ist der lebendigste, intensivste und *unmittelbarste Erlebnisverkehr mit der Welt selbst . . .* d.h. mit den Sachen, wie sie sich ganz unmittelbar im Er-leben im Akte des Er-lebens

a rejection of the limits imposed on reason by Kant, and an exuberant exhortation to his contemporaries to abandon their self-imposed immaturity and dare to know the infinite richness of human experience.

In opposition to rationalists and empiricists, Scheler insisted that philosophy must liberate itself from being the handmaid of the natural sciences. Once having gained this autonomy, the philosopher could fulfill an important function for modern man. Disabusing himself of the prejudices of positivism, the philosopher could penetrate behind all phenomena to their essential structures (*Wesenheiten*). He could then describe these structures in such a way as to awaken modern men to the poetic dimensions of reality that were imperceptible to the methods of science. Scheler's philosopher was to take on the role of poet and priest, evoking in modern man a sense of wonder and joy at the beauty and sacred mystery of God's universe.

If modern man could but learn to look at the world once more with the loving, trusting, wondering gaze of a child, Scheler felt, he would rediscover that he and nature were brothers, linked by an invisible band, the band of love, the bond of being. Scheler likened the epistemological confines of modern philosophy to the walls of a prison that shut out all the beauty in the world. Once he threw away the blinders of scientific rationalism, modern man would feel "like a man who after spending most of his life in a dark prison was suddenly set free in a flowering garden." This garden was "God's colorful world which we see opening before us and greeting us brightly, if only from a distance."[59]

---

geben, und in ihm und nur in ihm 'selber da' sind. Durstig nach dem Sein im Er-leben wird der phänomenologische Philosoph allüberall an den 'Quellen' selbst, in denen sich der Gehalt der Welt auftut, zu trinken suchen. Sein reflektierender Blick weilt dabei allein an der Berührungs-stelle von Er-leben und Gegenstand Welt — ganz gleichgültig, ob es sich dabei um Physisches oder Psychisches, um Zahlen oder Gott oder sonst etwas handelt. Nur was und sofern es in diesem dichtesten, Lebendigsten Kontakt 'da' ist, soll der Strahl der Reflexion zu treffen suchen."

59 *Vom Umsturz der Werte*, p. 325.

6

H A D   I T   N O T been for his wife, Scheler might have stayed on in Jena where he had gradually acquired a small circle of devoted students and friends. However, Amelie was a highly nervous woman who was prone to fits of jealousy. Knowing Scheler, she probably had good grounds for her jealousy. Nevertheless, when she slapped the wife of the publisher Eugen Diedrichs at a university party and publicly accused her of having an affair with Max Scheler, the incident caused such a scandal that the young philosopher had to leave Jena.[60]

Fortunately, Scheler was able to secure a post in his home town at the University of Munich. Graf von Hertling, later to be Germany's first Catholic chancellor in 1917, held the senior professorship in philosophy at Munich,[61] but he spent much of his time in the Reichstag where he served as one of the leaders of the Center Party. Therefore, the professor under whom Scheler worked was Theodore Lipps who taught psychology. Edmund Husserl, whom Scheler had met earlier, wrote to Lipps recommending Scheler and the appointment was secured. After spending the summer semester visiting friends in Heidelberg and Berlin, Scheler moved to Munich to become one of Lipps' assistants in the fall of 1907.

In every way Scheler found Munich exciting. Professionally he came into his own, attracting a small but devoted group of students with his lectures on ethics and psychology.[62] At the University of Munich he became acquainted with several of

60 Oral testimony of Dietrich von Hildebrand who became acquainted with Scheler soon after he moved to Munich in the fall of 1907.

61 In a letter to Hertling sent from Berlin on April 27, 1906, Scheler indicated his developing interest in phenomenology, his break with Eucken's neo-Kantianism, and his desire to transfer to Munich, which was already becoming a center of phenomenological studies. This letter was published after Scheler's death by Heinrich Finke in *Internationale Wissenschaftsbeziehungen der Görres-Gesellschaft* (Cologne, 1932), pp. 48–51.

62 Spiegelberg, *op. cit.*, I, p. 231.

his illustrious elder colleagues including the economist Lujo Brentano. Scheler enjoyed frequenting his old haunts in Schwabing, but found even greater pleasure in joining the social circles of the art city that opened to him through his university connections.

At the turn of the century Munich was extremely cosmopolitan for a German city. Some of the established society occasionally opened their houses to visits from young artists and intellectuals. One circle met at the home of Hugo and Elsa Bruckmann. This group favored the well-known anti-Semite Houston Stewart Chamberlain as well as some members of the Stefan George circle including Ludwig Klages, Rudolf Kassner, and Alfred Schuler. Another group met at the home of the prominent sculptor Adolf von Hildebrand. His five daughters held bachelor afternoons to which bright young men were invited to have tea and to discuss their ideas. Although Scheler was not a bachelor and was older than the usual visitors, he came to these parties through his acquaintance with Adolf von Hildebrand's son, Dietrich. The historian Karl Alexander von Müller who also attended these gatherings recalled that Scheler held forth on these afternoons like a Savonarola.[63] Through von Hildebrand, Scheler met the young woman who was to become his second wife, Maerit Furtwaengler.

In his professional and social life, everything seemed to be going well, but at home Scheler's wife cast a dark shadow over his whole life. After a year of continued difficulties the couple finally separated. However, the woman was bitterly jealous and conceived a way to avenge herself on her unfaithful husband. She contacted the editor of the Munich socialist newspaper, *Die Post,* and informed him that her husband had gone into debt to pay for his affairs with other women, leaving his wife and children in dire poverty.[64] The editor, Kurt Moeller Vollmar, was probably delighted to publish this bit of scandal as an example of the decadence of the bourgeois academic world.

[63] Karl Alexander von Müller, *Aus Gärten der Vergangenheit* (2nd. ed., Stuttgart, 1958), p. 501.

[64] Testimony of Dietrich von Hildebrand. See *Die Münchener Post,* Oct. 2, 1909.

Scheler tried to ignore the insults, but the articles produced such a scandal that the University of Munich ordered an investigation. Meanwhile, to clear his name, Scheler decided to sue the paper for libel. The testimony of friends might have enabled him to win his suit had not the newspaper's lawyers produced a hotel register showing that he had checked into a hotel with a shopgirl whom he had claimed was his wife. It was also alleged that he had borrowed money from his students without reimbursing them, but this could not be proved. However, the scandal was too great for him to be able to continue teaching at the university. He was asked to resign and was deprived of the right to teach (*venia legendi*) at any other German university. The investigation by the university authorities took place in April, 1910, shortly before the beginning of the spring term.[65]

Depressed, lonely, and unsure what his future might be, Max Scheler moved from Munich to Göttingen in the spring of 1911. Separated from his wife, and having no income, Scheler moved in with Dietrich von Hildebrand who had transferred from the University of Munich the year before. The attractions of Göttingen for both Scheler and von Hildebrand were Edmund Husserl and Adolf Reinach who had gathered around them a group of enthusiastic young students of phenomenology that included Theodor Conrad, Hedwig Conrad-Martius, Moritz Geiger, Jean Hering, Roman Ingarden, Fritz Kaufmann, Alexander Koyré, and Edith Stein.[66] Although he had no official position at a university, Scheler had found his way to the center of the phenomenological movement in Germany.

Scheler soon established himself in Göttingen as a master phenomenologist.[67] Dietrich von Hildebrand, who had attended

---

[65] See the anonymously published report on the investigation, *Der Fall Scheler*, Munich, 1910.

[66] Spiegelberg, *op. cit.*, I, p. 169.

[67] Alexander Koyré described Scheler's sparkling brilliance in Göttingen as one of the high points of his educational career: "'Scheler Sekt' disons nous alors, et la contagion de cette pensée, perpetuellement en acte, nous grisait d'une griserie féconde et lucide qui nous élevait au-

Scheler's lectures in Munich, rented a hall and encouraged some of Edmund Husserl's students to attend Scheler's private lectures. Scheler soon attracted a small band of dedicated followers, provoking the ire and jealousy of Husserl, who had been on good terms with Scheler as long as the latter had remained in Munich. Husserl had even helped Scheler out of his difficulties in Jena by recommending him for the Munich post. When he lost it after the investigation, however, Husserl became disgusted, feeling that a man who led such a confused and uncontrolled life could not be trusted either as a teacher or a scholar. At this time Husserl was still in a difficult position, trying to win a place for himself and his new approach to philosophy, which was under attack from positivists and neo-Kantians. Soon he began to see in Scheler more of a danger than an asset to his own aspirations to establish phenomenology as a rigorous science.[68] Nevertheless, Scheler became one of the four original coeditors of Husserl's phenomenological journal, although he never took a very active part in its management.

The differences between Scheler and Husserl were as much temperamental as philosophical. Husserl was shy and retiring, a better researcher than a lecturer; Scheler was a flamboyant showman who could easily capture an audience and hold them spellbound for hours. The fact that Scheler chose a café for his lecture hall in Göttingen is symbolic. Here he was in his element. Restless in the quiet of a library or study, he preferred the bustle of chattering people and the clink of glasses, even for his most serious writing. Because he did much of his "research" in restaurants and cafés, his notes scribbled on the back of a menu or a letter, he found it difficult to trace the sources of many of his ideas. As a result, he seldom acknowledged his intellectual debts. A scholar like Husserl, who found himself quoted without being cited, criticized him for his sloppiness and irresponsibility and accused him of intellectual charlatanry.

---

dessus de nous-mêmes et nous rendait capable de participer à cette agilité de voir et même de trouver nous-mêmes des choses que nous n'aurions jamais pu découvrir sans lui." "Max Scheler," *Revue d'Allemagne*, X (August, 1928), p. 98.

[68] Spiegelberg, *op. cit.*, I, p. 229.

It is likely, however, that Husserl's anger was sparked as much by jealousy of Scheler's charisma as by concern for Scheler's scholarship. The tension between the two men became so great that at the end of the semester Scheler moved from Göttingen back to Munich where Maerit was waiting for him.

Scheler was now thirty-six years old. Two thirds of his life was over, and he was a failure. Henceforth, as long as the German Empire lasted, he would be denied the possibility of a further academic career. He had prepared himself for nothing else; so, at this juncture, he did not know where to turn. He had been alienated from his family since his adolescence. His sister, with whom he had been quite close, had been murdered. His wife, who had been a constant thorn in his side, had finally left him, but nevertheless she had managed to ruin his professional career. Faith in his new love, Maerit Furtwaengler, and in his close friend, Dietrich von Hildebrand, alone probably saved Max Scheler from a nervous collapse. With their help, he gradually recovered himself in the next few years and launched a new career as a free-lance writer and critic of German culture and society.

2

The Critic of Bourgeois Civilization

MAX SCHELER grew up in a period of tremendous social and intellectual change in Germany. As one might expect, like other young men of his generation who expressed their contempt for the "bourgeois world" of their fathers by joining the youth movement and idolizing Nietzsche and Stefan George, Max Scheler developed a permanent hostility to nineteenth-century positivism and liberalism. Throughout his life he considered the "bourgeois human type" to be the epitome of decadence.

It is not difficult to understand Scheler's hostility to the modern world and to the bourgeoisie who made and controlled it. This mood of disgust with the dirty cities and the big factories that heavy industry brought in its wake was common in Wilhelmian Germany. With many other Germans, Scheler longed for the "good old days" when people lived together with a sense of shared values and common life-patterns. To Scheler, medieval society represented this ideal. The harmony of medieval life had been ruptured by the rise of capitalism and the bourgeoisie during the Renaissance. The Reformation had completed the break that had already begun in the social and economic sphere.

Catholic and rural Bavaria provided a social environment that encouraged Scheler's romantic social phantasies. Isolated and jobless in Munich in 1911, Scheler became increasingly disgusted with his world and pessimistic about its future. In an atmosphere that was seething with criticism of modern industrial society, Scheler began work on *Ressentiment* and other essays explaining how modern society had gone wrong and how it might be set right by returning to pre-capitalistic Christian communal ideals.[1]

This chapter will analyze Max Scheler's critique of modern civilization, and explain how and why his critique reflected and intensified the feelings of many Germans in the prewar years. The reader may see the mood of pessimism and resentment as a product of Scheler's personal and professional failures. Such a conclusion is only part of the story, however, for it just so happened that Scheler's personal depression corresponded to a general mood of dissatisfaction that swept through the German Empire in the years immediately preceding the outbreak of World War I. Scheler's personal circumstances placed him in a position to express the moral and psychological malaise of his nation.

[1] Scheler's "Über Ressentiment und moralisches Werturteil, Ein Betrag zur Pathologie der Kultur," was first published in the *Zeitschrift für Patho-psychologie* I, Nos. 2 and 3 (1912), but it was soon reprinted along with other essays in culture criticism he wrote between 1911 and 1914 in a volume of collected essays, *Abhandlungen und Aufsätze* (Leipzig, 1915). Scheler retitled the later editions of this collection, *Vom Umsturz der Werte*. We have used the fourth edition, which was published as Vol. 3 of the *Gesammelte Werke* (Bern, 1955). Unless otherwise noted, the references to *Ressentiment* are to the English version translated by William Holdheim, edited with an introduction by Lewis Coser (New York, 1961).

THROUGHOUT Scheler's writings one finds an idealization of medieval feudal society and a hostility to modern industrial society. What repelled Scheler most in modern society was its encouragement of individualism that had begun with the rise of capitalism in the Renaissance and had culminated in bourgeois liberalism in the nineteenth century. To Scheler, the bourgeois spirit of individualism extolled by modern liberals had destroyed the sense of moral and social solidarity that had characterized feudal society. Capitalism had failed to generate such new "community building powers" as commonly shared values and a sense of identity, or participation in and acceptance of the capitalist social order by all its members. Bourgeois capitalist individualism had produced a society torn by class conflict rather than one united in ideological consensus and social solidarity.

Scheler attributed the anarchy of modern life to the lack of a metaphysics of community in which men could perceive how their individual social activities were integral and necessary cooperative functions of that larger organism we call society. He wrote in 1921:

The sociological picture presented by a society in which metaphysics is lacking as a cultural integrating function is that of an unbounded *anarchy of specialization* devoid, even in the "University," of all universality of spirit. . . . As metaphysics introduces the possibility of replacing sociologically an assemblage of specializations with a *unity* of spiritual culture, it alone also provides the *common intellectual platform,* an atmosphere in which adherents of different positive religions and churches can confer together or with skeptics, and try to win the other party over to their cause. . . . Finally metaphysics is the necessary medium through which *nations* may come to understand one another in the world of knowledge. . . . It is only in the interaction of metaphysical ideas, their fruition and mutual *approfondissement,* that the high converse of national temperaments is engaged and ravelled out.[2]

2 Scheler, *On the Eternal in Man* (London, 1960), p. 300.

Because men had abandoned a commonly shared reliance on metaphysics to provide for the integration of all types of knowledge and experience, each of the individual sciences had developed metaphysical pretensions and attempted to provide an integrating world view. Naturally, they had all failed, said Scheler, because metaphysics alone was the medium through which individuals, states, nations, religions, and even civilizations could understand one another. True cooperation, involving the whole being of man, could only take place on the metaphysical level. "In default of metaphysics the highest spiritual commerce of nations in a common forum is paralyzed and the unity of mankind's spiritual world becomes a lost cause.[3]

Scheler held up to his readers a romantically conceived picture of the medieval social order. Medieval society, in Scheler's romantic scheme, had functioned as a cohesive unit because every person knew his place in the social order and accepted it. Peasants obeyed their masters joyfully because they felt that servitude had both a divine and a natural sanction.[4] In modern society, on the other hand, men had lost any sense of participating in and being a part of a social organism. With no external objective norms against which to measure their personal merit, men had come to adopt the labor theory of value according to which a man's wealth and productivity became the only measure of his personal worth.[5]

Modern liberals and socialists were completely wrong to consider man's concern for his material welfare and security as the primary motivation of human behavior. This lower motive was subordinate to higher spiritual motives, Scheler said. Values themselves could be arranged in an ascending hierarchy according to whether they satisfied man's animal or his spiritual needs. Men themselves could also be arranged in a hierarchy of types, Scheler argued, the noble being superior to the base.[6] It was only

3 *Ibid.,* p. 301.
4 *Ressentiment,* p. 56.
5 *Ibid.,* p. 139 ff.
6 Scheler explained his conception of the objective hierarchy of values, and the parallel human types, in his monumental ethics: *Der Formalismus in der Ethik und die materiale Wertethik* (1916).

modern value-blindness that had led to widespread acceptance of the false doctrine that all men are created equal.[7]

The highest values of culture and politics were never intended for the masses. They were created by and for a political and cultural elite. The modern proletarians were dissatisfied because they had lost the Christian view of their function as workers in the social hierarchy. They must be brought to recognize that only a minority could ever govern a society and that the majority of men were destined by God to work for and to follow a cultured elite.[8] The materialism that was rampant in bourgeois society had led the workers to expect more than destiny intended for them. Unless they were soon made aware of their proper place, Scheler feared that they would overturn the whole social order because of their unjustified dissatisfactions and unrealistic expectations.

Only the Christian conception of society as a hierarchy of interdependent corporations could provide the proper social perspective to heal the divisions of modern German society, Scheler said. It offered men a conceptual framework wherein they might feel themselves to be working for a common spiritual objective: the glorification of God. Motivated by love for the deity, men from all classes would forget the selfish rivalries highlighted by Marxism with its false doctrine of class conflict. The love of God would bind men together in solidarity and community more firmly than the loyalties to class, or nation, or international associations ever could.[9]

Scheler believed that the solution to the social problem, the problem of the proletariat in modern society, lay in transforming the class-conscious proletariat back to an estate. Scheler admired "estates" as opposed to "classes" because an estate was something stable, a standing wherein a man was self-sufficient. "To know one's estate is to be truly at home in the state, assured

7 *Ressentiment*, p. 143.
8 *Ibid.*, p. 140. Compare the similar argument in Scheler's first published article, "Arbeit und Ethik," *Zeitschrift für Philosophie und philosophische Kritik*, CXIV, No. 2 (1899), reprinted in *Liebe und Erkenntnis* (Munich, 1955), pp. 91–128.
9 *On the Eternal in Man*, p. 301.

of lawful rights on which no one may trespass."[10] Whereas estate-society promoted a spirit of love and pride in one's work, class-society engendered a spirit of competition and alienation.

Scheler's Catholic corporatism which he called Christian solidarism was drawn largely from the economic and social theories of the Jesuit social theologians Gustav Grundlach and Heinrich Pesch, and from the Encyclical of Leo XIII, *Rerum Novarum* (1891). The latter advocated a hierarchical scheme of occupational estates drawn together in economic councils that would provide a framework for industrial self-government and supplement parliamentary government in economic and social affairs. Pesch and Grundlach condemned atomistic competition because they argued that it inevitably led to periodic depressions. Instead of an uncontrolled economy, they believed that the government should determine general economic goals using corporative organizations that would have immediate jurisdiction over their respective industries.[11]

Most Catholic corporatists were reformists, and Scheler was no exception. He hoped to use the existing occupational and professional groups in Germany and gradually to transform them into estates by infusing a new ethos in them. When mobilization in the war produced a new spirit of cooperation and participation in the national community, Scheler argued that the spirit of Christian corporatism, coming from above, should join the spirit of mutual cooperation coming from below to produce a new society. The Christian's task was to attempt to lead these two streams to confluence so that "they might unite in a *single moral force*, the lower discovering its moral dignity in the light shed by the higher."[12]

10 *Ibid.*
11 See Heinrich Pesch, *Liberalismus, Sozialismus und christliche Gesellschaftsehre* (Freiburg at Breisgau, 1901).
12 *On the Eternal in Man*, p. 380. Here we already find adumbrated the central thesis of Scheler's later sociology of knowledge: ideas must combine with powerful economic, social, and instinctual tendencies if they are to become effective in history.

A L R E A D Y in Scheler's first published essay, "Work and Ethics," one can see the strong hostility to modern industrial civilization and the idealization of feudal society that recurs in his later writings. In this first essay, written while he was still very much under the influence of his teacher, Rudolf Eucken, Scheler insisted that modern society had been going downhill ever since men had ceased to believe in the objective hierarchy of values recognized by medieval Catholic theology and reflected in the feudal social order.

Why did men no longer recognize the objective hierarchy of values and organize themselves accordingly? Scheler traced the development of modern utilitarian value attitudes, and particularly the labor theory of value, to the rise of capitalism and to the bourgeoisie who created it.[13] However, Scheler rejected the Marxist argument that the capitalist mentality was a result of capitalist forms of social and economic organization. Prior to the capitalist era there were proto-capitalists, but they were the exception not the rule. When "Jewish rights and laws became general laws and were proclaimed as proper ways of value estimation," a *moral* revolution took place.[14] This moral revolution brought about the destruction of medieval society.

In *Ressentiment,* an essay devoted to explaining the origins of modern decadence, Scheler described the situation of contemporary man as follows:

With the development of modern civilization, *nature* (which man had tried to reduce to a mechanism for the purpose of ruling it), and *objects* have become man's *lord* and *master*. The *machine* has come to dominate *life*. The "objects" have progressively grown in vigor and intelligence, size, and beauty, whereas man, who created them, has become increasingly no more than a cog in his own ma-

13 Scheler, "Arbeit und Ethik," p. 91.
14 *Vom Umsturz der Werte,* p. 349.

chine. Perhaps there is no point on which there is more general agreement among sensible and right minded contemporaries.[15]

Scheler went on to say that this "generally acknowledged fact" was due to a fundamental *subversion of values:* Its source was *ressentiment,* "the victory of the value judgements of those who are vitally inferior, of the lowest, the pariahs of the human race!"[16] Everywhere he looked, Scheler saw that through the agency of *ressentiment,* bourgeois utilitarian values had replaced aristocratic vital values. Modern humanitarianism and love of mankind had replaced true Christian love. The artificial ties of atomistic society expressed in Adam Smith's system of free competition had become the ideal of a society increasingly rationalized, mechanized, and reduced to uniformity. The feeling of trust of one's neighbor, which Scheler believed to be characteristic of primary communities, had been replaced by a spirit of suspicion and selfish striving to get ahead of everyone else. The latter was, according to Scheler, but an expression of the desire of the anxious parvenu to escape from his own feelings of insecurity. The anxiety that beset modern man resulted from his alienation from God, nature, and his inner self.[17]

If the mechanistic world view was a subversion of the true hierarchy of values, and an "intellectual symbol of the slave revolt in morality,"[18] how did this transvaluation of the true tablets of value take place? Scheler agreed with Nietzsche that *ressentiment* was the source of modern morality and values, but he objected to Nietzsche's application of this concept to what he termed the true Christian ethos.

Nietzsche ignored the fact that love in the Christian sense is always primarily directed at man's ideal spiritual self, at man as a member of the kingdom of God. Therefore he equated the Christian idea of love with a completely different idea which has quite another historical and psychological origin; *the idea and movement of modern universal love of man,* humanitarianism, or love toward every mem-

15 *Ressentiment,* p. 172.
16 *Ibid.*   17 *Ibid.,* p. 114 ff.
18 *Ibid.,* p. 172.

ber of the human race. We agree with Nietzsche that *ressentiment* was the real root of this idea.[19]

Taking his cue from Nietzsche's description of *ressentiment*,[20] Scheler defined the psychological phenomenon as follows:

Ressentiment is a self-poisoning of the mind . . . caused by the systematic repression of certain emotions and affects which, as such, are normal components of human nature. Their repression leads to the constant tendency to indulge in certain kinds of value delusions and corresponding value judgments. The emotions and affects primarily concerned are revenge, hatred, malice, envy, the impulse to detract, and spite.[21]

These repressed emotions and affects "blossom into *ressentiment*" only if there is neither a moral self-conquest (such as genuine forgiveness) nor some other form of adequate emotional expression, *and* if this restraint is caused by "the *awareness of impotence.*"[22]

As in Scheler's earlier essay, "Work and Ethics," his real target was not so much the organizational form of modern society as its value system — what he called its *ethos*. To Scheler the atomistic, mechanistic, individualistic world view that he called "the bourgeois ethos" was both un-German and un-Christian.[23] He decried the modern Faustian man, like himself, who was forever restless, forever striving for new goals; and he praised medieval man who, he believed, had been content with his permanent status as a member of an estate in the social hierarchy.[24]

According to Scheler's fanciful interpretation of history, the social dislocations which followed the move to the urban centers and the rise of the bourgeoisie in the thirteenth century

[19] *Ibid.*, p. 114.
[20] Nietzsche, *The Geneology of Morals*, tr. Francis Golffing, (New York, 1956) p. 149 ff.
[21] *Ressentiment*, p. 45.
[22] *Ibid.*, p. 48. [23] *Ibid.*, p. 50.
[24] *Ibid.*

brought the common man into direct contact with men of more heroic caste. The comparisons that ensued nourished feelings of envy and *ressentiment* in the hearts of the plebean petty bourgeoisie.[25]

Scheler actually believed that the feudal aristocracy was "biologically" as well as "spiritually" superior to the petty-bourgeois common man.[26] The aristocrat inherited power and position and was born and bred to rule. Scheler contrasted the two types as follows: The aristocrat was heroic, loved uncertainty and danger, and had a spontaneous sense of his own worth and a general trust in life. He was generous, joyful, and ready to sacrifice himself. He valued men for their *being*, not for their achievements for the common good.[27] In contrast, the common man was slavish, servile, calculating, self-seeking, filled with anxiety, grasping, greedy, and distrustful of others and of life in general. Because he was insecure, he was constantly seeking security, regularity, and guarantees for the morrow. He trusted no one, not even himself.

We have said that Scheler spoke of the differences between the common man and the natural aristocrat as manifestations of a biological difference. He believed that the inferior type was gradually driving out the superior one through blood mixture (*Blutmischung*).[28] Throughout his life Scheler continued to believe that the ultimate cause of great cultural transformations — such as the decline of the Roman Empire, the shift from the medieval to the modern capitalist world, and the transition from capitalism to whatever would succeed it — were the results of blood mixture.

Over and over we find Scheler lamenting the biological and erotic decadence of modern bourgeois man. He looked to the youth of Europe, and in particular to the German *Jugendbewegung* as a source of renewal, bringing new blood and vitality into the world. He never explained how they had escaped

25 "Der Bourgeois," in *Vom Umsturz der Werte*, p. 355.
26 *Ibid.*   27 *Ibid.*, p. 357.
28 *Ibid.*, p. 356.

the "inferior blood"[29] of their bourgeois parents, though this would seem to be a crucial question.

Scheler's whole discussion of *Blutmischung* is as ill-defined and obscure as the concept itself. He sensed the indefiniteness of the idea and generally only broached the subject in occasional asides with such statements as:

Those who are familiar with many basic human types, who can recognize the psychic unity of action, word, and gesture in a particular human type, will not let anyone say that these are simply a product of education, environment, or adaptation to a milieu.[30]

Scheler's belief in a "natural aristocracy" conditioned his view of society in which he considered it to be inevitably divided between the leaders and the led.[31]

Historically, Scheler thought, *ressentiment* was not the product of the feudal aristocracy nor did it grow up in the hearts of the *grand bourgeoisie*. *Ressentiment* was the typical emotion and attitude of the common man, the shopkeeper, the artisan, the salesman, and the low-level administrator.[32] Scheler contrasted the aristocrat with the common man in the following manner:

The noble man experiences value *prior* to any comparison; the common man *in* and *through* a comparison. In fact, for the latter, the *relation* is the precondition for his apprehension of any value. Every value is a relative thing, "higher" or "lower" than his own. He arrives at value judgments by comparing himself to others and others to himself.[33]

Scheler admitted that most men, at one time or another, were inclined to compare themselves with their fellows, but he insisted that the correct attitude on such occasions was to accept the superiority of one's betters and to strive to emulate them.

---

29 "Die Zukunft des Kapitalismus," in *Vom Umsturz der Werte*, p. 391.
30 "Der Bourgeois," p. 356.
31 "Die Zukunft des Kapitalismus," pp. 386–387.
32 *Ressentiment*, p. 54.
33 *Ibid.*, p. 55.

When I see a man who naturally has superior ability and excellence, I will prefer him to the man who must work hard to acquire these qualities provided that my attention is oriented to the *values themselves*. I will be happier and gratefully acknowledge the fact that the former already has what the latter must acquire and is, therefore, already closer to the ideal of perfection. *How* he acquired it is a different question. He, after all, who sets out on life's journey with greater moral talents can, through effort, attain a higher level [of perfection] than the less gifted.[34]

On the other hand, when the common man compares himself with his betters, he "cannot bear" the original distance between them.[35] He suffers from the comparison, and *ressentiment* sets in and inspires him to deny the value of those qualities that he sees in his betters but does not possess himself.[36] Precisely, these motives of envy and *ressentiment* had inspired the transvaluation of values perpetrated by the petty bourgeoisie in modern times, Scheler said.[37] Modern values were bourgeois values, so much so in fact that men now denied that any objective hierarchy of absolute values even existed.

In his essay, Scheler traced a number of ideas which he considered to be characteristic of the "bourgeois mentality" back to their psychological roots in *ressentiment*. These ideas were: (1) universal love of mankind, (2) the labor theory of value, (3) individualism, and (4) utilitarianism.

Scheler contrasted the so-called active and spiritual quality of Christian love with the passive feelings of humanitarian love of mankind which arose largely through psychic contagion.[38] Christianity was the religion of the strong, humanitarianism that of the weak:

The pathos of modern humanitarianism, its clamor for greater sensuousness happiness and its revolutionary protest against all institutions, traditions, and customs which it considers as obstacles to the increase of sensuous happiness — is in characteristic contrast to the luminous, almost cool *spiritual enthusiasm* of Christian love.[39]

---

34 *Ibid.*, pp. 138–139.
36 *Ibid.*, p. 140.
38 *Ibid.*

35 *Ibid.*
37 *Ibid.*, p. 117.
39 *Ibid.*, p. 117.

Citing the British moral philosophers Smith, Hume, Hutcheson, and Bain along with the French moralist, Rousseau, Scheler complained that during the course of the seventeenth and eighteenth centuries, in theory and practice, Christian love was transformed into benevolent sentiment.[40] Spencer and Darwin had finally completed the *reductio ad absurdum* by viewing love as nothing more than sensual lust implanted in nature for preserving the species. The desire to pull love down from the lofty heights to which Dante and Saint Bonaventure had elevated it in the Middle Ages, when it had been considered as the primary spiritual activity of man and God, was inspired by the *ressentiment* of the spiritually impotent, Scheler said. The common man had imposed his plebeian values of equality and humanitarianism on the naturally superior military and religious aristocracy.[41]

The same influence of *ressentiment* might be discovered in the genesis and development of the labor theory of value, Scheler insisted. In the bourgeois world, said Scheler, "*Moral value pertains only to those qualities, actions, etc., which the individual has acquired by his own strength and labor.*"[42] "Work," in fact, was now considered to have the power of endowing being and action with value. The emphasis no longer lay on the objective qualities of value, but on the subjective process of "work."

Scheler had already attacked the labor theory of value in "Work and Ethics" where he maintained that value was not created by man but was given by God. In *Ressentiment* he spelled out the social implications of his value theory. According to their natural gifts and abilities, some men were superior to others. The labor theory of value had been created by the inferior men who resented the superior natural endowments of their betters, and therefore claimed that "there is moral value

---

[40] *Ibid.* Compare Scheler's *The Nature of Sympathy,* tr. Peter Heath (London, 1954), p. 180 ff.

[41] *Ibid.,* p. 118. Compare the similar analysis of the sociological origins of the bourgeois *Weltanschauung* in Scheler's later work, *Die Wissensformen und die Gesellschaft* (2nd ed. Bern, 1960), pp. 101, 117, 122 ff.

[42] *Ibid.,* p. 138.

only in that which *everyone* — even the least gifted — can do."[43] All human beings were designated as "equal" by the weak who now set the criterion of value for all. The superior man was deprived of his rights by the statement that his gifts were not due to his own merit and were, therefore, without the slightest moral value.[44] Scheler thus considered the labor theory of value to be the ideology of the "have nots," the "moral proletarians" who increased their own sense of self-esteem by dragging the gifted few, who stood as a living reproach to them, down to their plebeian level.

What he could not bear, the surpassing importance of the "superior nature," has now been fundamentally devaluated. The sweat and tears of his moral "toil" are now shining in the light of highest value! Through this transvaluation, his secret thirst for revenge against the better man has now been quenched.[45]

Scheler claimed that the theories of property and value of the English political and economic theorists, John Locke, Adam Smith, and David Ricardo, merely formulated and conceptualized the negative value attitudes of the unpropertied common man who was resentful and envious of the inherited wealth of his superiors.[46] By making utility the only standard of value, the British economists were able to question the ownership rights of property acquired through inheritance, donations, and war, the means of distribution practiced by the European feudal aristocracy.[47] "Who cannot see that this 'theory' has sprung from the laboring classes' *envy* of groups that did not acquire their property through work?"[48] Scheler asked. He later glorified the power and property that could be acquired through the heroic activities of the warrior when Germany went to war in 1914, greedy for annexations.

Individualism, another characteristic attitude of "the bourgeois mind," was also a product of *ressentiment* in Scheler's

---

43 *Ressentiment*, p. 139.
44 *Ibid.*, p. 140.   45 *Ibid.*, p. 139.
46 *Ibid.*, p. 140.   47 *Ibid.*
48 *Ibid.*

eyes. "Modern morality," Scheler argued, "is founded on *distrust* of men, particularly of their moral values. The merchant's fear of being cheated by his competitor has become the basic category of the very perception of others."[49] Scheler contrasted the distrust of one's fellow man characteristic of bourgeois civilization to the sense of trust and mutual solidarity which he believed to be characteristic of medieval society.[50]

Individualism resulted from the dissolution of the social and ideological ties of feudal society, he said. When men lived together, sharing a common sense of values, when they were concerned about the achievement of commonly shared goals through mutual cooperation among themselves, the question of who realized these goals and values was of no consequence.[51] Scheler believed that the primary ties of trust and brotherhood characteristic of medieval society, which was essentially rural and economically self-sufficient, were broken down by the distrust that capitalistic economic practices and social relationships brought into the hearts of men.[52] We shall return to Scheler's analysis of the moral and psychological consequences of the transition from feudal to bourgeois society, but first we will briefly consider his bête noire, utilitarianism.

Scheler believed that utilitarianism was *the* basic philosophy of bourgeois man. It was also the "chief manifestation of the *ressentiment* slave revolt in modern morality."[53]

The most profound perversion of the hierarchy of values is the *subordination of vital values to utility values* which gains force as modern morality develops. Since the victory of the industrial and commercial spirit over the military and philosophical-theological spirit (i.e., the feudal aristocracy and the clerical hierarchy) this principle has been penetrating ever more deeply, affecting the most concrete value judgments.[54]

Scheler complained that in modern times the "noble" had been subordinated to the "useful." He defined *noble* as standing for

49 *Ibid.*, p. 143.
50 *Ibid.*
51 *Ibid.*, p. 142.
52 *Ibid.*
53 *Ibid.*, p. 154.
54 *Ibid.*, pp. 154–155.

those qualities that constitute the value of life in living organisms. After the French Revolution, as the merchants and representatives of industry triumphed, their symbols and conceptions of the ultimate nature of things replaced the older religious symbols, and everywhere their utilitarian criteria became the criteria of morality in general.[55] For the bourgeois, the will to work was the primary motivation; he looked upon the world as a potential factory. "Being against bravery, gallantry, and the will to power and sacrifice, how else could he define life than as Herbert Spencer did?" Scheler asked.[56]

Scheler rejected Comte's and Spencer's social theories as too "static."[57] They reduced all vital activities to "reactions to environment" thereby ignoring the heroic creative thrust of the life force itself. "We must learn to see historical man as something moving, not moved, building and seeking his milieu, not being formed by it,"[58] Scheler wrote in 1914. His glorification of the war, when it came, was largely a result of his belief that it would once and for all break down the arbitrary ties of modern life and produce more vital chthonian ties between man and man. Life, so long stifled by the bourgeois calculating ethos would burst forth bringing new vitality to decadent modern man. The weak would go down in the struggle; the strong would survive. Scheler was a kind of social Darwinist in his own right!

3

AS HISTORY, Scheler's construction is fantastic and pure mythology. His analysis of "bourgeois decadence" only makes sense if we apply it to the German middle class who

---

[55] *Ibid.*, p. 155.
[56] "Versuche einer Philosophie des Lebens," in *Vom Umsturz der Werte*, p. 317.
[57] *Ibid.*, p. 318. Compare Scheler's critique of Spencer's and Comte's "static philosophy of life" in *Der Genius des Krieges und der Deutsche Krieg* (Leipzig, 1915), pp. 34–35.
[58] *Der Genius des Krieges*, p. 34.

were politically impotent vis-à-vis the feudal aristocracy that ruled Germany in the nineteenth and early twentieth centuries. To successfully challenge this feudal rule, the German burghers would have had to rely on the help of the Social Democrats, and they were afraid to be dependent on the socialists.

Scheler's observation that *ressentiment* flourishes particularly in situations where "strong pretensions must remain concealed" because they are "coupled with an inadequate social position"[59] *is* applicable to the German Empire. There the Prussian aristocracy and bureaucracy controlled and governed the Reich and the bourgeoisie were looked down upon by the military aristocracy as socially inferior. The German financiers, bankers, and great industrialists were tremendously successful in business, but they were *failures* politically. The few industrialists such as Alexander Ballin and Walther Rathenau who *were* admitted to the imperial court were simply the exceptions that proved the rule. Even they had no real political influence on the kaiser.

Before one can understand Scheler's hostility to the bourgeoisie, one must be aware of the political impotence of the middle class in the German Empire. In Germany, as in France after 1870, the heavy industries and agriculture joined together under the banner of protective tariffs.[60] They were also brought together by their common dependence on the soil and other natural resources, as heavy industry required coal and iron. The German industrial magnate often lived outside the urban centers, increasingly shared the convictions of the aristocratic landowner, and identified more with this class than with the class of bourgeois merchants and bankers.[61] Gradually the old aristoc-

[59] *Ressentiment*, p. 50.

[60] On the rapprochement between the aristocracy and middle class in Germany through *commercium* and *connubium*, see the extremely stimulating work by E. Kohn-Bramstedt, *Aristocracy and the Middle-Classes in Germany: Social Types in German Literature 1830–1900* (2nd rev. ed., Chicago, 1964), See also Max Weber, *Politische Schriften*, ed. Johannes Winckelmann (2nd rev. ed., Tübingen, 1958), p. 233 ff.

[61] Karl Brinkmann, *Wirtschafts-und Sozialgeschichte* (Berlin and Munich, 1927), p. 40.

racy was being replaced by a ruling class of feudal and bourgeois agricultural and industrial entrepreneurs who became the backbone of German nationalism and *Weltpolitik* in the Wilhelmian period. At the same time, the prestige of the aristocracy remained higher in pseudoconstitutional Germany than anywhere else in Europe.[62]

Ralf Dahrendorf has commented on the manner in which a feudal tradition set the tone in a highly industrialized society:

This odd combination of modernity in economic affairs and backwardness in social affairs — unique at the time — had important political effects. Representative government was the indispensable instrument for a bourgeoisie advancing a claim to power. Only by equal representation could it hope to make its voice heard. . . . But the German bourgeoisie did not advance a claim to political power. Rather it permitted the authoritarian state to survive industrialization: a state resting on the assumption that certain individuals, by virtue of very special insight and guided by the "well understood interests" of their subjects, are called upon to make all the political decisions. Not without reason has this state been described as "paternalistic": as in the Wilhelminian family, the authority of the father, harsh in punishment but genuinely concerned with the welfare of his subjects, was all-pervading.[63]

The dualism of economic strength coupled with political weakness in the German upper middle class often resulted in feelings of inferiority that expressed themselves in the burgher's oscillation between excessive authoritarianism in the home and obsequious submissiveness in public affairs. In Britain and France, the industrial revolution had been preceded by a bourgeois revolution, but Germany's rapid industrialization in the second half of the nineteenth century came after the failures of 1848. In Germany, industrialization was not accompanied by a demand for political power, and therefore it did not lead to the social and political hegemony of a new entrepreneurial class. Instead, the older aristocratic ruling class, consisting largely of Prussian civil servants, officers, diplomats, and landowners strengthened its position. Members of the upper middle class

---

62 Kohn-Bramstedt, *op. cit.,* p. 228.
63 Ralf Dahrendorf, "The New Germanies—Restoration, Revolution, Reconstruction," *Encounter,* XXII, No. 4 (April, 1964), p. 50.

regarded the landed aristocracy with a mixture of scorn and admiration. Acknowledging it as their social superior, they sought to imitate it by acquiring honorary titles – a *von* before one's name or *Hofrat* were prizes thought to be of far more value than parliamentary representation, which was meaningless because of the Reichstag's impotence. At the same time, the burghers looked upon the aristocracy with contempt for its economic backwardness. Furthermore, they reproached the aristocracy for immorality and lack of middle-class virtues. Not a little envy and resentment were mixed into this amalgam of hostility and admiration.

In England, the aristocracy maintained contact with the other strata of the nation by sending its younger sons into business and conferring peerages on successful middle-class businessmen, but in Germany the process was totally one-sided. Although wealthy industrialists and bankers were sometimes admitted into the feudal stratum, the aristocracy held itself proudly aloof from middleclass occupations. Despite the fact that they were being utterly ruined economically, the German aristocracy still enjoyed great social importance. Any aristocrat could belong to the society surrounding the emperor's court in Berlin. Meanwhile, the prosperous German bourgeois, no matter how many honors he might buy, always retained the stigma of social inferiority and political impotence.

The average German *burgher* might occasionally be dissatisfied with the mistakes of the governing class, but he felt certain that he could do no better. Political apathy was the usual pose of the German businessman whose attention was absorbed by his economic achievements. Everyone had his specialty, he felt: the aristocracy could govern best, while he could manage business best. The *burgher's* forefathers had failed to seize political power through a successful bourgeois revolution, and he would not accept political responsibility even if it were offered him on a silver platter. Thus he rationalized his political apathy. He surrounded himself with material comforts and with *Kultur*. His goals became personal rather than public.

Recent studies of Wilhelmian society have stressed the dichotomy between ideals and interests in the prewar years.[64] Although most Germans were proud of the unity of the Reich and of its military might and aggressive imperialistic foreign policy, all of which seemed to guarantee a continuance of material prosperity, many felt that despite the show of wealth and power, Germany was suffering a severe moral decline.[65] International capitalistic expansion in the seventies, and again in the nineties, caused an economic boom in Germany that was accompanied by a marked disintegration of commercial morality. Furthermore, the Empire lacked any inspiring ideal which might have encouraged the citizenry to work for something other than their own selfish profit. Hugo Preuss, one of imperial Germany's most outspoken democrats, recognized the lack of a unifying ideal in the Empire. Writing in 1915, Preuss attempted to explain why, when the war broke out, a deep sense of relief had swept through the German people and they had come to see in it the "birth pangs" of some apocalyptic new era. Preuss found the explanation for this exaltation with the war in the fact that Germany lacked any "great and clear sense of purpose which might have inspired, oriented, and united our public opinion."[66]

After the establishment of the German Empire, this basic deficiency was at first not felt because of the momentousness of the national events themselves; then it was concealed by general preoccupation with all manner of incidental developments. But for some time now this lack of goals has resulted in an oppressively sterile sense of emptiness. Self-preservation and maintenance of what has been achieved is the precondition, but cannot be the sole content of the international and domestic political life of a creative people.[67]

---

64 See, for example, Andreas Dorpalen, "Wilhelmian Germany—A House Divided Against Itself," *Journal of Central European Affairs*, XI (1951), p. 42 ff.

65 Fritz Stern, *The Politics of Cultural Despair, A Study in the Rise of the Germanic Ideology* (Berkeley and Los Angeles, 1962) p. xxviii. See also Georg Steinhausen, *Deutsche Geistesgeschichte von 1870 bis zur Gegenwart* (Halle, 1931).

66 Hugo Preuss, *Das deutsche Volk und die Politik* (Jena, 1915), p. 5

67 *Ibid.*, p. 6.

Within Germany, Preuss warned, this absence of positive, integrating political values and goals had led to catastrophic political results. The rapid development of German industry had created economic and social divisions which, when imposed upon the already existing, unreconciled political animosities, had brought about a political stalemate between uncompromising ideological (*weltanschauliche*) parties. The only ideal behind which all parties would unite was aggressive nationalism, as had become evident in 1914. The country was not borne up by a deep faith in humanity such as that which motivated the French and the English. Instead it saw its primary mission in the preservation and expansion of its power (*Machtdrang*).[68]

In particular, the Germans lacked an adequate conception of the state and its positive and creative role in promoting the common good. If a state is to be more than an agency of protection and domination, it must be part of a nation which instills into it ideals transcending these functions. The Germans had failed to develop a sense of community transcending social cleavages. The Prussian military *Obrigkeitsstaat* had been imposed from above, but it did not represent the fulfillment of the aspirations of the German people and was too narrow to capture the imagination of the whole people. Preuss noted that authoritarianism had constantly throttled the political aspirations of the German people, but he hoped that the advent of democracy would awaken untapped energies and foster an allegiance that the authoritarian state had failed to inspire.[69]

Preuss represented the best side of German liberalism. Unfortunately, most German liberals were content to accept "handouts" from "Father State" and state guarantees of protection against foreign competition and social democracy. Their political immaturity made them almost incapable of creative leadership when the Empire collapsed in 1918.

Scheler himself applied the concept of *ressentiment* directly to Wilhelmian society at several points in his essay. He began by analyzing the sociological background of *ressentiment* and

---

[68] *Ibid.*, p. 8.   [69] *Ibid.*, p. 12.

its diffusion in a society. *Ressentiment* spreads, he said, when there is a "discrepancy between the political, constitutional, or traditional *status* of a group and its *factual power*."⁷⁰ The decisive factor in determining the degree of *ressentiment* likely to develop in a society was the distance between *status* and *power*. Thus, social *ressentiment* would be slight in a democracy because democratic societies tended toward equality of property and social status as well as political rights.⁷¹ *Ressentiment* would probably also be slight in a society that was organized in terms of sharply divided classes or in a hierarchy of estates. In the first case, *ressentiment* would not build up because class hatred and antagonism would be dissipated in strikes or revolutionary violence.⁷² In the second case, that of medieval feudal society, or Hindu society, which was organized according to a strict caste system, *ressentiment* would be unlikely to develop because the members of a hierarchical or caste-society were consciously aware of their places and functions in the social order.⁷³

On the other hand, *ressentiment* would tend to manifest itself in a society like modern Germany where the bourgeoisie lacked political *power* commensurate with their socio-economic *status*, where, as Scheler noted "approximately equal rights (political and otherwise) or formal social equality, publicly recognized, [went] hand in hand with wide factual differences in power, property, and education."⁷⁴ While each had the "right" to compare himself with everyone else, he could not do so in fact. As a result, Scheler found that "independently of the characters and experiences of individuals, a potent charge of *ressentiment*" had been gradually "accumulating in the very structure of [German] society."⁷⁵

Ressentiment was not equally present in all groups in Germany, however. The aristocracy, for example, were not prone to *ressentiment*.⁷⁶ If they became impoverished, the aristocrats could always marry wealth, and they had the greatest political

---

70 *Ressentiment*, p. 50. My italics.
71 *Ibid.*   72 *Ibid.*
73 *Ibid.*   74 *Ibid.*
75 *Ibid.*   76 *Ibid.*, p. 55.

and social status in the Empire. In fact, the German junker governed the Reich through his influence on the kaiser, his participation in the higher echelons of the bureaucracy, the army, and admiralty,[77] and through the Bismarckian constitution which gave the junker control of the Reichstag.

Clearly, Scheler admired the German aristocracy and was loath to criticize it. His one complaint, typical of the supine German bourgeois, was that the aristocrats did not always live up to their noble traditions of being above commerce and industry. Scheler was offended to see that in recent times so many noblemen had become corrupted by the bourgeois lust for material wealth and accumulation of capital. He liked to think of his noblemen romantically living off their lands and heroically protecting their peasants in time of war with a touching sense of paternal responsibility.

When hard-pressed, Scheler had to admit that a certain amount of corruption and decadence had crept into the German nobility during the nineteenth century, but he attributed this decadence to the influence of the bourgeoisie, who had corrupted the aristocracy through intermarriage. It was this mixture of blood (*Blutmischung*) that had lowered the quality of the aristocracy, which Scheler believed was based on a superior biological type.[78] The bourgeoisie had further corrupted the aristocracy by making them almost superfluous economically.[79]

Scheler was greatly concerned about the rehabilitation of a viable aristocracy in modern Germany. He attributed the decadence of the German nobility to the lack of such proper principles of selection as the athletic contests of Greece or the jousting tournaments of the Middle Ages. "Modern civilization is alone in lacking such vital techniques,"[80] Scheler lamented, thinking that these had helped to cultivate and preserve a natural aristocracy in earlier periods of European history. He

---

[77] See Lysbeth Walker Muncy, *The Junker in the Prussian Administration Under William II, 1888–1914* (Providence, Rhode Island, 1944).
[78] *Ressentiment*, p. 143.
[79] *Ibid.*, p. 57.   [80] *Ibid.*, p. 159.

felt that the result of the abolition of these vital techniques was cultural decadence. "Vital and spiritual asceticism has become incomprehensible," Scheler moaned. "Chance governs everything."[81] With "even the last remnants of a social hierarchy" disappearing, Scheler feared that Germany was becoming increasingly atomised, a trend which he was certain could only lead to cultural suicide.[82] The capitalistic socio-economic order produced fine fat merchants and industrial tycoons, but it had brought about a degeneration in the old aristocracy that had no meaningful role in the bourgeois world.

Instead of concluding, as did Max Weber, that if the aristocracy no longer performed a useful socio-economic function, the groups that were more productive in the capitalistic order should acquire political power commensurate with their socio-economic status, Scheler lamented the trend of modern social development as hopelessly decadent. The only solution, Scheler felt, was to reverse the wheels of history and restore the importance of the aristocracy in society.[83] How this might be done remained a moot question. Scheler was unsure himself whether the existing aristocracy could be saved or whether a new "spiritual aristocracy" would have to be cultivated out of the German youth movement. When the war came, Scheler welcomed it as the perfect purge of decadence. War would awaken the leadership potential in both the German aristocracy and among the Germany youth, he hoped.

The sowers of discord, dissatisfaction and *resentment* were to be sought in the lower strata of German society. Scheler felt that these leaders of the "slave revolt in morals" were to be found among the socialists, suffragettes, and social reformers.[84] Scheler was particularly resentful of the latter type: "the 'social politician' who troubles his head about everything except himself and his own business."[85] This "type," which he feared was on the increase, he criticized as "nothing but a poor and empty human being fleeing from himself."[86] The social politician

81 *Ibid.*, p. 160.
82 *Ibid.*
83 *Ibid.*
84 *Ibid.*, p. 126.
85 *Ibid.*
86 *Ibid.*

preached "love of mankind" because he hated himself and was really unable to love either himself or his fellow man!

If the people concerned with social politics, feminism, and socialism were the leaders who stirred up *ressentiment* and fanned the flames of discontent in Germany, who were their followers? Scheler shrewdly observed that "in present-day society *ressentiment* is by no means most active in the industrial proletariat . . . but rather it is rife in the disappearing class of small artisans, in the petty bourgeoisie, and among small officials.[87] Although Scheler held the social politicians in contempt, he did not hesitate to use their findings to prove his point. From the report of the *Verein für Sozialpolitik* on "Training and Advancement of Workers in the Different Branches of Large Industry,"[88] Scheler learned that year by year, as the numbers of skilled industrial workers increased, the skilled workers were being pushed down the ranks of the unskilled because of a relative paucity of jobs demanding skilled labor. This proletarianization of the more highly trained workers, Scheler noted, produced a smoldering mood of bitterness, envy, and *ressentiment* among them.[89] Members of this socio-economic group felt helpless and unable to combat the squeeze in which they were caught. They found solace in Marxian deterministic economic theory.[90]

It was inevitable that capital should gradually become consolidated in fewer and fewer hands, Marx had said. The suffering proletariat should find consolation in the knowledge that the worse conditions became, the sooner they could expect socialism to replace capitalism as a product of natural and inevitable development. If the transition to socialism was inevitable, then reforms were not only unimportant, but there was the danger that they might impede the progress of society to socialism. The radical wing of the Social Democratic Party

[87] *Ibid.*, p. 66.
[88] "Untersuchungen über Auslese und Anpassung der Arbeiter in den verschiedenen Zweigen der Grossindustrie" (Leipzig, 1911), cited by Scheler in *Ressentiment*, p. 63.
[89] *Ressentiment*, p. 57.
[90] *Ibid.*

retained these Marxist ideas right up to 1914, but the revisionists had conquered the main body of the party in the first decade of the twentieth century.[91]

Scheler was aware of the split in the Socialist Party and analyzed the appeal of the extremist or orthodox Marxist plank to the proletarianized skilled workers as being a product of their exasperation and feeling of inability to work through the labor unions, as their unskilled comrades were able to do.[92] Scheler felt that *ressentiment* motivated these dissatisfied workers to indulge in irresponsible criticism of the German Empire. This peculiar kind of *ressentiment* criticism was not inspired by a desire for real improvements in the conditions criticized, Scheler said. Quite the contrary, these men did not want reforms because they gained subtle satisfaction and revenge simply from the activity of criticizing. To improve or reform the criticized conditions would cause even greater discontent, he said, for reforms would destroy the pleasure this group had discovered they could derive from indulging in invective.[93]

The satisfaction derived from indulging in irresponsible criticism was not limited to the radical socialists, however, Scheler felt. The petty bourgeois social politicians, bureaucrats, and the members of most of the bourgeois parties would also be annoyed by a partial satisfaction of their demands or by the constructive participation of their representatives in public life, for such participation would decrease the pleasures they had found in pure oppositionism.[94] The evils that were criticized by the members of the parties were very often nothing but a pretext for indulging in the delights of irresponsible criticism, Scheler said: "We all know certain representatives in our parliaments whose criticism is absolute and uninhibited precisely because they count on never being ministers."[95]

[91] On the schism in the German Social Democratic Party, see Carl Schorske, *German Social Democracy 1905–1917: The Development of the Great Schism* (Cambridge, Mass., 1955).

[92] *Ressentiment*, p. 57.

[93] *Ibid.*, p. 51.   [94] *Ibid.*, p. 52.

[95] *Ibid.*, p. 51.

Although it would be a gross exaggeration to say that all of the criticisms of the Reich, particularly those of such circumspect men as Barth, Naumann, Preuss, and Weber, were motivated by *ressentiment*, Scheler was quite right to castigate the socialist and bourgeois parties for indulging in irresponsible criticism rather than cooperating in a common program of reform. Scheler was also shrewd enough to predict that the political criticisms and reform proposals of the SPD would lose their pungency once they became positively associated with the authority of the state.[96] One of the tragic weaknesses of the Reichstag in imperial Germany was that it did not have sufficient power to inspire in its members a sense of high purpose and responsibility. As Scheler pointed out, the Reichstag, being little more than a debating society, attracted the man of words rather than the man of deeds.[97]

In a footnote added to the text in 1915, Scheler commented:

Our present-day semi-parliamentarianism in the German Empire is conducive to the inner health of the people, since it serves as a discharge mechanism for accumulated *ressentiment*. On the other hand, to the degree that the parliament is eliminated from the function of selecting those men of the nation who have the strongest will and the most acute political intelligence, it attracts only a certain section of the men of *ressentiment:* those who accept that their votes of nonconfidence strengthen the position of the ministers rather than weaken it.[98]

Scheler may have been filled with a certain degree of *ressentiment* against modern society, democracy, and humanitarianism, but perhaps precisely because of his alienated or hostile attitude to the semi-parliamentarianism of the Empire, he became a perceptive critic of two of its chief weaknesses: the irresponsibility of the German political parties, and the deficiency of the Bismarckian constitution for inspiring creative leadership in the German middle classes.

Familiarity with such conservative revolutionaries as Paul

96 *Ibid.*, p. 52.   97 *Ibid.*
98 *Ibid.*, p. 177.

de Lagarde, Julius Langbehn, Oswald Spengler, and Moeller van den Bruck, indicates similarities between Scheler's critique of modernity and their ideas. Like them, Scheler found the modern world decadent and uninspiring, filled with hypocrisy and selfishness. Like them, he idealized a romantic feudal past, and like them he found science, parliamentary institutions, and other attempts to make the social and natural order predictable outrageously offensive. Despite these and other similarities, however, there was one fundamental difference between Scheler and the exponents of the conservative revolution. Scheler's Bavarian Catholic background gave him a Catholic corporatist perspective that prevented him from ever accepting racialist nationalism, the cult of blood and soil, cosmic pantheism, and glorification of chthonian vitalism which provided the pseudo-religious background of the conservative revolutionaries.[99] The similarities between Scheler and the conservative revolutionaries resulted from their common quest for community and from their common belief that human beings needed to experience some closer solidarity than that provided by modern urban industrial society. Like the conservative revolutionaries, Scheler felt that modern society was decadent and in need of renewal; like them, he looked to the youth of Europe as a possible rejuvenating force; but unlike them, Scheler never considered the power of renewal to lie in the Germanic *Volk* or race as such.

4

SCHELER'S analysis of the social psychology of *ressentiment* and of its sociological basis in German society won him the respect of several of Germany's leading sociologists, including Georg Simmel, Max Weber, and Ernst Troeltsch, to say

99 On the ersatz religion of the conservative revolutionaries, see both Fritz Stern, *The Politics of Cultural Despair* (Berkeley and Los Angeles, 1961), and George L. Mosse, *The Crisis of German Ideology* (New York, 1964).

nothing of Werner Sombart who drew upon Scheler's *Ressentiment* in his book, *The Bourgeois,* that Scheler greatly admired.[100] The desire for more intimate contact with these scholars, particularly with Sombart, led Scheler to transfer his locus of operations from Munich and Göttingen to Berlin in 1912.

As usual with Scheler, however, an amorous motive played a role in his decision to move to Berlin, where he became a free-lance journalist and culture critic. During the year after his trial, Scheler's relations with his first wife, Amelie von Dewitz, rapidly deteriorated from embittered separation to outright hostility.[101] One can easily understand Scheler's desire to divorce himself completely and totally from any further connection with this woman. She had successfully ruined his promising career twice, first in Jena and again in Munich. Furthermore, while in Munich, Scheler had fallen in love with Maerit Furtwaengler. Separation from Maerit in 1911, enforced by her mother after the trial, had simply drawn the lovers closer together. Max Scheler corresponded with Maerit throughout the year, while she was living in Berlin, and they decided to marry as soon as he could secure a divorce from Amelie.[102]

It was during this period of waiting, when Scheler knew what he wanted, but was impotent to achieve it, that he wrote *Ressentiment.* Finally, toward the end of 1911, Amelie realized that she could not get Scheler back. They had already been living apart for several years. She therefore determined to make his escape as difficult as possible.

Amelie set the couple an almost impossible task which they had to achieve in a very short time if Max wished to win his freedom.[103] She insisted that Maerit hand over to her the 60,000 gold marks (approximately $30,000 by today's standards)

---

[100] See his review of Sombart's book, *Der Bourgeois,* reprinted in *Vom Umsturz der Werte,* pp. 343–361.

[101] Oral testimony of Maerit Furtwaengler.

[102] This account of Scheler's courtship and marriage to Maerit Furtwaengler is based on the autobiographical sketch that she wrote for us in 1962.

[103] Oral testimony of Maerit Furtwaengler.

which her father had willed to her at his death several years before. The difficulty was that Maerit was to come into her inheritance on August 22, 1912 (her twenty-first birthday). Amelie knew this arrangement, and therefore, insisted that the money be paid by the beginning of February, 1912. She vowed that if he did not have the cash by February, she would never agree to a divorce. Scheler sought everywhere to borrow the money, but he was not a good risk, considering his reputation, and it seemed as though he was not going to be able to meet the deadline set by his wife. At the last minute, Baron von Gebsattl, a close friend of Scheler's in Munich, informed him that a person who wished to remain anonymous had been fascinated by the little melodrama and had decided to put up the money, provided that Scheler promised to pay back the loan on August 22, when Maerit came into her inheritance.[104] He took the money, payed off Amelie, and then initiated divorce proceedings. In the divorce settlement, Scheler agreed to let Amelie keep their young son, Wolfgang. In August, Scheler wired his old friend Dietrich von Hildebrand: "Divorced and engaged! Debt paid. Alleluia!"[105]

During 1912, Scheler lived on advances for *Ethics* from his publisher, Max Niemeyer, but as he wanted to marry Maerit before the end of the year, Scheler had to seek employment where he could find it. He had received a letter from Werner Sombart earlier in the year complimenting him on his analysis of the bourgeois ethos in *Ressentiment*.[106] He decided to visit Sombart, in the hope that Sombart could help him find a teaching post in Berlin. Scheler wrote Maerit a disheartening letter from Berlin; Sombart could offer nothing unless Scheler could regain his *venia legendi* (*right to teach*) which had been suspended after the trial in 1910. Scheler was unable to persuade the Prussian Minister of Culture, Dr. Elster, to return his "union card," and he had to find another occupation.[107]

104 Oral testimony of Baron von Gebsattl.
105 Oral testimony of Dietrich von Hildebrand.
106 Oral testimony of Maerit Furtwaengler.
107 *Ibid.*

After much searching, Scheler finally hit upon journalism. A wealthy Dresden business tycoon who had read *Ressentiment* and been highly impressed by it met Scheler through Sombart and suggested that he edit a high-class cultural review. Temperamentally Scheler was not cut out for the day-to-day responsibilities of editorial work, but he needed a job badly, and the offer seemed attractive. The Dresden tycoon would pay him a good salary and subsidize the review until it got on its feet. There was only one catch, which Scheler found highly offensive. The review was to carry pictorial advertisements of Dresden china and other products that might be bought by the magazine's readers. Scheler obstinately refused to participate in the venture if there were to be any advertising; he felt that by printing these pictures beside or below his articles he would be indirectly acting as a salesman by giving the impression that he personally endorsed the commodities advertised. He explained in a letter to Maerit that from his point of view it would be immoral and a tragic squandering of the talents God gave him to compromise himself in this fashion.[108] He assured his bride-to-be that although they faced an insecure future, he was confident that he would find something else more suited to his own background and ideals. He refused to bring her into contact with the business world — so foreign to them both — in which they could only stumble gropingly like the blind.[109]

When the Dresden merchant realized that Scheler would not cooperate in launching the review as a commercial venture, he withdrew his offer, and Scheler had to resume his job-hunting. The idea of working in journalism apparently appealed to him, for he continued to seek work in this area, and finally secured a post writing abstracts for a sociological journal edited by a Dr. Beck.[110] At the same time, he met Kurt Wolff, the

[108] This information comes from an unpublished letter Scheler sent to Maerit Furtwaengler from Berlin, November 9, 1912. This letter is quoted in my unpublished doctoral dissertation, "Max Scheler: Philosopher, Sociologist, and Critic of German Culture" (University of California at Berkeley, 1965), p. 149.

[109] *Ibid.*

[110] Oral testimony of Maerit Furtwaengler.

publisher of *Die Weissen Blätter,* and agreed to write several studies on the pathology of bourgeois culture along the lines of *Ressentiment* during the next year. One of these articles was Scheler's review of Sombart's *The Bourgeois,* mentioned above.

With these good prospects in the offing, Scheler returned to Maerit in Munich. The couple were married in the Catholic Church across from the University of Munich in Schwabing, but the wedding was depressing. Maerit's marriage to Max Scheler had been bitterly opposed by her family. Ludwig Curtius, an archeologist, voiced the feelings of the family when he toasted: "Thank God that the bride's father is dead and her brother is away in Africa so as not to be present here today."[111] Although he left Munich under this curse, Scheler took his fairy princess on a short honeymoon trip to Salzburg and Prague and stole away with her to Berlin, their home until the outbreak of the war.[112]

Before going on to Scheler's activities during World War I, we will recapitulate his intellectual development between 1910 and 1914. In 1910, having lost his academic post in Munich, Scheler moved to Göttingen where he presented his ideas on phenomenology and value-theory to an admiring circle of students outside the halls of the university. His belief in an absolute and objective hierarchy of values inspired him to analyze modern value attitudes in order to explain modern man's skepticism regarding the existence of any objective absolute value standards. Scheler's desire to unmask modern skepticism as a product of extratheoretical motives — as the result of *ressentiment* among the petty bourgeoisie against their moral superiors, the aristocracy — led him to confront ever more directly the sociological and psychological origins of the *Reichsverdrossenheit* (*weariness of empire*) that beset all classes of German society until the outbreak of the war.

Scheler's contempt for the German bourgeoisie, his hostility to capitalism, and his ambivalent feelings toward the military and feudal aristocracy were typical attitudes of a large

---

[111] *Ibid.*   [112] *Ibid.*

segment of the German middle class before the war.[113] Scheler expressed their self-contempt and their romantic longings for power and prestige commensurate with their economic and social status in his prewar culture criticism. A failure himself, he became the mouthpiece of the dissatisfactions, hopes, and fears of the German burgher who had never succeeded in throwing off the tutelage of the aristocracy and taking upon himself the responsibilities of self-government.

[113] See, for example, the remarks of Theodor Wolff, liberal editor of the *Berliner Tageblatt* in the Wilhelmian period, in *The Eve of 1914*, tr. E. W. Dickes (New York, 1936), p. 312 ff.

3

The Genius of the War

ONE OF THE novelties of World War I, in contrast to previous wars, was the extent to which all the major nations involved relied on the use of propaganda not only to keep up morale in the field and on the home front, but also to win the support of the neutral countries. The problem of fabricating a credible ideology to justify the tremendous demands put upon the nation by the war and to win foreign sympathy was particularly difficult for Germany, because even before the war, in contrast to the Allies, Germans lacked a sense of national purpose. They were not united behind the kaiser as were the British behind the crown and the Russians behind the tsar. Nor could they take pride in a revolutionary–republican tradition such as inspired the French and the Americans. As a result, the Germans met the outbreak of war in 1914 with boyant enthusiasm; it appeared to have welded the nation together. In the so-called war experience many Germans felt that at last they had discovered Germany's world-historical mission. The intellectuals glorified the war as a German revolution, and as a victory within the German soul of the ideas of 1914 over the ideas of 1789.[1]

The ideas of 1914 were an ideological counterpart to the *Burgfrieden* (*domestic peace*) proclaimed by the kaiser in August, 1914. Intellectuals from all sides of the political spectrum found in them a common basis for agreement regardless of their differences over specific war aims. The term *ideas of 1914* was coined by Johann Plenge who welcomed August 4 as the "day of German rebirth," the "day of awakening of a new spirit of common social, economic, and political action in the service of the fatherland."[2] His ideas of 1914 were ideas of German organization and cooperation in which prewar class conflicts were transcended.

In an essay written during the war the historian and philosopher, Ernst Troeltsch, compared the "ideas of 1914" to the "ideas of 1813" and the German national awakening provoked by the Napoleonic occupation.[3] Like the Wars of Liberation, the 1914 war inspired deep ruminations among Germans about their national destiny. The blockade isolated Germany not only commercially but also morally, forcing her to discover untapped inner resources. Compelled by Allied propaganda to consider what they were fighting for and to proclaim their ideals to the world, the Germans came forth with the "ideas of 1914."

Actually, there were not many *ideas* of 1914. One might more accurately speak of the *spirit* of 1914 or the war-experience, for the term *ideas of 1914* really referred to the experience of cooperation and national unity when Germany was mobilized in 1914. As Troeltsch put it: "The profound sig-

---

[1] A good general discussion of the "ideas of 1914" may be found in Hermann Lübbe's *Politische Philosophie in Deutschland, Studien zu ihrer Geschichte* (Basel and Stuttgart, 1963), pp. 173–238. The best account in English appears in Klemens von Klemper's book, *Germany's New Conservatism: Its History and Dilemma in the Twentieth Century* (Princeton, 1957), pp. 47–59.

[2] Johann Plenge, *Der Krieg und die Volkswirtschaft* (Münster, 1915), p. 187.

[3] Ernst Troeltsch, "Die Ideen von 1914" (1916), *Deutscher Geist und Westeuropa*, ed. Hans Baron (Tübingen, 1925), pp. 34–35.

nificance of August, 1914, was that under the pressure of
danger the whole nation was drawn together into an inner
unity such as we had never known before."[4] For Germans who
had deplored the political and ideological disunity of the prewar Reich, the feeling of togetherness brought by the war
seemed to be a religious experience. Troeltsch recalled that in
the autumn of 1914 "Germany prayed . . . and our weapons
were blessed by our prayers."[5] Along with the national awakening and the rediscovery of spirit, Troeltsch felt the most outstanding part of the war experience was "the discovery of the
masses, not merely as a statistical object, but as living human
beings."[6] The war seemed to have healed all the cleavages in
German society. The ideas of 1914 were the expressions of
these new feelings of national unity and community.

Without a doubt the most effective weapon in the allied
propaganda arsenal was the charge that the Central Powers
were aggressive militarists who had violated Belgian neutrality.
Disregarding their Russian ally, the British and French claimed
that the war was a struggle of democracy all over the world
against the Central European authoritarian monarchies. German publicists waged a counterattack against the Allies on two
levels. On the one hand they attempted to present an appealing
image of Germany as the land of poets and philosophers,
musicians and scientists, and as the defender of Western
Christian civilization against the barbaric East. On the other
hand they glorified the German sense of duty and spirit of
cooperation, which they contrasted with the selfishness and
excessive individualism of the Western democracies. These
ideas, contrived to repel the allied propaganda attack, were
propounded by such outstanding German intellectuals as
Thomas Mann,[7] Johann Plenge,[8] Friedrich Meinecke,[9] Werner

4 *Ibid.*, p. 43.   5 *Ibid.*, p. 38.
6 *Ibid.*, p. 41.
7 Thomas Mann, *Betrachtungen eines Unpolitischen* (Berlin, 1919).
8 Plenge, *op. cit.*
9 Friedrich Meinecke, *Die deutsche Erhebung von 1914: Vorträge und
Aufsätze* (Stuttgart and Berlin, 1915) and *Probleme des Weltkriegs: Aufsätze* (Munich and Berlin, 1917).

66 Sombart,[10] and Alfred Weber.[11] One of the most articulate and influential proponents of the ideas of 1914 was Max Scheler.

The War was undoubtedly one of the most important experiences of Scheler's life. His military service took place more in the realm of ideas than on the battlefields of the Marne, the forests of the Argonne, or the Masurian Lakes; nevertheless, the war experience shaped Scheler's evolving political consciousness profoundly, and through his war writings he became a renowned public figure. Before the war, he had made a small mark in the academic world with the first volume of his *Ethics* (1913), and he had reached a somewhat larger public with his neo-Nietzschean critique of bourgeois decadence published in various scholarly and literary journals in the prewar decade. For these readers, Scheler's first widely read book, *The Genius of War*, probably came as no surprise. They might have expected that he, like so many other German intellectuals, would rally to Germany's cause. For most Germans, however, Max Scheler did not exist until they read his eulogy of war in 1915. Having found that Scheler expressed the spirit of 1914 so well, many Germans eagerly awaited his further publications. They did not have to wait long. After 1915, he produced books, articles, and speeches on Germany and her fate in a steady stream that seldom subsided until his untimely death in 1928.

1
———

THE CLOUDS that had long been gathering on the European horizon finally broke in August 1914. When the war came, Max Scheler, like many of his contemporaries, welcomed it with a sense of relief and exaltation. In fact, he later recalled the period of mobilization as a soul-shaking experience:

We could feel in those hours how a peculiar national fate touches the heart of every man — the smallest and the greatest. . . . The

10 Werner Sombart, *Händler und Helden: Patriotische Besinnungen* (Munich and Leipzig, 1915).
11 Alfred Weber, *Gedanken zur deutschen Sendung* (Berlin, 1915).

great course of world history and the innermost desires of the individual were suddenly tied together. Miraculously they became dependent on each other. No more were we what we had been for so long: *alone!* The broken contact between individual, people, nation, world, and God was suddenly reestablished. The interchange of these forces was intensified more than it ever had been by any poetry, philosophy, prayer, or ritual.[12]

Stefan Zweig captured this mood particularly well in his autobiography:

As never before, thousands and hundreds of thousands felt what they should have felt in peace time — that they belonged together. All felt that they were participating in world history, in a moment which would never recur. Each man was called upon to throw himself into the glowing mass, there to be purified of all selfishness. All differences of class, rank, and language were flooded over at that moment by the rushing feeling of fraternity. Strangers spoke to each other in the streets, people who had avoided each other for years shook hands; everywhere one saw excited faces. Each individual experienced an exaltation of his ego, he was no longer the isolated person of former times. He had been incorporated into the mass, was part of the people, and his own person, hitherto unnoticed, had been given meaning.[13]

As Scheler put it, "the fresh air of war has replaced the musty fog of peace, the air of history has replaced the smog of the social situation."[14] *The Genius of War* expressed not only his own elation, but the mood of a good part of the German nation at the war's outbreak. Scheler dismissed any pretense that war might have been avoided; it could only have been postponed, he said, because war between the Central Powers and the materialistic West as well as the barbaric East was inevitable. Germans of every class and profession agreed with Scheler's ideas. His book was not only widely quoted; parts of it were anthologized. *The Genius of War* soon became a minor classic, widely read and beloved by the war generation.

Perhaps a part of the obvious joy and enthusiasm over war

[12] Max Scheler, *Der Genius des Krieges und der deutsche Krieg* (Leipzig, 1915), p. 1.
[13] Stefan Zweig, *The World of Yesterday: An Autobiography* (New York, 1943), p. 223.
[14] *Genius des Krieges*, p. 2.

68 which pervaded the book can be explained by the conditions under which Scheler wrote it. In September 1914, he tried to enlist, but was already forty, and was told that younger men would be called first. Scheler was convinced that the war would be over before he could ever get into it. If he were to take part in the war effort in any way, he would have to do something immediately, before the German armies swept through Paris and wound up the war on the western front. Waiting and hoping to be called every day, Scheler set himself to writing a short piece on "The Spirit of War." It was published in October in *Die Neue Rundschau.*[15] He was probably surprised to find that the armistice had not already been signed before his essay appeared. He sent his wife home to her mother in Munich. The war was going to last longer than he had thought, and he would get into it, he was sure. It was only a matter of days. While he waited, he continued to work out his ideas. By Christmas he had expanded his first article into a 440-page book. *The Genius of War* was dedicated both to the soldiers at the front and to the "unfortunate ones" who had to stay at home.[16]

In Berlin, Scheler had become acquainted with several Jewish writers and thinkers including Max Brod, Gustav Landauer, and Martin Buber. These men were pacifists, and they freely aired their views to Scheler at his home where they occasionally gathered. One evening, Max Brod recalled, the discussion of the causes of war and peace continued long into the night. Scheler listened intently, drawing the others out, but saying little himself. In fact, he concealed his own views so well that his guests assumed that he agreed with them and were

[15] As *Die Neue Rundschau* was one of the most widely circulated cultural journals of the Wilhelmian epoch, many educated Germans had a preview of Scheler's book before it appeared in 1915. This may partly explain its immediate success. By 1917, it had reached a third edition.

[16] Scheler was finally drafted in March, 1915, but was soon discharged because of his poor eyesight. Later in the war, when he might have been inducted despite his eyes, he was absolved from bearing arms because of his lectures in Austria, Holland, and Switzerland for the division of psychological warfare headed by the Catholic Reichstag Deputy, Matthias Erzberger. See the Scheler File in the German Foreign Office Archives at Bonn.

shocked to discover his true position a few days later when his article appeared in *Die Neue Rundschau*. Brod was so incensed at Scheler's duplicity that he wrote a short dramatic sketch as a rebuttal to Scheler's "spiritual militarism" which he called "The Genius of Peace."[17] He gave a copy to Scheler, but the book was never published, because it was so hostile to the popular mood of the hour which Scheler's work had expressed.

Scheler welcomed the war for several reasons. It represented a release of the tensions in Europe, and at the same time it was a scourge of God inflicted upon a sick society, corrupted by the alien spirit of capitalism which had infiltrated Germany from England. In contrast to the atomism of modern life, the war was a return to the "organic roots of human existence."[18] War was not mere physical violence; it was a deeply spiritual thing; in fact, it was the creator of all human progress and even of civilization itself.[19] Peace, on the other hand, was "a constant danger to civilization." "Peace does moral and spiritual damage to the soul and to all civilization, destroying the ethos-bearing vitality of the community which only war can heal."[20]

To understand Scheler's eulogy of war as a "civilizing agent" it must be remembered that his view reflected the cult of strife and violence which ran strongly through German thought since Hegel. According to Hegel, reality is only apparently stable. Actually it is in continual flux, as the contradictions within it continually struggle against each other; it is only natural therefore that nations and individuals should be forever locked in combat. In fact, they are most themselves when they are fighting. War draws out of man his full potential. He becomes the instrument of the Absolute realizing itself through struggle.[21]

If Hegel contributed the idea of self-realization through struggle, Nietzsche, Scheler's mentor in so many things, offered

---

[17] Max Brod, *Streitbares Leben: Autobiographie* (Munich, 1960), p. 89.
[18] *Genius des Krieges*, p. 8.
[19] *Ibid.*, p. 46.   [20] *Ibid.*, p. 103.
[21] See Shlomo Avineri, "The Problem of War in Hegel's Thought," *Journal of the History of Ideas*, XXII, No. 4 (1961), pp. 463–74, and Hans Kohn, "Political Theory and the History of Ideas," *Ibid.*, XXV, No. 2 (1964), p. 303 ff.

the view of war as the great purifier, the antidote to decadence. Disgusted with the materialism and lack of heroism in nineteenth-century Europe, Nietzsche welcomed "all signs that a more manly, a warlike, age is about to begin, an age which, above all, will give honor to valor once again."[22] Nietzsche believed that only war could produce a new elite that might overthrow and replace the "sand and slime of our present civilization and metropolitanism." For Nietzsche all intellectual and cultural activity was a form of sublimated combat. The healthy man was he who constantly struggled to transform himself into what he wished to become. Thought, for Nietzsche, was not the quiet occupation of scholars, but a valorous struggle carried on by "men who are bent on seeking for that aspect in all things which must be *overcome*." "Believe me," Nietzsche told the thinker, "the secret of the greatest fruitfulness and the greatest enjoyment of existence is: to *live dangerously!*"[23] Knowledge was a world of risk, full of dangers and victories.

Scheler found nourishment for his bitterness toward modern society and his delight in the will to power in two other German writers, both more concretely concerned with international affairs than were Hegel and Nietzsche. In his lectures on politics at the University of Berlin, Heinrich von Treitschke popularized Hegel's concept of the state as *power*. Scheler quoted him often in *The Genius of War* as the ultimate authority on *raison d'état*. War was not only an institution ordained by God, and therefore a fundamental characteristic of human history, as Treitschke had written, but it was history's driving force, said Scheler. "War, too, has its nobility, it is the mover of human history." This phrase, taken from Schiller's "The Bride of Messina," adorned the frontispiece of *The Genius of War*, summarizing Scheler's view as he reflected on the war that had galvanized his country into a new sense of solidarity.

22 Friedrich Nietzsche, "The Gay Science," Aphorism 283, in *The Portable Nietzsche*, ed. Walter Kaufman (New York, 1954), p. 97.
23 *Ibid.*

In addition to Trietschke, the political analyst Scheler most admired was General von Bernhardi.[24] War is not only a necessary element in the life of a nation," the General wrote in 1911, "it is an indispensable factor in human civilization and, indeed, the highest expression of the strength and life of truly cultured peoples."[25] For the Germans, Bernhardi was convinced, there was only one alternative: world power or destruction. Scheler agreed. However, in his eyes it was not only world power that was at stake, but the German spirit itself. If the Germans did not recover their lost vitality and heroically drive the British out of Europe and off the seas, the spiritual creativity of the German nation would be smothered forever in bourgeois materialism, greed, and decadence.

War and peace were for Scheler part of the natural rhythm of life, "like inhaling and exhaling, the flow of the tides, storm and sunshine."[26] Throughout the course of history, war had brought men closer together, unifying them far more than the artificial ties of international agreements made during peacetime. War was thus both natural and good. If the world went without war too long, *ressentiment* and hatred began to smolder in the hearts of the nations. Dialectically viewed, peace became the ultimate cause of war. "It is a proven fact that the bourgeoisie is driven to war through long peace, as a sad frantic flight from itself,"[27] asserted Scheler, quoting Dostoevsky. And the advent of war in a decadent era, Scheler believed, could offer only grounds for hope, for war would purge the peoples and clear away the soft comforts accumulated during peacetime. Out of the war a new European man might be born.

[24] Friedrich von Bernhardi (1849–1930) published his book, *Deutschland und der nächste Krieg*, in 1911. It created a sensation abroad as well as in Germany and reached a sixth edition by 1913.

[25] Quoted by Koppel Pinson in his *Modern Germany, Its History and Civilization* (New York, 1954), p. 309.

[26] *Genius des Krieges*, p. 102.

[27] Quoted in *Genius des Krieges*, p. 16.

2
_____

SCHELER'S BOOK was filled with a running diatribe against England. Anglophobia was already a common attitude among many German intellectuals in the late nineteenth century.[28] One of the most vituperative Anglophobes in Germany in 1914 was one of Scheler's friends, Werner Sombart. In his slim volume, *Hawkers and Heroes* (*Händler und Helden*) Sombart contrasted the English commercial attitude with the heroic German spirit, insisting that everything which even resembled European ideas was a definitely un-German phenomenon.[29] Before the war, he had despaired of Germany's ever escaping the encroaching bourgeois spirit, but the war brought him new hope. "The miracle happened; the war came. A new spirit surged forth out of a thousand sources."[30] He gloried in Germany's isolation brought on by the blockade. Now Germans could meditate on the "inexhaustible wealth of Germanism which included every real value that human culture could produce." Germany had a spiritual world-historical mission not simply to purify and revivify herself, but to insure the very survival of human civilization. "Germany is the last dike against the muddy flood of commercialism which threatens to cover all other people because none of them is armed against this threat by the heroic *Weltanschauung* which alone provides protection and salvation."[31]

Although he gradually modified his extremism as he came to understand the war, during the opening six months of the war, Scheler expressed sentiments closely akin to Sombart's.

[28] Pauline Anderson, who wrote *The Background of Anti-English Feeling in Germany, 1890–1902* (Washington, D.C., 1939), found that German Anglophobia was as much a product of Germany's special intellectual and cultural traditions as it was a result of resentment of British maritime supremacy, commercial rivalry, and competition for empire.

[29] Sombart, like Scheler, drew his inspiration from Nietzsche. For a comparison of Sombart's views on war with Nietzsche's, see Hans Kohn, *The Mind of Modern Germany* (New York, 1960), p. 297 ff.

[30] Quoted in Kohn, *op. cit.*, p. 299.

[31] *Ibid.*, p. 300.

Not only was *The Genius of War* filled with bitterness against England and English commercialism; at the end of the book, Scheler included a fifty page appendix "on the psychology of the English ethos and its cant" complete with a table of categories by which the heroic German might best translate British moral concepts. According to Scheler, the British tended to identify "culture with comfort, the warrior with the robber, thought with calculation, reason with economy, God's eternal order with the interests of England, nobility with wealth, power with necessity, [and of course] community with society."[32] The latter category gives a clue to the sociological origins of Scheler's *ressentiment*-laden hatred of England. As in the case of his earlier analysis of the bourgeois human type, Scheler projected onto a seemingly identifiable object all his hatred and misunderstanding of the modernization of German society that took place during his own lifetime.

To Scheler, "regardless of the opinion of the diplomatic corps about its origin, the war was first and last a German-English war."[33] The real goal of Germany's fight with England was to free human civilization itself from the stranglehold of capitalism and its attendant life forms which England had spread across the world. Scheler agreed with Troeltsch that the calculating capitalistic mentality grew up in England under the favorable auspices of the Calvinist ethos in which worldly profit was interpreted as a symbol of God's favor.[34] In the late nineteenth century, Germany had been dragged into economic competition with England with the result that German values and heroism were corrupted by the English calculating spirit.[35]

However, the efficient Germans had beaten the British at their own game. Benefiting from Britain's mistakes, the German industrialists had built upon their own native corporative cartel tradition rather than adopting British laissez-faire policies. By the turn of the century they had not only equalled

---

[32] *Genius des Krieges*, p. 413.
[33] *Ibid.*, p. 73.
[34] Compare Ernst Troeltsch, *The Social Teachings of the Christian Churches* (1912), tr. Olive Wyon (New York, 1960), II, 576 ff.
[35] *Genius des Krieges*, p. 73 and p. 440.

British productivity in numerous commodities, but were threatening to surpass it. Furthermore, the British Empire was rapidly becoming obsolete. The colonial peoples, awakened from centuries of slumber, were now beginning to throw off the British yoke. The real cause of the war, then, was Britain's feeling of insecurity as a world power.[36] British industry felt challenged by German competition. The British Empire was on the verge of disintegration. Even the British fleet of dreadnoughts was becoming obsolete with the advent of the German submarine. Seeing their hegemony threatened by the German competition they had provoked, the British were determined to go down fighting. Hence war between England and Germany was inevitable.

On the other hand, Scheler believed that in the East, Germany and Russia were doomed to eternal conflict. Here he faced a real problem. Where was the greater enemy — in the West where perfidious Albion selfishly ruled the seas, or in the East where Russian autocracy crushed the individual person and reduced men and women to slavery? In the West, Scheler saw an excess of individualism; in the East, he believed there was no sense of individualism at all. He constructed these ideal types in order to contrast them with the so-called true sense of individualism represented by the German idea of freedom.[37]

In actual fact, his images bore little resemblance to the political-social realities of either Great Britain or Russia. By 1914 England had undergone a social revolution in which the nation as a whole had become a progressive state with universal suffrage extended to all citizens over twenty-one. Through reformist social legislation, the injustices of nineteenth-century British capitalism had been significantly eliminated. Fabian socialism seemed to be growing stronger, and a sense of solidarity had developed in the working class that closely resembled the estate-consciousness which Scheler considered to be the prerogative of the German soul.

Russia, likewise, through the process of industrialization

---

36 *Ibid.*, p. 11.   37 *Ibid.*, p. 12.

and modernization, had become increasingly similar to its Western European neighbors. In the last quarter of the nineteenth century, Russian heavy industry and steel production mounted rapidly. French capital spurred investment in new industries. The growing economy drew the raw masses off the land into the cities. By 1905 the labor force was sufficiently organized to carry out a series of successful mass strikes. These workers had grown up in the cities, children of the first generation who had poured into the cities in the 1870's and 1880's. They bore little resemblance to the simple peasants portrayed in the novels of Dostoevsky, Tolstoy, Gogol, and Turgenev from which Scheler, like most Germans of the period, drew his knowledge of Russian society.[38] Scheler's whole analysis of Russian life and character was based on a metaphysical conception of the Russian soul as irrational and instinctual. Beginning from this premise, Scheler believed that Russia and the West were doomed to face each other in eternal conflict.

In an article entitled "Eastern and Western Christianity" published in *Die Weissen Blätter* in 1915, Scheler more fully explored the metaphysical and religious differences between Russia and the West; he believed these were the ultimate causes of inevitable conflict between the two "culture spheres."[39] He was convinced that "a clear understanding of Russian Christianity and its ecclesiastical structure" was more important for understanding Russian thought and politics than knowledge of contemporary intellectual currents in Russia. "Next to the Russian language itself, Orthodoxy alone is the basis of that central

---

[38] In his article "Die Auffassung Dostojewskis im Vorgriegsdutschland," *Zeitschrift für Sozialforschung*, III (1934), pp. 344–381, Leo Löwenthal showed how this conception of the "Russian soul" provided a happy escape for Germans in the prewar years as they watched their society become ever more rationalized. In Dostoevsky's novels, political and social problems were transposed into questions of self-consciousness. To Scheler and his contemporaries, the folk-community and peasant Christ portrayed by the Rusian writers represented the sense of togetherness that the war had awakened in Germany.

[39] Max Scheler, "Über östliches und westliches Christentum," *Die Weissen Blätter, eine Monatsschrift*, II:4 (October, 1915). Reprinted in Scheler's *Schriften zur Soziologie*, pp. 99–114.

unity we call Russia."[40] Scheler was so convinced that Orthodoxy was the primary expression of the "Russian soul" that he assured his readers that even if the tsar and autocracy should be overthrown by a revolution, Orthodoxy would remain. For the Russian, according to Scheler, "Orthodoxy precedes and lies at the basis of all forms of social and political organization." "The act of ruling is felt by both ruler and ruled to be rooted in God, who alone can overcome the burning shame that one person should rule another."[41] *God and the Tsar* not *Russland Russland über alles* was the formula in which the Russian understood his unity. Rejecting the Marxist interpretation of Orthodoxy as an ideology used by the Russians to mask their imperialistic designs, Scheler reversed the relationship. He interpreted Russian nationalism and pan-slavism as ideologies cloaking the real Russian "organic Christianity and its missionary thrust."[42]

Russia's fateful mission was to expand into Constantinople and the Balkans to protect the Orthodox believers who had lived there ever since Ivan III had brought his Byzantine bride home in 1483 and had placed the two-headed Byzantine eagle on his shield.[43] On the other hand, it would always be Germany and Austria's historical fate to stand as the bulwark of Western civilization against the onslaught of the barbaric Slavic hordes into the Balkans.[44] Scheler had no illusions about pan-Slavism. The threat was from Russian nationalism, and all pan-Slavist propaganda was nothing but an ideological mask imported by westernized Russian intellectuals to justify Russia's spiritual and imperial mission. Therefore, armed conflict in the East was inevitable. The longer Germany and Austria waited to strike, the more dangerous would Russia and her allies become.

However, neither this war nor a series of wars could ever settle the basic conflict between East and West symbolized in

---

40 *Schriften zur Soziologie*, p. 99. Compare *Der Genius des Krieges*, p. 268.
41 Scheler, *Schriften zur Soziologie*, p. 99.
42 *Ibid.*, p. 100.
43 *Genius des Krieges*, p. 169.
44 *Ibid.*, p. 170.

the Eastern question.[45] Here Scheler saw traces of the tragic nature of history, and ultimately of human existence. Both sides were "right" from their respective points of view, and neither could ever compromise or abandon its claims without betraying its own God-given mission embodied in its whole cultural and religious tradition.

As the conflict in the East was irreconcilable, the situation in the West was all the more important. France, after all, shared in the spiritual and cultural tradition of western Christendom. Germany's disagreements with France and Belgium were primarily political, and spiritual only to the extent that these western democratic nations were heretics, traitors to the true Christian monarchic tradition which Germany was heroically defending.[46] No matter who won the war, France and Germany would later reconcile their differences in the face of the Russian threat.[47] France would be easy to bring around, for her conflicts with Germany only went back a generation, to 1870. When the rule of this generation passed, new ties would be developed again.

With England, however, matters stood differently. The differences between Anglo-Saxon *civilization* and German *Kultur* went back more than a century. Scheler questioned whether in the postwar world England could be included in the European community or whether she might not better strengthen her ties with her materialistic leviathan offspring across the Atlantic.[48] No matter how hard the Russians bled her, Germany must avoid the temptation of making peace in the West; her mission, above all, lay in purging France and England of the spirit of *pleonexie* (*greed*) that had begun to spread and threaten Western European civilization.[49]

Should Germany betray her mission, the results would be

---

45 *Ibid.*, p. 172.   46 *Ibid.*, p. 173.
47 *Ibid.*, p. 174. Scheler believed that although he could not yet point to a real European consciousness, the war would create this awareness on the part of European man. Europe would then become the defender of western values against the Russian drive toward the West.
48 *Ibid.*, p. 175.   49 *Ibid.*, p. 178 ff.

catastrophic.[50] The globe would be divided into three huge empires: (1) a Mongolian empire under the leadership of Japan with the motto "Asia for the Asians"; (2) a Russian empire expanding over the West in which some elements of European civilization might be preserved; and (3) a more or less mechanized America that, having abandoned Europe as its model and wise old conscience, would rapidly run through all its special cultural potentiality and burn itself out as a technocracy. England might at best become a politically free tool of a Russian Europe! Germany, Austria, France, and Italy, crippled politically as well as culturally would probably join Spain who would do nothing but look back wistfully at her once glorious past. Like the Indian in Ruth Benedict's famed parable, Europe would then only gaze astonished at the broken potsherd that once was her living culture.[51]

3

D U R I N G the first months of the war, German intellectuals continued to justify Germany's imperialistic drive for world power in the same terms they had used during the long cold-war period before 1914. Germany had been chosen to "liberate" Europe from the yoke of English maritime hegemony and to re-establish a more "realistic" balance of power in Europe.[52] Gradually, however, the conduct of war on the European continent produced great confusion in Germany's spiritual armory which had been largely a rationalization of German naval expansion. The German publicists had been able to present Germany as the advocate of the underprivileged nations across the seas, but how could they possibly justify invasion of Belgium

---

[50] *Ibid.*, p. 247.

[51] Ruth Benedict, *Patterns of Culture* (8th ed., New York, 1958), p. 34.

[52] On the whole problem of Germany's justification of her aggressive policies both before and during the war, see the excellent study by Ludwig Dehio, *Germany and World Politics in the Twentieth Century*, tr. Dieter Pevsner (London, 1959).

with the same propaganda and expect to be believed by the nations of Europe? German public opinion agreed on the ultimate aim of freedom of the seas, which meant the destruction of English maritime supremacy, but on the immediate war aims there was great confusion.[53]

Much of the discussion of German war aims was complicated by the fact that whereas the broad masses of the population wanted a peace by mutual consent, the military aristocracy which ruled Prussia wanted a victorious peace in which they saw a guarantee of their privileges.[54] Although most Germans accepted the kaiser's proclamation that Germany was fighting a *defensive* war, in 1915, as military successes bolstered their confidence, middle-class Germans supported the expansionism of the ruling elite. German professors and other civil servants jointed their voices to the general hue and cry for conquest of territory from Belgium, to the Baltic, to the Balkans. In May came the Petition of the Six Associations and, in July, the Petition of the 1,347 Professors, Diplomats, and Government Servants. These remarkable documents conjured up visions of mountainous indemnities; long years of military occupation of allied territories, a Germanized Belgium, Poland, and Baltic; possession of Belfort, Verdun, the coast of Flanders, Longwy, and Briey; as well as the destruction of England's power overseas. At times these terms were characterized as the prize of

[53] On German war aims, see the now classic work by Hans Gatzke, *Germany's Drive to the West: A Study of Western War Aims During the First World War* (Baltimore, 1950); and the recent controversial study by Fritz Fischer, *Griff Nach der Weltmacht* (Düsseldorf, 1961). On German plans for expansion in the East, see Henry Cord Meyer, *Mitteleuropa in German Thought and Action, 1815–1945* (The Hague, 1958), p. 198 ff.; and Werner Conze, "Nationalstaat oder Mitteleuropa: Die Deutschen des Reiches und die Nationalitätsfragen Ostmitteleuropas im ersten Weltkrieg" in *Deutschland und Europa: Historische Studien zur Völker und Staatenordnung des Abendlandes* (Düsseldorf, 1951), pp. 201–232; and Erwin Hölzle, *Der Osten im ersten Weltkrieg* (Leipzig, 1944).

[54] Arthur Rosenberg, *The Birth of the German Republic, 1871–1918*, tr. Ian F. D. Morrow (New York, 1962), pp. 88 ff. Rosenberg interprets the expansionist war aims of the German military leaders and large industrialists as an attempt to "erect a barricade against the demands of the working class" (p. 89).

victory, compensation for losses; at other times as an insurance, required by strategy, against another war.[55]

In contrast to the confusion in German war aims, from the very beginning of the war the Allies proclaimed their stirring demands for German evacuation of Belgium, Strassbourg, Trieste, and Constantinople. Already in the winter of 1914 the British had launched a vigorous propaganda campaign against the Central Powers.[56] Britain's propaganda was designed to shore up her own soldiers' morale and to win the sympathy of the neutral nations for the allied cause. In England, the Germans were portrayed as unscrupulous warmongering barbarians in both the popular press and in scholarly books and articles designed to appeal to the general public. Taking advantage of an already existing dislike for the Germans in the world-at-large, the British publicists argued that the destruction of Germany was not only to the general interest of humanity, but the moral inferiority of the Germans demanded it as well.[57]

The collection of essays entitled *War and Rebuilding*, which Scheler published in 1916, analyzed Germany's mission in relation to the other European nations.[58] Specifically, Scheler took up the allied criticism of Germany as "militaristic." The author of *The Genius of War* not only accepted the appelation of militarist, he revelled in it,[59] rejecting the excuses offered by

55 Frank P. Chambers, *The War Behind the War, 1914–1918: A History of the Political and Civilian Fronts* (New York, 1939), p. 124. Compare Gatzke, *op. cit.*, p. 37, and Klaus Epstein, *Matthias Erzberger and the Dilemma of German Democracy* (Princeton, 1939), p. 100 ff.

56 On allied propaganda during World War I see George G. Bruntz, *Allied Propaganda and the Collapse of the German Empire in 1918*, Hoover War Library Publications No. 13 (Stanford, 1938) and the earlier German account by Hans Thimme, *Weltkrieg Ohne Waffen, Die Propaganda des Westmächte gegen Deutschland, ihre Wirkung und ihre Abwehr* (Stuttgart and Berlin, 1932).

57 Typical examples of the British critique of German barbarism were: J. W. Allen, *Germany and Europe* (London, 1914); J. C. Cramb, Ramsey Muir, *Britain's Case Against Germany* (Manchester, 1914); and the collection of essays by R. W. Seton-Watson, J. Dover Wilson, Alfred E. Zimmern and Arthur Greenwood, *The War and Democracy* (London, 1914).

58 *Krieg und Aufbau: Aufsätze* (Leipzig, 1916). Most of this book is reprinted in *Schriften zur Soziologie* (2nd ed. Bern, 1963).

59 Max Scheler, "Über Gesinnungs-und Zweckmilitarismus. Eine Studie zur Psychologie des Militarismus," *Schriften zur Soziologie*, p. 187.

moderate liberals who claimed that Germany had developed a strong army only in order to hold the frontier against the barbarians in eastern Europe. Scheler admitted that geographical factors may have played a role, but the decisive factor in the development of German militarism was *spiritual*. Militarism was simply the natural organic form in which the Prussian spirit expressed itself[60] By *militarism* Scheler meant not simply *aggressiveness*. Militarism was the combination of the German heroic spirit and the Prussian spirit of discipline and order. Scheler characterized the Prussian spirit, which he believed had become the *German* spirit after 1870, not as aggressive and warlike, but as "the spirit of order, duty, organization, punctuality, discipline, and thoroughness." Being warlike was not peculiar to Prussia; it was a characteristic of the German people in general. Through Prussian influence this natural vitality had been disciplined. Scheler cited as proof that "Germans are warlike by nature" the fact that during the periods of their history when they had no one else to fight with, they fought with each other. As the Empire was ruled largely by members of the Prussian military aristocracy, it was only natural, Scheler argued, that militarism became the common spiritual attitude (*Geisteshaltung*) of the German people. The spiritual was so much more influential than the geographical, he believed, that even if the Germans lived in the British Isles, their fundamental Prussian-German attitude would not change one iota. According to Scheler's social theory, the moral and intellectual attitude of the ruling class set the moral tone for the whole society. In England, the commercial adventurer was the culture-ideal; in Germany, the heroic disciplined military leader was the social model for the elite, and therefore, in turn, for the society.[61]

Scheler considered German militarism to be a "work of art," the highest cultural expression of the German soul.[62] Military men in the allied nations tried to emulate German

60 *Ibid.*, p. 189.
61 "Militarismus," p. 187.
62 *Ibid.*

discipline and order, but they inevitably failed because they lacked the German military spirit. Their militarism was merely a utilitarian construct, thrown together in times of national crisis.[63] Bourgeois comforts had so softened the British that they had lost even the ideal of a heroic warrior caste. The French, closer to the Rhine, were not quite so badly off. Before the war, members of the French youth movement, like their German neighbors, had begun to cast off the cloying comforts of bourgeois civilization, seeking to return to a more manlike existence. During their long sojourns in the mountains and forests, hiking, singing, and vowing eternal fidelity to one another, the youth of both countries had rediscovered a heroic view of life.[64]

In 1914 these young men had found themselves on opposite sides of the battlefield, but in the war they would discover their common European heritage and their common enemy, the European bourgeoisie. The "patriotism of Europe" would be born out of the blood and iron of the war. It would lead to a spiritual revolution and the birth of a new type of man.[65] German militarism, as a spiritual attitude and a way of life, could point the way to this new heroic human type. Having purged Europe of the calculating, comfort-loving capitalistic spirit, the French and Germans would join hands as spiritual brothers. In prophesying this moral revolution, Scheler was not alone. Such German intellectuals as Ernst Jünger, Oswald Spengler, and Walter Flex believed that militarism as a way of life was the wave of the future.

Scheler argued that Germany's *spiritual militarism* (*Gesinnungsmilitarismus*) offered less of a danger to world peace than the *instrumental militarism* (*Zweckmilitarismus*) of the Western democracies. The military in these nations was at the beck and call of the ruling class of industrialists and financiers who lacked the sense of discipline and restraint of the Prussian military elite.[66] In the last forty years, Germany's politics had

---

63 *Ibid.*, p. 188.
64 *Genius des Krieges*, p. 277.
65 "Militarismus," p. 199.
66 *Ibid.*, p. 192.

been "strictly the politics of preparedness and of peace more than any other European nation."[67] Before the war, the emperors William II and Nicholas II had worked harder than any of the Western bourgeois diplomats for peace. Thus, Scheler idealized autocracy and military aristocracy as if he were living in the age of Frederick the Great. Monarchs had been trained in the art of ruling. They had not wanted the armaments race which led to the war. The responsibility for this lay squarely on the shoulders of the Western bourgeoisie.[68]

To British propaganda that the war was essentially a struggle of world democracy against the forces of reaction, Scheler replied that the concept and practice of democracy was not uniform everywhere but varied widely from country to country. Every country, including Germany, developed that form of democracy which was consistent with its own national character. The Western nations would be as wrong in imposing their form of democracy on the Central Powers as would the Germans in imposing their form of militarism on the West.[69]

Whereas Scheler's first war book was directed against England, his second was aimed primarily at France. Written in the second half of 1915, the year in which the Central Powers attained their most spectacular military victories, the essays in *War and Rebuilding* reflected Scheler's confidence in a German victory. Before the German cannons had been turned on Verdun in 1916, Scheler had leveled his intellectual artillery on the citadel of the French spirit, the idea that the French national mission was to spread bourgeois democracy across the world, an idea exemplified in the writings of Emil Boutroux, philosopher and president of the French Academy.

On May 29, 1915, Boutroux had delivered a lecture in Lausanne, Switzerland, on "the French National Idea,"[70] one of many sponsored by the French propaganda bureau. It was

---

[67] *Ibid.*   [68] *Ibid.*
[69] Scheler, "Der Geist und die ideellen Grundlagen der Demokratien der grossen Nationen" (1915), *Schriften zur Soziologie*, p. 161.
[70] Cf. Emil Boutroux, "La conception française de la nationalité," *Bibliothèque Universelle et Revue Suisse*, LXXX, No. 238 (1915).

published, widely circulated, and reached Scheler's attention during the summer. His reply appeared in *Der Neue Merkur* in August.[71] Boutroux had argued that the French stood for the freedom and equality of all nations in 1914 just as they had stood for the principles of liberty and equality in 1789. France's mission was to extend democracy and freedom across the world.

Scheler's critique of Boutroux was based on his opposition to the democratic idea of popular sovereignty. The nation was not simply the result of the collective will of its citizens, as Boutroux and many Frenchmen believed; it was a "spiritual personality" in its own right.[72] As such, it expressed itself primarily in the moral and intellectual sphere, in the realm of culture rather than in the realm of politics. The state, however, must have the power to guarantee the moral autonomy and freedom of the groups within it, the family, corporations, and the people. Under its protection, each of these was supposedly able to develop to its full potentiality. The state "draws forth out of the nation those powers slumbering deep within it, waiting to be awakened."[73]

The trouble with the French was that they denied any "objective value differences between nations." All nations were not equal in cultural value just as they were not equal in power.[74] The French would have liked to extend their idea of freedom and equality across Europe. They failed to recognize that their world mission would inevitably lead them into conflict with other nations who did not envisage their national essence in the French form. The Germans, on the other hand, believed "that nations deserve freedom and world power only to the extent that they represent vital community-building and spiritual culture."[75] As each nation's value was different, and there was no measure for respective values, only historical ac-

---

[71] Max Scheler, "Das Nationale in der Philosophie Frankreichs," *Der Neue Merkur*, II, No. 8 (August, 1915). Reprinted in *Schriften zur Soziologie, op. cit.*, pp. 121–157.

[72] *Schriften zur Soziologie*, p. 122.

[73] *Ibid.*, p. 124.   [74] *Ibid.*, p. 127.

[75] *Ibid.*, p. 129.

tion indicated a nation's value in the eyes of God.[76] Historical action never created a nation's value, however; it simply revealed it by giving it political or cultural expression.

The conclusion that Scheler drew was that France had no right to demand that the Central Powers adopt bourgeois liberalism and democracy. The German spirit was oriented toward diversity and cultural pluralism, as seen in the writings of the great German philosophers and poets. In contrast to France, Germany had not one great tradition, but many traditions.[77] He cited Leibnitz, Spinoza, Kant, Fichte, Goethe, and Lotze who held different metaphysical principles, but agreed that man, as a microcosm, contained within himself the whole diversity of reality. Nor did the Russian national idea fit into the French formula.[78] The Russians believed in a sentimental brotherliness, in the unity of an ecclesiastically and religiously directed world state in which Russia as an independent nation would disappear. The Russian national mission, then, was to sacrifice Russia for humanity.[79] Scheler feared the loving clutches of the Russian bear even more than Western aggressive expansionism. "If you won't be my brother, I'll clobber you," expressed the Russian spirit of brotherly love. Russia might not wish to lead or to rule the world, but nevertheless, Scheler did not relish Germany's being offered up as part of the "sacrifice for the establishment of the theocratic world state."[80] Regardless of whether Russian messianism adopted an authoritarian or a democratic covering, it remained inspired by the same brutal naïve barbarism and lack of respect for the individual. Scheler's attitude to Russia betrayed a combination of fear and admiration. Although he feared Russian messianic expansionism, he admired the sense of community which he believed to be characteristic of the Russian soul. In the West, a politics based on the spirit of brotherly love had been conservative and patriarchical throughout the nineteenth century; in Russia, the Chris-

---

76 *Ibid.*, p. 130. 77 *Ibid.*, p. 138.
78 *Ibid.*, p. 125. 79 *Ibid.*, p. 128.
80 *Ibid.*, p. 130.

tian spirit of love had inspired a revolutionary movement as well as the official policies of the Russian autocracy.[81] After the February revolution in 1917, Scheler hoped that Russian socialism would point the way to a new social order that would overcome both the individualism of western capitalism and the atheism of western socialism.[82]

What were Scheler's ideas of Germany's national mission? In *The Genius of War*, he waxed eloquent on the subject, but in the essays in *War and Rebuilding*, he betrayed doubts. The English, the French, and the Russians knew what they were fighting for. The Germans, Scheler noted with distress, were continually divided among themselves. Their cultural pluralism might provide a model for a postwar European federation, but as a people the Germans were too "simple, direct, and true" to have a national consciousness as well developed as the other nations. All one could say of the Germans was that they did not believe in the equal value of all nations. Looking for Germany's national mission, Scheler was forced on the defensive. "We Germans sincerely believe that nations, like individuals, have varied unique natures and are of varied value."[83] Germany was not out to impose its political and social forms on other nations, but simply to defend its own right to exist according to its own traditional forms.[84]

By the end of 1915, Scheler had abandoned the monstrous simplification of the war presented in *The Genius of War*. In his essays on nationalism, militarism, and democracy, although justifying the German autocratic system, he gave a less chauvinistic interpretation to the meaning of the war than he had held in 1914. In little more than a year, he had become disillusioned with Germany's "community-building and unifying powers" that he had eulogized in August, 1914. The *Burgfrieden*, declared by the kaiser at the opening of the war, had begun to dissolve. Faced with the reappearance of the old party

---

81 *Ibid.*, pp. 169–170.
82 *On the Eternal in Man*, p. 431.
83 *Schriften zur Soziologie*, p. 129.
84 *Ibid.*

antagonisms reflected in the discussion of war aims, Scheler moved away from nationalism and began to seek in the supranational church the "community-building powers" he had failed to find in the German nation.

In doing so, Scheler moved away from the mainstream of the ideas of 1914. Instead of justifying the German cause, he began to look for a way out of the war that was tearing European civilization apart. In 1914, he had welcomed the war as a *liberation from decadence.* Now he saw it as a *revelation of decadence.*[85] If Europeans did not quickly reaffirm the spiritual unity of European civilization and rebuild a new united Europe on their commonly shared Christian tradition, Europe would destroy herself in internecine strife.[86]

In *The Genius of War* Scheler spoke of the Asian criticism of the European war. He cited, for example, the writings of a Chinese conservative, Hung Ming Ku, whose book *The Spirit of China and the Road to Peace*, published in German in 1915,[87] warned of the impending collapse of European civilization. Hung Ming Ku attributed the war to excessive mob worship in Europe. In fact, it was this mob worship, imported to China from the West, that had brought on the revolution and the present nightmare of a Republic of China. The only thing that could wipe out this disease which had spread from Europe and begun to infect civilization everywhere was the adoption of the Chinese ethic of loyalty and obedience: "If you want to save civilization, don't call in the priest or soldier; call in the Chinaman. He is an invaluable asset to civilization because he is a person who costs the world nothing to keep in order."[88] Scheler agreed with this Chinese thinker that the revolt of the masses was threatening civilization, but he turned to Catholicism instead of to Confucianism for his solution. In short, Europe

[85] *Krieg und Aufbau*, p. 196.
[86] *Ibid.*, p. 347.
[87] Hung Ming Ku, *Der Geist des chinesischen Volkes und der Ausweg aus dem Krieg* (Jena, 1915). The English translation, *The Spirit of China* (Peking, 1915) is used here.
[88] *Ibid.*, p. 165.

could only be saved if European man repentantly returned to the loving arms of Mother Church as Scheler himself had done.

4

BECAUSE most of Max Scheler's thought and action during the remainder of the war was related to his Catholicism, a short account of his reconversion may be helpful here. Although Max Scheler had never formally abandoned the Roman Catholic faith, from the time of his marriage to the divorceé Frau von Dewitz, in 1895, until his separation from her in Munich in 1910, Scheler had withdrawn from participation in the sacramental life of the Church. His first step back had been his marriage to Maerit Furtwaengler at Christmastime in the magnificent Ludwig's Church, near the University of Munich, in 1912.

Just as his first approach to the Church had been largely emotional, stimulated by the lovely music and baroque pageantry of the Munich May Devotions to the Virgin, and by the sweetness of the young maidens who took him there,[89] so too in his second conversion *agape* was prompted by *eros*. Joy and peace welled up inside him, opening his heart to the Christchild once more, but it took several years of wedded bliss to soften his heart to the point of complete conversion.

Steeped in the writings of the early Church fathers, introduced to him through the works of the early nineteenth-century Tübingen theologian, Johann Adam von Möhler,[90] Scheler eventually found his way to the Benedictine Abbey of Beuron, near Freiburg-at-Breisgau where, in the winter of 1915, he made a general confession and re-entered the sacramental life of the

---

[89] For an account of Scheler's first conversion, see Oesterreicher, *op. cit.* (New York, 1953), p. 141. Father Oesterreicher seems prone to overestimate the seriousness of this first conversion, but his account of the circumstances of the conversion is accurate, as far as we have been able to determine.

[90] Johann Adam von Möhler, *Patrologie* (Regensburg, 1840) and *Symbolik* (Regensburg, 1832).

Church. Armed with the bright weapons of obedience and love, Scheler marched forth from his Benedictine retreat to attack the windmills of modern European civilization. Full of the enthusiasm of the repentant prodigal, Scheler asked himself, as he gazed at war torn Europe: "What guiding ideal emerges from a comparison of actual conditions with the eternal aspirations of Christianity?"[91]

From the beginning Scheler had been convinced that "the true meaning of the war must be sought on other than political and economic grounds."[92] Whereas in 1914 he had maintained that Germany's mission was to preserve the "spiritual unity of European civilization," he now proclaimed that the war represented "God's call to European man to turn from his sinful ways." A merely political and economic interpretation of the war failed to take account of "the purifying meaning of this first experience of the whole of mankind."[93]

Scheler never tired of pointing to the irony of the fact that the whole international communications network linking the remotest parts of the earth together had not preserved peace, as its creators had expected, but had simply provided a more efficient means of spreading self-righteous nationalistic propaganda and hatred. The war had brought all the nations together in hatred of the Central Powers. It was not so much a war against Germany, as a revolution against the spiritual values she was defending.[94]

By the end of 1915, Scheler had begun to doubt that Germany or any other single nation could provide the regenerative force necessary to overcome the national antagonisms expressed in the war. These conflicts were based on *spiritual* rather than merely political oppositions, and the entirely different world views involved could only be reconciled in a spiritual body transcending the particularism of national states. What worldwide organization could better serve this purpose than the Church Universal?

91 *On the Eternal in Man*, p. 363.
92 *Krieg und Aufbau*, p. vi.
93 *Ibid.*   94 *Ibid.*, p. 5.

During the last years of the war, Scheler became an influential spokesman in Catholic circles for the peace program of the Catholic parliamentary leader Matthias Erzberger.[95] Working for Erzberger's propaganda office, Scheler lectured to German-speaking Catholics in Switzerland and Holland, trying to win the sympathy of the neutral countries for the Central Powers. Speaking to large audiences in Vienna, Karlsruhe, and Berlin, Scheler lectured on such topics as "Germany's Mission and the Catholic World View,"[96] "The Contemporary Relevance of the Christian Idea of Community,"[97] and "The Renewal of European Culture."[98] These speeches, as well as a series of articles entitled "Sociological Reorientation and the Responsibilities of German Catholics,"[99] reached a large audience when they were published in *Hochland*, Germany's leading Catholic monthly review, edited by Scheler's friend, Karl Muth.[100]

95 Heinrich Lutz, in his book *Demokratie im Zwielicht. Der Weg der deutschen Katholiken aus dem Kaiserreich in die Republik 1914–1925* (Munich, 1963), showed that the evolution of Scheler's political views in 1916–17 corresponded to a general re-orientation of Catholic attitudes to the war. As far as we know, Prof. Lutz is the first person to have utilized the materials relating to Scheler's propaganda activities in the Scheler File in the German Foreign Office Archives. We are grateful to him for calling our attention to this file and for making his microfilm copy of it available to us. Letters in this file from Ago Freiherr von Maltzan, at the German Embassy in The Hague, to Imperial Chancellor Graf Hertling in July, 1918, indicate that Scheler's speeches boosted the morale of interned prisoners of war in Leiden and had a remarkably favorable effect among Dutchmen as well. Scheler's propaganda activities were effective enough for Maltzan to request permission to extend Scheler's stay in Holland for three more months.

96 "Deutschlands Sendung und der katholische Gedanke" was published in the series *Vom katholischen sozialen Geist, Programmschriften der Sozialen Frauenschule des katholischen Frauendienstes* (Berlin, 1918).

97 This speech, first presented to the Katholische Frauenbundes in Karlsruhe, Nov. 13, 1916, and published in *Hochland*, XIV (March, 1917), was reprinted in Scheler's study of the philosophy of religion, *On the Eternal in Man* (1921), p. 357 ff.

98 "Vom kulturellen Wiederaufbau Europas," *Hochland*, XV (Feb.–March, 1918). Reprinted in *On the Eternal in Man*, p. 403 ff.

99 "Soziologische Neuorientierung und die Aufgabe der deutschen Katholiken nach dem Krieg," *Hochland*, XIII (January–June, 1916). Reprinted in *Krieg und Aufbau*, pp. 196–373, and in *Christentum und Gesellschaft* (Leipzig, 1924).

100 For Scheler's relations with Carl Muth, see Carl Muth, "Begegnungen: Hinterlassene Notizen," *Hochland*, XLVI (October, 1953), pp. 13–17.

From the spring of 1917 until after the German surrender in November, 1918, Max Scheler's writings and speeches were filled with one basic theme: Europe must repent of the bourgeois revolt against God symbolized by the war and reunite in Christian solidarity. Only a general repentance of European man could provide the regenerative forces necessary for the redemption of European culture. This theme had already come to the fore in Scheler's "Sociological Reorientation" essays in *Hochland,* but in 1917–1918 it predominated all other considerations in his writings.

In the spring of 1917, Scheler called for a general confession of common guilt among all the belligerents. There must be a *universal repentance.* Europe had grown progressively decadent since the Renaissance and the advent of bourgeois man, but complete repentance could effect Europe's moral rejuvenation. The war had been God's punishment for man's greed. Restitution for the revolt against God had been made. If men would but confess their guilt, they could reunite and rebuild Europe on a cooperative basis. "Young forces, as yet guiltless, lay dormant in every soul, smothered by the tangled growths of oppressive guilt." If European man would but tear away the undergrowth, these regenerative forces would rise up of their own accord. The first step, however, was for European man to recognize his guilt. Too often he self-righteously blamed his enemy without recognizing his own guilty part in the conflagration. Scheler compared European man to Faust, storming through the world in secret flight from the burden of his own history. But "history comprehended frees us from the power of history."[101]

Of what must European man become conscious and repent? To Scheler the answer was clear. European man must recognize that Europe as a whole was no longer Christian. "Either one admits Europe's deep and widespread falling away from Christ and confesses that his representatives have made an inexcusable compact with the spirit of anti-Christ, or one confesses that

[101] "Zur Apologetik der Reue," *Summa,* I (1917), pp. 53–68. Reprinted in *On the Eternal in Man,* p. 33 ff.

Christianity is bankrupt!"[102] The question of distribution of war-guilt was minor. Both sides were guilty. "What do I care *who* is guilty among the members of a family when I can see from afar that the whole family is rotten to the core?" All the nations of Europe had been seduced into worshiping the false bourgeois gods of nationalism and imperialism.[103] If nationalistic passions, capitalism, the system of radical mistrust, the arms race, and imperialistic dividing up of the world regardless of European solidarity were compatible with the spirit of Christianity, then, Scheler admitted, Christianity was bankrupt. In fact, however, it was not Christianity but the bourgeois spirit that had been proved bankrupt by the war.[104] The first thing that could bring men to an awareness of their common guilt for the war would be the recognition that they had been led into the war because they worshiped false gods.[105]

Good Nietzschean that he was, Scheler set out to smash the idols of the "cultural philistines." Religion was not merely a complement to civilization. It was a strictly independent phenomenon. Scheler had to prove this belief, else he could not hope that religion might provide the regenerative force for decadent, war-torn Europe. Historically, he said, religion had usually *led* the way, *preceding* the evolution of a higher civilization and determining the general lines of its development.[106] Another distinct difference between religion and culture was that culture was "always the concern of an *elite*" whereas religion presented itself to *all* men as "*the* way of salvation." Culture was confined to national boundaries, whereas religion, in the forms of church, sect, school, and order rose above national divisions.[107]

If religion were once again to become the leading spirit of civilized humanity, so that it might deploy its unifying powers "from above" (without whose assistance all expectations of unity based on the powers of drives and interests "from below"

102 *On the Eternal in Man*, p. 123.
103 *Ibid.*, p. 125.   104 *Ibid.*, p. 126.
105 *Ibid.*, p. 125.   106 *Ibid.*, p. 322.
107 *Ibid.*

were doomed), then it must become aware of its *autonomy*.[108] The religious conscience of European man must be disentangled from the values and norms of bourgeois secular culture which the war had rendered questionable. Scheler demanded an uncompromising "radical break with a culture so hostile to religion at its core."[109] But religion, by itself, according to Scheler's metaphysics of history, was impotent, unless it was linked to some social force. The *powers from above* could inspire and guide the *forces from below,* but the latter were essential in order for the ideal to be actualized in the social world.

In October, 1918, the last month of the war, Scheler once again repeated his call for a general repentance. Looking around Europe, he observed a general sense of despair at the havoc wrought by the war. "All hearts, especially young hearts, were seized with the urge to take their fate in their own hands and join forces across all frontiers, to fly to each others' arms in mutual pardon and remorse, crying Brother! Brother!"[110] The heart of European man, frozen by bourgeois greed and hatred, had been melted, Scheler believed. After the war, the springs of Christian love might stream through Europe again, just as they had done in the precapitalist era.

Scheler welcomed the rupture of European man's moral orientations that the war had brought in its wake. The old idols of humanitarianism, liberalism, capitalism, and imperialism had been smashed for good. The World War had shattered the prewar positivistic faith in *humanity* as a substitute for genuine religion. The realization of the goals of world government and socialism represented by the establishment of a League of Nations and by the entrance of social democracy into political responsibility after 1917 meant the dissolution of the utopian affects attached to these goals. Freed from devotion to false gods, postwar man would be ready to embrace "true religion" if it were properly presented to him. Scheler felt called to fill the ideological vacuum left by the war, particularly among the working class. "No Christian thinker should allow himself to

108 *Ibid.,* p. 326.   109 *Ibid.*
110 *Ibid.,* p. 126.

neglect the opportunity of collaborating in the formation of the fourth estate's new ideology," he warned.[111]

After the war, the church in Germany would have to try to win back the masses who had fallen away from Christianity to the false idol of Marxism. Once they saw that the church had cut itself free from its alliance with the bourgeoisie, the people would be more likely to return to the fold, Scheler argued. The church could not, must not, rely on legal safeguards in the constitution to hold the masses. It should work for a real conversion of spirit, should try to awaken a renewed sense of spiritual mission on the part of the people. The fourth estate should be brought into alliance with the powers of "Christian cultural conservatism" against the "oligarchic plutocracy with its liberalism and rationalism."[112]

This Christian *solidarism* became the keystone of Scheler's program at the end of the war. Even the nations should overcome their political antagonisms and be reconciled in the spirit of European "solidarity." The masses should be reconciled with the church in a new Christian social program which would defend the interests and ideals of all Christian men against the discredited but still powerful heresies of liberalism and capitalism. Christian socialism was a contradiction in terms, Scheler believed, for socialism was tied to its antithesis, capitalism. Only Christian solidarism could offer hope to postwar Europe.

[111] *Ibid.*, p. 443.   [112] *Ibid.*, p. 401.

4

Education for Democracy

THUS FAR we have followed Max Scheler's intellectual development and political propaganda activities during the final years of the German Empire. We have analyzed Scheler's critique of bourgeois society and morality and observed his transposition of this critique from Germany to her enemies in World War I. Like most other German intellectuals, Scheler ratified every outrage of German imperialism not by direct assent, but by lofty values. He ran with the herd while deploring the herd, and supported the politics of the bourgeoisie while excoriating them as philistines. His whole life seems to have been dedicated to devising anti-bourgeois ideas to justify the bourgeois social order by the values of every other stratum — aristocratic, clerical, proletarian, and military — as their influences waxed and waned, always, of course, in the name of the highest culture.

Despite Scheler's shifting ideological allegiances before and during the war, his social function as a public figure in the German Empire was to provide a moral and spiritual covering for Germany's drive for world power. Furthermore, no matter what ideological trappings Scheler chose for Germany's *Machtdrang*, he always made certain that they would serve to justify the maintenance of power in the hands of the ruling elite against the demands for reform in a liberal direction coming from the socialist and progressive-liberal parties. Scheler was keen enough to sense the rising political currents and cross-currents in order successfully to ride the crest of the wave of enthusiasm for each group that rose and crashed on the rocks of the crumbling Empire. When the Empire finally collapsed, Scheler quickly became a loyal supporter of the newly formed Weimar Republic.

Like many other members of the German intelligentsia, Scheler accepted the overthrow of the monarchy as a *fait accompli*. A republic was not his ideal, but if it preserved Germany's traditional religious and cultural pluralism, and if it guaranteed the spiritual freedom of the individual, Scheler was willing to support it. In the war and in the revolution in which it culminated, both the middle class and the old aristocracy had failed to provide responsible leadership for the nation. Scheler now recognized that, faced with the threat of a German Communist revolution, only a compromise with the moderate socialists could save the bourgeoisie. The socialists would become less militant, Scheler hoped, once they recognized the magnitude of the problems of postwar reconstruction and bore the burden of responsibility for this task on their own shoulders. At the same time, the bitterness of the class struggle might best be alleviated, Scheler insisted, if discussion were focused on estate-consciousness and social solidarity rather than on class consciousness and class conflict. To succeed, the Republic must not be the property of one class, but must win the allegiance of all.

Before and during the war, an almost omnipotent German state had hidden the fact from most Germans that political life was constantly being determined by a multiplicity of political and social forces. With the collapse of the Empire, the problems of governing a pluralistic society were suddenly thrust upon the politically inexperienced German people. After Noske's volunteer army had put down the Kapp Putsch in March, 1920, the chaos of revolution soon gave way to the less dramatic routine of political compromise among the three parties of the Weimar coalition, the Catholic Center, the Social Democrats, and the Liberals. Behind the facade of the coalition, however, the deep antagonisms and divisions in German society, clefts that had been temporarily covered over by the *Burgfrieden* during the first two years of the war, again became apparent. They were to haunt the Republic as they had the Empire; their final resolution came only after Hitler "liquidated" or drove into exile the "recalcitrant" elements in German society, claiming thereby to have fulfilled the "German revolution."[1] Max Scheler's speeches and articles written in the postwar period betray a constant concern to find a way of reconciling the differences in German political life on a metapolitical level.

1

Scheler's post-mortem on the Empire that collapsed in 1918 appeared shortly after the signing of the Treaty of Versailles in the summer of 1919.[2] He protested against the Allied imputation of war-guilt to the Central Powers, reiterating the old theme he had developed when the war was going badly: that the whole modern world was equally guilty. What distressed him even more was the fact that, judging from the mood of despair in Germany, many of his countrymen seemed to agree with the Allies' verdict. "The tidal wave of the world's hatred has swept away Germany's self-respect to the point that Germans no longer realize that there are values in our national heritage for which they can be justly proud,"[3] Scheler moaned. Actually, the moral dissolution of the German people after the war was more the result of starvation, inflation, and the collapse of the monarchy than a reaction to the anti-Germanism of the Allies.

As usual, Scheler traced the *political* anarchy around him to *moral* causes. His article was entitled "Two German Mala-

---

[1] Karl Dietrich Bracher, *Die Auflösung der Weimarer Republik: Eine Studie zum Problem des Machtverfalls in der Demokratie,* 3rd ed.; Schriften des Instituts für politische Wissenschaft, Vol. IV (Stuttgart-Düsseldorf, 1960), p. 30.

[2] "Von Zwei deutschen Krankheiten" first published in *Der Leuchter,* VI (Summer, 1919). Reprinted in *Schriften zur Soziologie,* p. 204 ff.

[3] *Ibid.,* p. 204.

dies." These maladies, rooted in the German character, were: a tendency that manifested itself in a perpetual *oscillation* between aggressive self-assertion and abject self-abandon; and a tendency toward excessive *inwardness,* a cult of inner freedom that caused a terrible disharmony between *Geist* and *Macht,* culture and force, in German life. In contrast to the English and French who had worked out a relatively integrated spiritual and political life which admittedly was overly materialistic, the Germans alternated between idealizing culture and glorifying power.[4] Like Meinecke, Scheler had become disillusioned about the possibility of synthesis between the two.[5] During the war he had claimed that a powerful state was necessary to guard and preserve cultural values. But the collapse of the Bismarckian *Machstaat* in 1918 had left German culture in a shambles. The old spiritual and cultural values were discredited along with the old state. Like Meinecke, Scheler was sorry to see these go, and he, too, was concerned that *Geist* and *Macht* achieve a happier integration in postwar Germany.[6]

Watching the revolution that Max Weber wryly commented was more like a carnival than a real revolution, Scheler became terrified that the socialists who had risen to power would impose a "dictatorship of the proletariat," legalized by a sham constitution. Scheler felt that the Germans had rightly abandoned their abject servility before the German princes and military aristocracy, but they lacked a properly German democratic ideal to substitute for the discredited monarchical one. Instead, they had "simply turned the old German *Obrigkeitsstaat* on its head and called this democracy and freedom!"[7] This could only lead to a worse tyranny than before, the tyranny of the uncultured masses, said Scheler echoing de Tocqueville, Mill, Burckhardt, and other nineteenth-century thinkers who had warned of the tyranny of the majority.

4 *Ibid.,* p. 206.
5 On Meinecke's concern with the relation between *Geist* and *Macht,* see Richard W. Sterling, *Ethics in a World of Power: The Political Ideas of Friedrich Meinecke* (Princeton, 1958), especially chapter eight, "Defeat and Revolution: The Polarity of Power and Culture."
6 "Von Zwei deutschen Krankheiten," p. 206.
7 *Ibid.,* p. 218.

If Germany were to build a new society on solid foundations, her people must do more than react against the old ideals; they must seek to discover positive new ones. Before they could find new ideals, however, they would have to overcome the extreme specialization of German life and culture that industrialization had brought in its wake. "It takes well-rounded men, not narrow specialists (*Fachmenschen*) to govern and guide a democratic society."[8] Scheler complained that the tendency to narrow specialization in the civil service produced a bureaucracy of officials who could only obey orders but could never come up with any creative suggestions of their own.

The separate function of the official in the mechanism of government has taken precedence over the evolution of the statesman; specialized technologists have been produced to the detriment of the personal, supervising intellectual spirit that enables branches of knowledge to cross-fertilize each other; in economic matters the middle class has become so taken up with business that it has lost its sense of political community as much as its taste for a higher life of the mind.[9]

Each ministry had become so absorbed in its own interests that it failed to understand its role in the whole society. It simply obeyed orders unquestioningly.

If today we see a large part of the old middle class bureaucracy now working for the socialists serving their purposes just as loyally as they did the old order, German specialization is the cause of this.[10]

Specialization had caused the German people to dissolve into a bourgeoisie which was morally shocked and unready to take the lead in politics, on the one hand, and a band of socialists who, despite all their mistakes and poor education, were the only men (besides the aristocracy who had been discredited) who had the courage to take on the responsibilities of leadership.[11] The bourgeoisie had intellectual culture (*Geist*), but they were politically inexperienced and impotent; the socialists had

8 *Ibid.*, p. 218.
9 *On the Eternal in Man*, p. 427.
10 "Von zwei deutschen Krankheiten," p. 218.
11 *Ibid.*, p. 219.

power (*Macht*), but they lacked culture. The problem of post-war Germany would be to bring the two together, the vital energies which had given power to the working class, and the intellectual culture of the German bourgeoisie.[12] A spiritual revolution should go hand in hand with the political and social one, he cried. The socialists could not provide new spiritual ideals to awaken the latent energies in the defeated German nation. They should abandon their outmoded positivism and accept the spiritual leadership of their betters.

Obviously Scheler was preaching the old bourgeois values he had attacked before the war. The German middle classes were now said to be the bearers of true culture. Only a small fraction of them had really been corrupted by bourgeois values imported from the West. Most of them retained true spiritual values "in their hearts."[13] They had merely been demoralized by the defeat of the German *Machtstaat,* an idol that they had unwisely adored. Now that the idol was broken, they should turn within, repent, and rediscover new untapped spiritual energies. From the inner souls of all Germans, the guiding spiritual values of the new Germany would be born:

Give up the old system of ideals and goals and the world will appear otherwise. Your soul will create the courage and power not only of economic reconstruction but of culture creation as well.[14]

Scheler hoped that the crisis facing Germany after she received the harsh terms of the Carthaginian Peace would force the Germans to overcome their long-standing political and ideological differences and unite them in a new spirit of solidarity. The new cooperation, born of need, like the cooperation born in the war, would help the Germans to recover from the malaise of defeat.

Facing the new Republic, Scheler repeated the same old phrases: unity and solidarity. He felt that the great problem of modern Germany was the disunity of her people who were divided ideologically, politically, professionally, and religiously.

---

[12] *Ibid.,* p. 217.   [13] *Ibid.*
[14] *Ibid.,* p. 219.

Repentance and a will-to-unity would bring healing powers from above, Scheler hoped. The *spirit* of unity and solidarity would have to be sown in the hearts of the people before any political and social order could be viable in postwar Germany.

2

IN THE postwar chaos, as flocks of young men returning from the army flooded Germany's universities, it was not difficult for Christian Eckart, the rector of the newly re-established University of Cologne, to overlook the Munich indiscretions that had once blocked Max Scheler's academic career. In January, 1919, Scheler accepted an appointment to the Sociological Institute, because the new university, supported by Cologne businessmen rather than by state funds, could not yet afford the luxury of a chair for philosophy.[15] Since Napoleonic times, Cologne's famous medieval university, established in 1388, had been defunct. In 1906, the conservative Cologne business community had encouraged the development of a business college (*Handelschochschule*). Students who sought more heady fare still journeyed to the imperial university established by the Hohenzollerns in Bonn. However, Bonn, like the majority of German universities, was dominated by a strong anti-Catholic liberal tradition. Catholic parents in Cologne had long felt the need for a Catholic university in the Rhineland to protect their children's faith. The new Cologne University, established largely through the unflagging efforts of the city's Catholic mayor, Conrad Adenauer, was financed by local sources in order to preserve independence from the anti-Catholic Ministry of Culture in Berlin.[16]

15 Information on Scheler's activities at the University of Cologne, 1919–1927, is drawn from interviews with Maerit Furtwaengler, Maria Scheler, Paul Honigsheim, Helmuth Plessner, and Leopold von Wiese, and from the letters Scheler wrote to Maerit Furtwaengler during this period.
16 Willehad Paul Elkert, *Kleine-Geschichte der Universität Köln* (Cologne, 1961), p. 170 ff.

These conditions made Max Scheler a particularly suitable candidate. Considering the great reputation Scheler had acquired during the war and his spectacular return to Catholicism, Christian Eckart hired Scheler with the understanding that as soon as the university developed a philosophical faculty, he should have the first chair. Scheler probably welcomed the opportunity to teach again. His colleagues were Hugo Lindemann, an active Majority Socialist, and Leopold von Wiese, a Liberal. Thus, the Weimar coalition was represented in the faculty of the Sociological Institute.

In Cologne, Scheler became good friends with the leader of the Catholic Intellectual Union (*Katholischer Akademischer Verband*), Father Francis Xavier Munch. The group had organized before the war as part of a general movement of German Catholic renewal to upgrade the cultural level of Catholics.[17] Prior to 1914, the term *Catholic* in Germany had generally meant anything but catholic. German Catholics had not recovered from their defensive attitude toward German culture which they had developed during the *Kulturkampf*. Intellectuals, especially university professors, held Catholic scholarship in contempt. The Catholic Intellectual Union was designed to counteract this impression by encouraging Catholic intellectuals to become familiar with the general cultural issues of the day and to participate in a dialogue with their liberal colleagues who had up to then monopolized the field.[18]

Under the auspices of the Catholic Intellectual Union, in 1919–1921, Scheler lectured to large audiences all over Germany. Some of his lectures were concerned with problems of the philosophy of religion, but more often they dealt with the practical applications of the Catholic *Weltanschauung* to modern political and social problems.[19]

In view of the revolutionary origins of the Weimar Republic, it was particularly necessary for German Catholics to find a

[17] Robert Grosche, "Der geschichtliche Weg des deutschen Katholizismus aus dem Ghetto" in his book, *Der Weg aus dem Ghetto* (Cologne, 1955), p. 13 ff.
[18] *Ibid.*, p. 15.
[19] See Frau Maria Scheler's notes in *On the Eternal in Man*, p. 449 ff.

theoretical ground for conscientious approval of its beginnings in order to subscribe wholeheartedly to its constitution. After the ideological-political traditions of the monarchy had broken down in 1918, Max Scheler felt personally challenged to rethink the political implications of Catholic doctrine in order to inspire his cobelievers to participate in the rebuilding of Germany within the republican framework. He tried to disentangle the Catholic Church from its historical ties to the monarchical state. The alliance between throne and altar had been merely an accidental connection, he said; it was neither the only nor necessarily the best form of church-state relationship. Scheler spoke of separation between church and state as a tendency inherent in Christianity itself. "Not only does the church teach no correlation between church and state," he wrote; "since the French Revolution it has gradually disengaged itself from any ties to the state."[20] It is true that the nineteenth century witnessed a trend toward separation of church and state, but to say that the church *voluntarily* chose this path, as Scheler implies, is grossly to distort the facts. Along with the separation of church and State, Scheler insisted that Catholics be guaranteed the right to continue to educate their children in confessional schools.

Making the best of the realities of the Weimar coalition, Scheler tried to dissolve the ideological barriers between German Catholicism and German Social Democracy. Hoping that the anti-religious propaganda of the socialists might be curbed, Scheler emphasized the common sense of solidarity and spirit of cooperation which Catholics shared with the socialists. The church shared with socialism a positive spirit of organization in contrast to the anarchic nature of bourgeois liberalism. The new community would be a product of the cooperation between proletarians and Catholic corporatists. The socialists could provide the organizational experience; the Catholics would provide the ideology of solidarity, cooperation and brotherhood.[21]

Above all other considerations in the new era, Scheler

[20] *Ibid.*, p. 441.   [21] *Ibid.*, p. 444.

placed foremost a wholesale and complete purgation of the capitalistic spirit from all elements of the German population. Once they had overcome the prejudices engendered by the bourgeois ethos, German aristocrats, the middle class, workers, and peasants would recognize their common *solidarity* and would exchange class antagonisms for the joys of participation as brothers in the estate-order of society.

Scheler was not alone in hoping that a corporatist order might grow out of the revolutionary upheaval. Ernst Troeltsch noted in his *Spektator-Briefe* that during the "dreamland of the armistice period," that is, until the signing of the Treaty of Versailles in June, 1919, when the Germans were shocked out of their hopes for a millennium following the revolution, people from all classes "dreamed socialism."[22] Some Catholics hoped to use the *Rätesystem* (*worker's councils*) to establish an estate-order of the medieval pattern under strong ecclesiastical leadership. Another group dreamed of a new rational world order based not on democracy or equality, but on a system of functional differentiation such as that described by Plato in which each member participated willingly because he was conscious of his contribution to the whole community.

In 1919, Max Scheler, too, dreamed of socialism.[23] Although he disliked the term *Christian socialism* because of the atheism, materialism, and collectivism usually associated with the socialist movement, Scheler believed that Catholics could collaborate with revisionist socialists in developing a Christian social program for the postwar era.[24] The question of the relationship between Christianity and socialism was brought to the forefront of discussion among Catholics in January, 1919, when the German bishops distributed an episcopal letter prior to the National

[22] Ernst Troeltsch, *Spektator-Briefe, Aufsätze über die deutsche Revolution und die Weltpolitik, 1918–1922*, ed. H. Baron (Tübingen, 1924), p. 69. Compare Carl Landauer, *European Socialism. A History of Ideas and Movements* (2 vols., Berkeley and Los Angeles, 1959), I, p. 810.

[23] See "Prophetischer oder Marxistischer Sozialismus?" first published in *Hochland*, XVII, 1 (October, 1919). Reprinted in *Schriften zur Soziologie*, p. 259 ff.

[24] *Ibid.*, p. 261.

Assembly elections stating that "whoever is for socialism is against Jesus Christ."

Scheler believed that socialism represented the direction of German economic development after the war, and he was anxious to demonstrate to the Catholic world that there were many types of socialism in addition to the Marxian variety. Although the Christian should naturally oppose materialistic Marxism, cooperation between Christians and revisionist socialists was not only morally justifiable but morally imperative.[25] Why? Because if the Christian did not try to infuse socialism with the Christian spirit, socialism could never escape its spiritual limitations. Socialism had developed as a reaction to capitalism and individualism with the result that it was simply the negative counterpart to its enemy. Whereas capitalism was individualistic, socialism was collectivistic. Christian solidarism, on the other hand, rooted in the natural law tradition, recognized the value of both the person *and* the community without overemphasizing either one. It was the responsibility of Christians to imbue socialism with the spirit of solidarity and with the Christian community idea.[26]

Scheler further expounded his views on the possibilities of rapprochement between Christians and socialists in a lecture and discussion at the University of Münster in April, 1919. He debated there with Johannes Plenge, a Hegelian Marxist.[27] Scheler and Plenge agreed that orthodox Marxian socialism was too collectivist. Plenge believed that the advent of true socialism would mean the reorganization of society so that each individual would be more able to fulfill his full potentiality. Scheler agreed, and believed that Christian socialism, which he preferred to call *solidarism* because it was based on Catholic corporatism, represented a middle way between the extreme individualism of capitalism and the collectivism of socialism. Social evolution was bringing socialism in the wake of capitalism. The

[25] *Ibid.*, p. 268.   [26] *Ibid.*, p. 265.
[27] For Plenge's account of Scheler's lecture, see Plenge's essay "Christentum und Sozialismus" in *Zur Vertiefung des Sozialismus* (Leipzig, 1919), p. 218 ff.

Christian must strive to spiritualize this socialism by transforming it into solidarism.[28]

The Christian could agree with the Marxist in repudiating the abstractions of bourgeois economic theory as expressed by the Manchester School. Like the Marxist, the Christian could see that capitalism carried within it the seeds of its own destruction. However, from the Christian point of view, things would only get worse should Marxian socialism move in to fill the vacuum left by the dying old order. To Scheler, Marxian socialism was equally as abhorrent as bourgeois capitalism, because they were simply two sides of the same coin: the exploitation of man and nature for the sake of wealth. The Christian, on the other hand, argued Scheler, believed that every human activity should be integrated into a total picture in which God was the Alpha and Omega. Work was only a *means*, never an end. Creative labor was one of the means by which man could give glory to God.[29]

The Christian must be a prophetic socialist pointing out that socialism was coming, inevitably, as capitalism declined. Recognizing the order of the day, he must attempt to infuse it with the spirit of Christian love and to turn it to the service of Christ. To long for the old feudal order would be to waste time in idle dreaming. Socialism must be Christianized before it was Bolshevized.[30] The prophetic socialist might derive strength from his knowledge that not man alone, but man and God together make history. God would help him to turn whatever might develop to His service. In short, Scheler was resigned to the advent of socialism in 1919. Yet he hoped that this unexpected turn of affairs might be utilized by the forces working for solidarity as opposed to those working for collectivism.

The obvious lacuna in Scheler's program was a specific plan of action, and Plenge criticized Scheler on precisely these grounds. If the Christian socialist remained no more than a *prophet*, the world would pass him by. Scheler refused to offer a

---

28 "Prophetischer oder Marxistischer Sozialismus," p. 265.
29 "Arbeit und Weltanschauung" in *Schriften zur Soziologie*, p. 273 ff.
30 "Prophetischer oder Marxistischer Sozialismus," p. 268.

concrete plan, claiming that the Christian must be suspicious of all utopianism. Who could know the mysteries God had in store for man? Plenge rejected this idea as essentially a retreat from the world. Scheler could propose nothing more than that Christians should pray for the advent of a great new spiritual leader like Saint Francis or Saint Ignatius. "I don't know what Catholicism needs," snapped Plenge, "but as for society and Christian socialism, it needs men familiar with the world, not monks. It needs strong Christian laymen united in a brotherhood of organized labor."[31] Scheler, the moralist, had failed to see that Christian socialism must be more than prophetic; it must bring new social forces into action. This would require organization. Scheler admitted this, but, as always, he maintained that *moral* reform must precede and guide *social* reform.

3

IN AN ESSAY written in 1919 for a volume of articles by leading intellectuals intended to outline the new spirit of community which should characterize Germany after the overthrow of the old order, Scheler discussed his idea of the role of education in the Republic.[32] The problem seemed particularly pressing to Scheler because the new Minister of Culture, Adolf Hoffmann, a radical Independent Socialist had proposed a full-scale anti-religious educational program upon his advent to power in November, 1918. In opposition to any uniform educational and cultural program, Scheler appealed to the leaders of Weimar Germany to preserve cultural autonomy in the Republic. Only cultural freedom would make possible the full flowering of the German "cosmopolitan" spirit, he said.[33] Socialist culture was but one of the many forms of intellectual culture

31 Plenge, *op. cit.*, p. 252.
32 "Politik und Kultur," in *Der Geist der neuen Volksgemeinschaft Eine Denkschrift für das deutsche Volk,* ed. Zentrale für Heimatsdienst (Berlin, 1919), pp. 31–48.
33 *Ibid.*, p. 42.

possible to man. Particular historical conditions had produced an iconoclastic attitude toward other cultural traditions on the part of socialist leaders, however. They recognized that culture was related to class structure. but failed to draw the conclusion that their own culture was as incomplete and one-sided as the bourgeois culture they wished to abolish. Scheler looked forward to a cooperation between the various classes and religious groups in the Republic, believing that only the composite of all points of view could fully express the total vision of all the German people.[34]

Adumbrated here are the seeds of Scheler's later theory of the "sociology of knowledge."[35] Accepting the Marxist sociological analysis of intellectual systems, Scheler attempted to integrate this essentially relativistic approach into a metaphysical system in which the entrenched rights of traditional metaphysical and religious thought would be guaranteed. Culture was a continuum stretching back to the past and forward to the future, as well as deep in the collective unconscious of the race, he said.[36] To deny all of these dimensions and enforce one type of world view on the whole of German society would be to impoverish it terribly. Scheler could not prevent the parliamentarization of Germany on the political level, but he hoped, at least, to prevent the same process from occurring in the realm of intellectual culture. The threat to traditional religion and culture would pass, Scheler hoped, once the socialists had become accustomed to sharing the responsibility of governing the society instead of being a party in opposition.[37]

In order to understand Scheler's concern with the reform of education in postwar Germany, it is important to recall some of the problems the Weimar Republic faced in its early days. One immediately thinks of the pressures of the political parties and the emergence of movements with murky ideologies in the Republic. Coupled with these political pressures came the

34 *Ibid.*, p. 46.
35 See Chapter Six.
36 "Politik und Kultur," p. 47.
37 *Ibid.*, p. 48.

burden of economic insecurity and widespread impoverishment, which induced resentment and conspiracy against the Republic among the upper and middle classes.

In his history of German education, Professor Friedrich Lilge noted the impact of this social disorder on the German universities:

Even if a majority of professors continued to teach the life of reason, it was inevitable that the university as a whole should be affected by the insecurities and anxieties of the mass of students who began to flock to the institution in alarming numbers.[38]

Throughout the 1920's, the university and with it the strict *Gymnasium* which alone prepared students for university studies, remained the preserve of the middle classes. According to a study made in 1930, only 5.8 per cent of all German university students came from peasant or proletarian backgrounds.[39] The upper-middle class (big landholders, army officers, industrial magnates, high-ranking civil officials, and professional men) supplied 31.7 per cent. The majority, 60.7 per cent, came from the lower-middle class (bureaucrats, white-collar workers, school teachers, small shopkeepers, and farmers).[40] This lower-middle class had been impoverished and unnerved by the inflation in the early 1920's. Its members made desperate efforts not to sink down to the mass of proletarian workers. Young people from this class flocked to the universities not so much from a passion for learning as from the desire to save themselves from economic destruction. They hoped to climb to safety on academic privileges. The title of *Herr Doktor* would distinguish them from their proletarianized contemporaries.

In this situation of terrible overcrowding, the German universities faced a severe crisis. Whereas for most critics, the debate centered on whether to expand the existing facilities or to limit enrollment, Max Scheler proposed a total re-thinking and

---

[38] Friedrich Lilge, *The Abuse of Learning: The Failure of the German University* (New York, 1948), p. 145.

[39] Walter M. Kotsching, *Unemployment in the Learned Professions* (London, 1937), p. 57.

[40] *Ibid.*

reform of the whole German university system. Scheler's discussion of the problems of German higher education in the postwar period was stimulated by the establishment of an institute for adult education at the University of Cologne in 1920. His colleague at the Cologne Sociological Institute, Leopold von Wiese, edited a volume of studies on the sociology of higher education to which Scheler contributed the essay, "The University and Adult Education," [41] in 1921.

Scheler's views, which seemed quite progressive in the 1920's, stood in sharp contrast to those of his friend, Carl Heinrich Becker, who later became Minister of Education in Prussia (1925–1930). Like most German academicians, Becker admired the ideals of the early nineteenth-century pedagogues, Humboldt and Fichte. They believed that a university should draw together in one organization all branches of learning. Becker insisted that the universities should remain small, not allowing themselves to become overcrowded.[42] His conception of higher education was essentially elitist, based on the belief that culture was the preserve of the propertied classes.

Scheler was a reluctant democrat at best, but he recognized that under the new social conditions of mass democracy in Weimar Germany, the old style university could not possibly provide professional training for the many men and women who were now flocking to the universities.[43] He pointed out that the university had already been forced into becoming an aggregate of professional schools, but university administrators had failed to revise their ideas accordingly.[44] Instead of resisting the trend by clutching to an outworn ideal derived from an earlier, less-specialized age, Scheler suggested that the university should

[41] Scheler's essay, first published in the Cologne Sociological Institute volume, *Zur Soziologie des Volksbildungswesens*, ed. Leopold von Wiese (Cologne, 1921), was reprinted in Scheler's book on the sociology of knowledge: *Die Wissensformen und die Gesellschaft* (2nd ed., Bern, 1960), p. 383 ff.
[42] See Lilge, *op. cit.*, pp. 147–148 on Becker's idea of a university. Our understanding of Scheler's educational theory was greatly helped by this book and by several stimulating conversations with its author.
[43] *Wissensformen*, p. 387.
[44] *Ibid.*, p. 385.

divide itself into several separate institutions, each one designed to fulfill certain specific objectives. In other words, Scheler proposed that the universities should simply continue in the direction that they had been moving for several decades: division into specialized colleges and institutes.

According to Scheler's plan, professional training would be entrusted to experienced practitioners of law, medicine, and architecture. The university professors who considered themselves to be mainly research men would be relieved of their teaching duties, which they performed so begrudgingly, and freed for research.[45] The research institutes would be separate from the professional schools and the liberal arts colleges, because Scheler resented the pragmatic orientation which filtered into the colleges and research laboratories from the professional schools. He felt that their utilitarian and materialistic emphasis violated the principles and ideals of scientific freedom and severely hindered the progress of science.

As to liberal education, Scheler lamented the fact that humanistic studies had been subordinated to research and professional training. The German university had failed utterly in the important task of forming the human person.[46] According to Scheler, as indicated earlier, moral, aesthetic, and religious values — all values, for that matter — could not be communicated merely verbally. If values were to be taught, the teacher would have to inspire his students by showing them personal models from the past and present who embodied these values. The university could only succeed in its task of transmitting the *values* of Western civilization and culture to its students if it put a premium on dedicated and well-rounded teachers, rather than on specialists (*Fachmenschen*) and researchers who resented their teaching duties.[47]

Scheler proposed the establishment of separate liberal arts

45 *Ibid.*, p. 392.

46 The word *Bildung* which Scheler used means *personal cultivation* and *cultural development* as well as *education* in German.

47 *Wissensformen*, p. 398. Compare Scheler's caustic criticism of the German tendency to over-specialization in "Von zwei deutschen Krankheiten," p. 209 ff.

colleges modeled on the *Collège de France*.[48] Here the student might acquire a broad synthesis of knowledge which would enable him to see the matrix of conceptions and hypotheses within which all empirical knowledge lay ordered and embedded. He would be taught to see the universal in the particular. To Scheler this ability was the mark of the well-educated man, although not necessarily of the scientist or the scholar. The ultimate objective of liberal education was not to teach the individual how to predict and control events, but to teach him to know himself, and to see himself as part of an objective order which he could never control but which he could understand.

Through what Scheler called *knowledge of culture* (*Bildungswissen*) men could enter into communion with other minds, and, thus humanized, could learn to perceive the existence of a common moral order. Scheler hoped that through training in the liberal arts, men might come to agreement not only about matters concerning the material world, but also about moral and religious problems. The goal of liberal education, Scheler said, was to teach men what they were as men, that is, what they shared with all men.[49]

In particular, Scheler was concerned with the establishment of a common European university in which the youth of all European nations could become aware of their common cultural heritage and of the contributions which Europe, in contrast to America and Asia, could make to world civilization in the twentieth century.[50]

Scheler rejected the traditional ideals of German humanistic education as too one-sided. He had already broached this theme in his *Hochland* essay on "The Reconstruction of European Culture,"[51] in which he analyzed the values and shortcomings of Wilhelm von Humboldt's humanism. Although he admired the Humboldtian ideal, upon which he himself had been

---

48 *Wissensformen*, p. 398.
49 *Ibid.*, p. 399. Compare Lilge, *op. cit.*, pp. 150–153.
50 *Ibid.*
51 Scheler's essay, "The Reconstruction of European Culture" (1918), is reprinted in *On the Eternal in Man*, p. 405 ff.

raised, he felt that it overemphasized the classical heritage of Western man at the expense of the Christian:

> . . . in our view this ideal of *personal culture,* with the conception of antiquity which it embodies, contains *three* features which . . . require correction. Firstly, it isolates antiquity . . . from its *Asiatic* origins and no less from its transition into Hellenism and Christianity. Though sprung entirely from Christian soil, and secretly far more molded by Christianity than its originator would wish to concede, . . . Humboldt's ideal reads into the ancient a notion of pure "humanity" which is of *Christian* origin. . . . Secondly, Humboldt's ideal does not rise above the quasi-aesthetic individualism of striving to shape oneself into a "perfect specimen of humanity" — like a work of art — and of referring all individual relationships with the community to this endeavor as the highest goal. Thus in its internal assumptions, it [Humboldt's ideal] is as utterly remote as is the ethics of Kant and Hegel from the *solidarity* which I have developed elsewhere as the highest principle of social morality. . . . Thirdly, as an ideal of education it places so disproportionate an emphasis on the *inner* formation of the personality, that it neglects the individual's function and conduct in the frame of a highly developed community. It is, therefore, impossible to apply in our age.[52]

Modern liberal education should replace the Humboldtian ideal of *personality* with a "preponderantly *functional* ideal related to the community."[53] The trend of mass society was toward depersonalization. The individual was becoming merely a cog in the industrial machine. The old liberal individualistic ideal could not counteract this tendency, Scheler said, because it failed to awaken in the person a sense of belonging and participation in the community.

During the war, Eduard Spranger had suggested that the Humboldtian ideal of "personal culture" had proved inadequate because it did not develop a proper sense of citizenship and civic duty in students.[54] The study of the ancient classics should be supplemented, Spranger said, with training in civics that would teach the individual his proper place in the social order,

[52] *Ibid.,* pp. 424–425.   [53] *Ibid.*
[54] Eduard Spranger, *Das humanistische und das politische Bildungsideal im heutigen Deutschland* (Berlin, 1916), p. 34.

reminding him of his responsibilities and duties as well as his rights and privileges as a member of the German nation.[55]

Writing after the German defeat, Scheler warned that civics courses could too easily become nationalistic orgies of patriotism.[56] The chastened author of *The Genius of War* now eschewed fervent nationalism for more innocuous fare. The role of the citizen in the state should be taught within the context of a course in sociology, Scheler said. The sociologist could foster in the student "an intensified sense of community" without encouraging the aggressive nationalism that a patriotic civics teacher might engender.[57] In sociology the student would learn to consider all forms of human organization and community; he would learn that the state was simply one among many forms of society. Scheler's desire to play down the "community building powers" of the nation-state stood in marked contrast to his wartime eulogies to the German nation. His quest for unity and community in Germany now shifted from the state to the society. The goal of the social education which Scheler advocated was "to teach the student to play his part not simply in the state but in a multiplicity of communities coexisting in their own right each with its own aims and functions."[58]

Instead of direct civic education, Scheler suggested that instruction in the liberal arts should include an analysis of how a particular literature, philosophy, art, or science fitted into the state of the time, why certain groups of values stood outside the state, and which features of the thought were conditioned by the groups holding them. The students should also discuss the ideas and artistic forms that lay potentially in various cultural traditions but had not been developed. They should consider the extent to which the growth and development of an idea or artistic form was stimulated or frustrated by the prevailing

55 *Ibid.*
56 *Eternal in Man*, p. 425.
57 *Ibid.*, p. 426.
58 *Ibid.* For a discussion of the relevance of Scheler's ideas to education today, see Ernest Becker, *Beyond Alienation: A Philosophy of Education for the Crisis of Democracy* (New York, 1967), p. 268 ff.

political and economic conditions. By asking such questions, the students would learn that intellectual culture had never existed in a vacuum, but was always interlinked with particular political and social forms. They would thereby become aware of the importance of society in a more effective and meaningful way than they ever could through direct civic education.

Scheler was also vitally concerned with the social education of the masses who would never be exposed to university training. He realized that if democracy were to survive in Germany, it needed a broad base of commonly shared values.[59] Before the war, Catholics, Protestants, socialists, and humanists had all fostered their own adult education programs. Their schools simply reinforced the old ideological divisions among the German people. There had also been an old university extension movement, but it had incurred the resentment of the working class who considered it as a sop thrown to them by the bourgeoisie. Adult education would have to be freed from the aura of charity that had surrounded it, Scheler said. He was eager to allay the workers' suspicions that the bourgeoisie, entrenched in the universities, were using adult education as a means to counteract Marxism.[60] Therefore, he proposed that new independent *Volkshochschulen* (popular adult-education centers) should be established.[61] One of the primary objectives of these centers would be to help recruit leadership from the working class whose constructive powers had hardly been tapped. At the same time Scheler hoped that these schools might foster a sense of solidarity among the working men, overcoming their class prejudices and helping them to become responsible, active members of the new Republic.[62]

Scheler's adult education centers were to promote more than culture; they were to promote a sense of community. How was this objective to be achieved? Scheler insisted that the schools should not have a particular ideological or religious orientation; they should be ideologically neutral.[63] Neutrality

---

59 *Wissensformen*, p. 407.
60 *Ibid.*
61 *Ibid.*, p. 408.
62 *Ibid.*
63 *Ibid.*

would be difficult, Scheler admitted, but he felt that the difficulties could be overcome if the instructor would make a point of explaining the positions of the different ideologies regarding the same problem, state his own position, and then encourage general discussion. Scheler's centers were to offer specific courses in the theory of *Weltanschauungen* in which the different ideologies in contemporary Germany would be described and their social and historical roots explained.[64] Eventually, Scheler hoped, the student might be freed from the prejudices of his particular ideology and, recognizing the relativity of his and other positions, attempt to overcome his one-sidedness by returning to the facts with a more open mind.

Scheler was concerned that the adult education centers not become professional training schools as the universities had. The centers were to offer courses in the humanities as well as in the natural and social sciences in order to educate well-rounded and cultivated citizens. Culture should be made meaningful to the worker, but the instructors should make clear from the beginning that the work-world and the world of culture were not the same. Scheler opposed the idea of spiritualizing factory work. "Modern industrial labor, as such, cannot be spiritualized," he said.[65] The worker should be brought to the realization that the world of culture lay totally outside his daily work world, but that as a man, a German, and a citizen he had the responsibility to develop himself culturally as well as materially.

Thus, in the last analysis, despite the fact that the adult-education centers could serve the function of helping to bridge the divisions among the German people and reinforce a sense of solidarity, they also had another aim. "Pure human fulfillment" — the value and joy of pure intellectual achievement and the growth and enrichment of the soul must be the ultimate objective of all liberal education, said Scheler, and adult education was no exception.[66] Considered from this point of view,

---

64 *Ibid.*, p. 409.   65 *Ibid.*, p. 410.
66 *Ibid.*, p. 407.

the adult-education centers shared a common objective with the liberal arts colleges which Scheler hoped would be established separately from the professional training schools of the universities.

4

THE REVOLUTION had opened the way to a new social order devoid of the bourgeois spirit. For this reason Scheler had accepted the Republic without much difficulty. He claimed that his objective was to educate the inexperienced German people to a sense of responsibility in self-government.[67] The German people had been used to the old order in which they had become increasingly technicized and specialized, instruments of exploitation rather than free-thinking responsible members of a community whose goals they themselves determined. Until they had learned a sense of responsibility, they should accept the tutelage of a cultured elite who could help them to find new goals to replace the old ones which had been discredited by the war. Mere economic and political reconstruction would never succeed unless the stimulus of a new ideal were there to "unlock the energy hidden in the tired, defeated German people."[68]

Socialism could not provide the new goals because like capitalism, its opposite, it was tied to the materialistic bourgeois ethos,[69] said Scheler. Socialism was only a reaction to something rather than an independent creative force. What was needed was a new positive and constructive approach based on traditional Christian wisdom and a recognition of the needs of the present.[70] Only an intellectual elite, above the various interest groups and aware of the importance of Germany's cul-

[67] "Politik und Kultur," p. 38.
[68] *Ibid.*, p. 37.
[69] *Ibid.*, p. 35. See also "Arbeit und Weltanschauung," p. 274.
[70] "Arbeit und Weltanschauung," p. 275.

tural traditions could offer a suitable solution to the problems of the day.[71]

As usual, Scheler looked to the youth movement as a source of new vitality for the "sick, lethargic, defeated German nation." The leaders of the bourgeois world had become ever more corrupted by their endless striving for unlimited power and profits. By their profiteering in the war that they had caused, they had been discredited. There was hope, however. Even, before the war, German youth had withdrawn from the decadent culture of their society to re-form themselves into a spiritual heroic elite. Although many of their leaders had died in the war, members of the youth movement eventually would provide leadership for the new Germany.[72]

Contact with the youth movement meant hope to Scheler and other German intellectuals concerned with leadership in the new society. Until 1918, the movement was, for the most part, politically neutral.[73] After the revolution, however, it began to split into right and left factions. This politicization of the movement distressed Scheler, for he had visions of developing an elite out of the youth groups that would be above party allignments (*überparteilich*).[74] He urged the youth not to heed the dissolution of German society into conflicting classes. Instead they should study the great synthetic organization of medieval society in which the Christian idea of solidarity had prevailed. They should "abandon their cries of embitterment and aimless gesticulations of so-called psychic activism" discovering instead a strong self-discipline that would enable them to become the responsible leaders of Germany.[75]

Like Plenge, Scheler believed that raw enthusiasm was

---

71 "Politik und Kultur," p. 40.

72 Scheler spoke of the German youth as the hope of the future in almost every one of his speeches and essays in 1919–1922.

73 The literature on the German *Jugendbewegung* is extensive, but little of it is really of much use. We have used a recent book by Walter Z. Laqueur, *Young Germany* (London, 1962) and Howard Becker, *German Youth, Bond or Free?* (New York, 1941).

74 *Spenglerkritik* in Scheler's unpublished *Nachlass*. We were given access to this manuscript and several other essays on economics and philosophy of history through the kindness of Maria Scheler.

75 Preface to "Moralia" in *Schriften zur Soziologie*, p. 11.

inadequate to meet the problems of the day. The youth movement seemed "ripe for a deeper knowledge of the arts of recollection, silence, meditation, and tolerance."[76] To Scheler, self-mastery was a pre-requisite to the proper domination of the natural world. Unless the youth developed themselves spiritually *before* they entered the practical world, they would be tempted by the spirit of *pleonexie* (*greed*) and become corrupted by the bourgeois values of their parents.

In January, 1922, a meeting of the leaders of the various German youth groups took place in Cologne.[77] Scheler spoke to the group on solidarism, his perennial theme. It was the first time that Scheler and the youth groups that he idealized had really come together face-to-face. Both were disappointed. Whereas Scheler felt that the youth were undisciplined and irresponsible, they found him cynical, even Machiavellian, or at best a restoration-minded romantic.[78] Elizabeth Busse-Wilson, a young woman present at the meeting, later recalled that in describing the economic system that should develop after the demise of capitalism, Scheler tended to favor an economic dictatorship under one or two directors. She found him to be simultaneously a devotee of Saint Augustine and Hugo Stinnes, Thomas Aquinas and Bismarck. Apparently it was difficult to convince him that Bismarck could not serve as the ideal to the postwar generation who had seen Bismarck's creation topple in ruins. Romano Guardini, then the leader of the Catholic *Quickborn* group, criticized Scheler for his Machiavellian opportunistic approach. Whereas Scheler had argued for the necessity of calculation in politics, Guardini expressed the

---

[76] *Ibid.*

[77] For an account of the meeting, see Elizabeth Busse-Wilson, "Max Scheler und der Homo Capitalisticus," *Die Tat*, XIV (April, 1922), p. 179 ff. In the following issue, one of Scheler's disciples, the young Paul Ludwig Landsberg, wrote a letter criticizing Miss Busse-Wilson's characterization of the meeting, but as he offered no corrective account, hers is the only description available. Landsberg claimed that "Scheler was *not* surrounded by a Praetorian Guard of his students." Presumably if there were such a guard, Landsberg would have been at its head, as he was one of Scheler's most devoted pupils in 1922.

[78] *Die Tat*, p. 181.

idealism of the youth when he insisted that public and private morality could not be separated. Spiritual laws like natural laws could not be violated. Bismarck had begun the war of 1870 with the Ems telegram; he had received his answer fifty years later at Versailles.[79]

Scheler's interest in the youth movement was intensified by his awareness of Germany's need for new leaders in the postwar era. In his lectures at the University of Cologne in 1919, he discussed "the nature of leadership and the role of social models in history."[80] In later years he was to become increasingly concerned with the quest for new leaders and for a new elite to govern Germany.[81]

Examination of Scheler's theory of prophetic socialism has shown that Scheler attributed more importance to the *types of men* who direct a social system than to the form of the system itself. Any socio-economic system would be dehumanizing, Scheler believed, unless it were led by men filled with a spirit of love and a sense of human solidarity, the responsibility of each man for all men.[82]

The question of the nature and selection of leaders was no mere theoretical problem in postwar Germany. The nation had been robbed of leadership in all areas of life. Therefore, Scheler addressed himself to this question in his lectures to the young men returning from the war who entered the University of Cologne in order to prepare themselves for leadership in the new society.

It is no coincidence that Max Weber chose to lecture on similar themes at the University of Munich in 1919 or that Oswald Spengler's metaphysical reflections on "the Decline of the West" were widely read all over Germany immediately after

79 *Ibid.*, p. 182.

80 These lectures were edited by Frau Maria Scheler and published in *Schriften aus dem Nachlass, Band I: Zur Ethik und Erkenntnislehre* (2nd ed., Bern, 1957), p. 255 ff. (Hereafter referred to as *Nachlass Schriften*).

81 See the essays written between 1925 and 1928 published as *Philosophische Weltanschauung* (Bonn, 1929); tr. Oscar A. Haac, *Philosophical Perspectives* (Boston, 1958); discussed in Chapter Seven.

82 *On the Eternal in Man*, p. 393.

the war. Germany's old leaders either had been killed or discredited by the war and revolution. New leaders were needed. One of the great weaknesses of the Weimar Republic was that the groups that had been excluded from governing in the Empire were unable to develop enough dynamic responsible leadership to lead the German people out of the mood of despair, which followed the collapse, to a new sense of Germany's mission as a democracy. Of the leaders who rose to prominence in the major Weimar parties, it is difficult to name one who had not already established himself politically before the war. Whereas German society had been transformed in the war and revolution from a feudal autocracy into a parliamentary democracy, the leaders of the Weimar Republic remained men of the old order.

The generation that might have provided new leadership and new ideals by the late twenties had been physically and emotionally decimated on the battlefields of Europe. Those who returned were disgusted with the work of their fathers, but lacked the incentive to try to do better themselves. Cynical and disillusioned, they shunned responsibility, seeking to escape through action in the Free Corps and other paramilitary organizations which offered them the sense of importance and mission that they could not find in the monotonous work of rebuilding and consolidation that the Republic demanded.

Germany's leading liberals after the war, such men as Hugo Preuss, Ernst Troeltsch, Friedrich Naumann, and Max Weber, all registered their exasperation and feelings of despair at the paucity of leadership potential in Germany. The socialist historian, Gustav Mayer, pointed out that the

very decency and strict adherence to traditional tactics which were a source of pride to SPD leaders and held their middle aged supporters, were inadequate to win over the new proletarianized and pauperized masses attracted by the extreme right and left. [Mayer also admitted] that there was scarcely a single figure in the entire leadership cadre of the SPD who, measured by a strict standard, aroused within me any profound ethical respect and admiration.

Petty bourgeois pedantry was combined in many of them with egotism and ambitious place-hunting.[83]

Walther Rathenau expressed a similar pessimism in his speech to German youth in 1919:

No statesman, nor act of parliament, nor even a change of organization can help us now. . . . Can you find the *men* and bring them together? Do not forget that even if we could establish a German earthly paradise today, we should not have the men to administer it. Look around you at these parliaments, offices, academies—everywhere. . . . I lose heart. Where are the men?[84]

Although Scheler claimed that his lectures on the nature of leadership were intended to be "an objective and strictly scientific study," he admitted quite frankly that he was distressed by the paucity of leadership after the war and that he hoped that his lectures might help the young men and women in his audience to choose good, responsible leaders when they had the opportunity to do so. Like Max Weber, Scheler was distressed to see the young flocking around the "false prophets" of the day.[85] Like Weber, he insisted that he had no desire to be taken for a leader; his role as teacher was simply to provide them with the intellectual training so that they might, through a deeper understanding of the nature of leadership, choose their leaders more wisely.

Scheler's general theory of leadership was based on his elitist conception of society. "All groups of any kind are divided into a small number of leaders and a large number of followers," he said. This law was supposed to be "rooted in the

[83] Quoted in Koppel Pinson, *Modern Germany, Its History and Civilization* (New York, 1954), p. 415.

[84] Graf Harry Kessler, *Walther Rathenau, A Biography*, tr. W. D. Robson-Scott and Lawrence Hyde (New York, 1930), p. 240.

[85] Scheler cited the following groups to which the youth were turning in their quest for new leaders: the psychoanalytic sects; the religious socialists; the Communists; the solidarists, represented by Eduard Stadler's ultra-conservative journal, *Gewissen;* Count Hermann Keyserling's School of Wisdom in Darmstadt; Rudolf Steiner's Circle of Anthroposophists; the circles around Stefan George, the poet, and around his heretical ex-followers; the group around the prophet, Johannes Müller; and the group associated with Eugen Diederich's journal, *Die Tat.*

very nature of organic life itself."[86] Drawing the familiar analogy of the social group to the living organism, often popular with conservative social theorists, Scheler compared the leaders in the social hierarchy to the central nervous system that directs the hierarcy of organs, each of which has its own particular function.[87]

For those who refused to accept the organic analogy, Scheler offered another proof for the "iron law of oligarchy." Sociologically it was a proven fact that "in every conscious human group there is, from the outset, a small number who rule."[88] This law applied as much to a republic as to a monarchy. Robert Michels had proved this fact in his sociological study of the oligarchic tendencies in modern political parties. What Michels had baptised as "the iron law of oligarchy" was a codification of a practical truth that he had discovered through personal experience: political organizations through the internal necessities of discipline and administrative continuity, inevitably become closed and self-perpetuating oligarchies.[89] As elites were inevitable, even in a democracy, to Scheler the crucial question became: how do elites rise to power?

Given the fact that Scheler believed, or rather hoped, that the bourgeois leaders of Europe were on the way out, Scheler's real question was "how can we gradually replace the decadent elite with a creative one?" Scheler found the answer to his question in the distinction he made between leaders and models. Agreeing with the old maxim that "a people gets the

[86] "Vorbilder und Führer," *Nachlass Schriften*, p. 260. For his discussion of the nature of leadership, Scheler relied heavily on the theory of elites developed by the neo-Machiavellians, Michels, Mosca, and Pareto.

[87] *Ibid.*

[88] Scheler was quoting the Austrian economist-sociologist, Friedrich Freiherr von Wieser, who had proposed this "law of the minority" in his Salzburg lectures, published as *Recht und Macht* (Salzburg, 1910). Scheler cited von Wieser's law frequently in his *Formalismus in der Ethik* as well as in his later sociological works. On von Wieser's life and work, see Ewald Schams, "Friedrich von Wieser und sein Werk," *Zeitschrift für die Gesamte Staatswissenschaft*, LXXXI (Tübingen, 1926), pp. 432–448.

[89] Robert Michels, *Political Parties: A Sociological Study of the Oligarchical Tendencies of Modern Democracy*, tr. Eden and Cedar Paul (New York, 1959), pp. 389–390.

leaders it deserves," Scheler asserted that the choice of leaders in a society depended on the ideals held by that society. These ideals are embodied in the "social models" who are the society's culture heroes and saints, imitated by both the rank and file and the leaders alike. "It is the effective models which determine the choice of leaders, and above all the quality of leadership in a society."[90] Thus, social models act as the intermediary link between the ideals of a society and its members. Given this premise, Scheler concluded that the best way to teach the youth to choose the best kind of leaders was to talk not about leaders, but about models.

As might be expected, Scheler did not think of the possible types of social models as purely arbitrary. As there was an eternal hierarchy of values, and a corresponding hierarchy of societal forms, so also Scheler postulated a hierarchy of social models. These models, corresponding to his four ranks of values, were "the connoisseur, the hero, the sage, and the saint."[91] There were, of course, great men in history who might claim more than one rank. There was the hero-sage, such as Friederich II of Hohenstaufen, and the sage-saint, such as Saint Augustine and Saint Thomas Aquinas. These model types existed eternally, Scheler believed, in the realm of "ideas." However, to have any influence in the world they had to become embodied in real men living in a particular culture and epoch.[92]

Although the types were eternal, Scheler admitted that their historical expressions differed in different cultures. The ideal of the man to whom living was an art varied from the

---

90 *Nachlass Schriften*, p. 263.
91 *Ibid.*, p. 269. Compare *Formalismus*, p. 586 ff. It may be helpful to the reader at this point to see Scheler's hierarchy of model types in the context of his other hierarchies:

VALUES	SOCIETAL FORMS	MODELS
the pleasant	the primitive horde or tribe	the connoisseur
the vital	the organic community (*Gemeinschaft*)	the hero
the intellectual (*geistige Werte*)	the atomistic society (*Gesellschaft*)	the sage
the holy	the Church Universal	the saint

92 *Ibid.*, p. 262.

English *gentleman,* to the Japanese *samurai,* to the Italian *cortegiano.* Furthermore, the peasant, townsman, and knight in the medieval period each had a different heroic ideal or model. In the multiplicity of professions characteristic of modern society, there would be even more variations of the hero type; each professional group had its own hero-ideal. Scheler correlated the model types to the value hierarchy. Just as lower values were tied to bodily instincts or emotions, so the lower social models were more dependent on social structure. The higher social models, on the other hand, he considered to be freer of outer circumstance. For example, a slave would seldom be a connoisseur or hero, but he might as easily be a saint as might a king.[93] Despite the fact of "accidental historical variations," however, Scheler insisted that the hierarchy of model types itself was part of the eternal order of things. This gap between the ideal eternal forms and their accidental historical expressions runs throughout Scheler's thought. It left him with the problem of mediation between the ideal and the real worlds. In his social theory this role was fulfilled by the *elite.*

As noted earlier, Scheler was convinced that history was always shaped by a small minority of men: those who led and inspired the majority. For the eternal hierarchy of values to be fully actualized in a particular society, the members of the society must see these values embodied in social models whom they would be inspired to imitate.

What type of man might be the model for the postwar world? In a memorial speech for the industrialist-intellectual Walther Rathenau after his assassination in June, 1922, Scheler gave his answer.[94] The coming era demanded a new elite of men skilled in industrial management and technology, yet at the same time not blind to spiritual and heroic values. Scheler

[93] See the discussion of this point in Oesterreicher, *op. cit.,* p. 165.

[94] Walther Rathenau was murdered by a band of youthful assassins on June 24, 1922. A memorial service was held at the University of Cologne on July 16, 1922. Scheler's speech, along with those of two other professors from Cologne, Arthur Baumgarten and Eduard Heimann, was printed in a pamphlet by the university, reprinted in *Schriften zur Soziologie,* pp. 361–376.

126 presented Walther Rathenau as a model for the youth of Germany, but he emphasized the fact that Rathenau should not be considered a martyr *for* the Republic. Scheler's Rathenau was no utopian democrat. "He had always realized that some men were destined by God to lead, the rest, to follow."[95] Rathenau was an elitist at heart, although he *had* dedicated his life to the Republic in his last years.

In many ways Rathenau, whom Scheler knew personally, was Scheler's ego-ideal. He was the intellectual who did not live in an ivory tower of eternal ideas, but was thoroughly familiar with the mechanics of high finance and industry and sought to spiritualize the work world. Such a combination had been Scheler's ideal ever since he had studied with Rudolf Eucken.

5

IN HIS concluding lectures in the leadership course, Scheler came down to earth. From talking about the ideal model types, he moved to a discussion of types of political leadership. A comparison with Max Weber's speech to the Munich students on the same subject will help point up Scheler's position.[96] For Scheler, as for Weber, politics was the realm of the possible. The best statesman was he who could meet the demands of the hour. In these situations, a man with "principles" was out of place.[97] Scheler quoted Bismarck: "A man with principles [in politics] is like a man who walks through the forest with a tall walking stick." Like Weber, too, Scheler was critical of the

---

95 *Schriften zur Soziologie,* p. 370.

96 "Politics as a Vocation" by Max Weber was presented in the winter of 1918–1919 at the University of Munich. The speech is printed in English in *From Max Weber: Essays in Sociology,* ed. Hans Gerth and C. Wright Mills (Oxford, 1946), pp. 77–129.

97 *Nachlass Schriften,* p. 342; Weber, "Politics," pp. 110 and 120 ff. Although Weber insisted that the politician could not abide by an "absolute ethic," he believed that the political leader should adhere to an "ethic of responsibility" to the society which he served.

German parliamentarians who indulged in irresponsible criticism but were unwilling to take over the reins of power and try to do any better themselves. In fact, Scheler found the man with principles and the man who was afraid of political responsibility to be two of a kind. Because these types predominated in the Reichstag, Scheler refused to consider it the proper training ground for statesmen.

Scheler's ideal of the political leader, the statesman, as opposed to the party politician who "merely applies the party program," was Bismarck. The cult of Bismarck flourished in the 1920's among men of Scheler's generation who had witnessed Germany's political decline under the irresponsible leadership of William II. Bismarck had not been committed to any party, but had stood above parties, playing one off against the other so that the resulting power alignments seemed almost "accidentally" to conform to his political objectives.[98] Scheler's image of the statesman who was above parties also was a typical idea among the German middle classes in the Empire. The problem with this view was that it harkened back to the pre-party days when the statesman held his authority by appointment from the absolute sovereign. Scheler had not yet arrived at the pragmatic views of Weber who believed that the politician's primary responsibility was to his constituents. To Scheler the constituents were but the pawns which the statesman used to achieve his own ends. Ultimately the statesman was responsible only to himself and to God for securing the welfare of the nation. However, unlike the diplomat who necessarily had to be deceitful, the statesman had to be honest, trustworthy, and deeply rooted in the spirit of his nation. To this spirit, above all, he must be true. He must devote himself to drawing forth the creative energies of the nation instead of wasting himself in "yea-saying to the masses."[99]

Scheler's statesman, responsible only to himself, God, and the national spirit, could easily be a demagogue. Surely Hitler believed that he acted in responsibility to this triad in meeting

---

98 *Nachlass Schriften*, p. 342.
99 *Ibid.*, p. 343.

the "demands of the hour." Scheler was aware of the potentialities for demagoguery in his theory of political responsibility. He even admitted that "the statesman in a parliamentary republic must also be a great demagogue," but he insisted that the truly great statesman would "subordinate his demagoguery to the creative art of statesmanship."[100] Unfortunately, in history the great men of the type Scheler admired have been few. If there be no other check than the politician's sense of "the creative art of statesmanship," God preserve us from leaders who lack this sense! However, in Scheler's eyes "the great men of history have always scorned the masses rather than flattered them."[101] Although the statesman might despise the masses, he should not despise men, Scheler felt, for he could only draw forth the nation's potential when he manifested a faith in the real possibility of human achievement. In this matter, Scheler preferred Baron von Stein to Bismarck as a model because Bismarck had despised all men, not just the masses. Scheler warned that the statesman must count on all men, but put himself at the mercy of none. Whereas the demagogue might flatter the masses, the real statesman would know instinctively that "the mass is a creation of the moment, moody like a nervous woman,"[102] easily won but easily lost. Firmness of will against the perfidious desires of the masses, Scheler insisted, was essential to the statesman. "He must reckon with public opinion as with other factors, but not give in to it."[103]

Furthermore, Scheler rejected the rationalistic ideal that the statesman should directly seek the best for the whole world. This idea was but an English and French camouflage for disguising their own national self-interest. Scheler was not fooled. He thought it best to admit openly that the statesman should seek the interest of his nation first. To the statesman, the interests of the European community would naturally appear secondary to the national interest. Just as the statesman should direct his attention to fulfilling the concrete needs of the hour rather than trying to implement abstract party principles, so

100 *Ibid.*, p. 344.
102 *Ibid.*

101 *Ibid.*, p. 341.
103 *Ibid.*

he should be devoted to the concrete needs of his nation rather than to the abstract goals of humanity.

Thus we see that for Scheler the statesman was an artist, working with the masses, molding them to his political objectives as a sculptor works his clay. The sculptor could draw out of the clay its potentiality for higher form; the statesman could do the same with the people in his hands. Although he was responsible only to his creative genius and to God, he was conscious of his responsibility for the whole society and its citizens. He would have to be consciously oriented toward *power*, because he would need power in fulfilling his vocation to spiritualize and perfect the masses. Thus the hero-statesman, unlike Scheler's other models, was an intermediary between the worlds of drive (*Trieb*) and spirit (*Geist*), the realm of power, and that of spiritual culture. Whereas the sage and the saint should remain far from power, the statesman should seek power with a deep sense of responsibility to the whole society, knowing that only through the attainment of power could he draw forth and realize the potential energies of the nation.[104]

Scheler's political theory was marred by a serious weakness to which we have already alluded. Although he admitted that the statesman must be responsible to the highest moral and religious authorities on earth as well as to his own conscience, Scheler so despised the ignorance of the "masses," that he was loath to see the hands of the statesman tied by political responsibility to the electorate. His view of the relationship between the leader and the led presumed "enlightened" leadership. In the final analysis, it was not very different from Plato's theory of the society ruled by "philosopher kings." In fact, because Scheler believed that all societies were inevitably controlled and guided by a small elite, he believed that his social function as a philosopher was to educate an elite of new leaders for postwar Germany. During the last decade of his life, Scheler sought out opportunities to present his views in public lectures at the Institute for Politics, the Lessing Institute, and the Army Officer's Training Academy, Berlin academies where

104 *Ibid.*, p. 344.

Germany's future leaders were being formed. That Scheler should have chosen this road to political influence follows from his theory of political leadership. If the "masses" simply imitate their leaders in all things, then the man who forms the character of the leaders has a hand in shaping the culture and society of the future.

But the questions still remain: Where do new elites come from? How are they formed? How do they attain power, and what guarantee do we have that, once they have attained it they will use it responsibly? Such questions did occur to Scheler, occasionally. But as he gazed at the shambles of Germany after the war, the practical problems seemed so overwhelming that it was easy for him to project them to cosmic dimensions. As the present slipped out of focus, Scheler's speculations moved to the grandiose problem of the meaning of history itself. Never adept at thinking a concrete problem through to its practical solution, Scheler was soon lost in the misty clouds of hope and despair as he ruminated over the ultimate meaning of world history.

6

LOOKING AT modern society, Max Weber, like Spengler, became pessimistic as he observed that bureaucracy was gradually replacing individual initiative in all spheres of life. Weber called this process "the routinization of charisma." The trend toward bureaucracy seemed inevitable to Weber. In fact, he considered it simply a part of the general tendency of Western civilization toward rationalization, that is, toward the elimination of all magical and unpredictable elements from man's life. Weber viewed the total process with mixed feelings, but he felt only pessimism and despair at the disappearance of charismatic leaders from the worlds of politics and religion.[105]

---

105 *From Max Weber: Essays in Sociology*, pp. 51–55. For Weber's discussion of the "routinization of charisma" see *Ibid.*, p. 245 ff.

Whereas many of the younger generation were filled with confidence that a new religion would develop and guide them in the postwar world, Scheler agreed with Weber that the very structure of modern society worked against the development of a new religion. Like Weber, Scheler believed that religion had its origin in a special type of charismatic personality. In his book, *On the Eternal in Man* (1921), Scheler called this type the *homo religiosus*.[106] He quoted Weber to the effect that increasing specialization and the predominantly technical concerns of modern life had led to a "decline in the human capacity for religious knowledge of transcendental forces."[107] As modern life became increasingly rationalized and secularized, the advent of new saints, or religious leaders, became ever more unlikely. These "great men of religion, on whose emergence there hangs the whole history of religion," could not be "manufactured" by education, politics, or any modern forms of organization. *Homo religiosus,* as a type, could only be "grown" by a society at a particular stage in its evolution. The social structure at this stage was based on close communal ties (*Gemeinschaft*) rather than on the arbitrary contractual relationships (*Gesellschaft*) which Scheler believed governed modern social life. During the course of modern industrial development, the social conditions and forms of life requisite for the rise of new religions had been gradually destroyed by the very progress of civilization.[108] To seek a new religion in the present day would be futile, wrote Scheler, because the social conditions militated against the growth of religious leaders who could found and inspire such a new faith. The task of contemporary man was more modest: "this older, more sophisticated humanity must imprint into the tractable stuff of the world the values which an earlier, younger, more spiritually alive humanity saw and sensed."[109]

[106] *On the Eternal in Man*, p. 356.
[107] *Ibid.*, p. 355. See also Scheler's discussion of "the holy man" as a model human type in "Vorbilder und Führer," *Nachlass Schriften*, pp. 274–288.
[108] *On the Eternal in Man*, p. 355.
[109] *Ibid.*, p. 356.

The decline in man's "organs of religious cognition" in modern society was only a part of a much more general decline characteristic of the transition from communal (*Gemeinschaft*) to associational (*Gesellschaft*) forms of social life.[110] Looking toward the future from the shambles left by the war, Scheler could see little hope. The general trend described by Spengler, the tendency of modern society to eliminate all heroic and aristocratic virtues, coincided with Scheler's own prognosis in *Ressentiment*.[111] What Spengler described as merely a "cultural" phenomenon, however, Scheler, with characteristic boldness of generalization, projected into cosmic dimensions: Man, as a biological species, was withering and gradually heading for extinction. "Even if the various parts of mankind — races, peoples, and civilizations — exist in different phases of the process — the vital law of withering and death still holds for mankind as a whole just as it does for the individual."[112]

In the second edition of his book *On the Nature of Sympathy* (1922), Scheler explicitly rejected any view of history that would interpret it in terms of a linear "progressive" evolution:

Our conceptions of life as everywhere "evolving" towards the human, and of man himself as progressing throughout his history towards present-day civilization, have been profoundly modified in one essential respect: we now realize that in this evolution, life and mankind have not only *acquired* essential capacities but have also *lost* them. Thus man has all but lost the animals' capacity for specialized identification, and many of their instincts, thanks to the hypertrophy of his "intellect"; just as the civilized man has all but lost the primitive's capacity for identification and the adult that of the child. . . . It seems as though certain kinds of knowledge can be acquired only in youth or not at all. . . . This is evidently how civilized man has lost his sense of the "supernatural" in religion, so that he has to "keep the faith" and "trust" in what his forebears could still discover and see for themselves (it being "natural" to them).

110 *Ibid.*, p. 244 ff. Scheler cited Ferdinand Tönnies's *Gemeinschaft und Gesellschaft* (1887), as the pioneer study which had interpreted the direction of modern social development.
111 See Chapter Two.
112 *On the Eternal in Man*, p. 240.

Indeed, the modes of knowledge appropriate to particular types of object seem to be necessarily related to specific phases of development and to no others. Every advance in intellectual capacity involves an increasingly extensive decline in these other powers. The ideal to aim at would be a *synthesis* between progress and the maintenance of tradition — including the revival of what threatens to become extinct — together with an integration of the sequence of tasks assigned to each stage of development, from animal to man, primitive to civilized, child to adult.[113]

Scheler spoke of woman, for example, as a being who possessed powers of intuition that had atrophied in man.[114] Woman also had unique powers of identification and sensitivity to the needs of others that grew out of her maternal instincts. This intuitive approach to life could be cultivated and encouraged among Western men as well as women. As a result, Scheler hoped men would begin to rediscover the primary ties which he believed bound all human beings together in solidarity.

Needless to say, Scheler did not believe that science and technology could provide a way of combating the trend toward decadence and the eventual extinction of humanity. Since modern science had begun to cut down the infant mortality rate, the process of natural selection was ceasing to function. The lower forms of humanity were on the increase. In a footnote to the 1922 edition of *Sympathy*, Scheler commented: "In contrast to the previous optimism concerning racial matters, the recent Conference on Social Biology held in New York in 1922 unanimously agreed that European man is in the throes of a racial decline for which there is no present remedy."[115] Furthermore, in the twentieth century, world population was increas-

113 *On the Nature of Sympathy*, tr. Peter Heath (London, Routledge and Kegan Paul, 1954), pp. 31–32.
114 *Ibid.* The reader familiar with the works of D. H. Lawrence, may recognize a parallel to Scheler's ideas in Lawrence's novels. Lawrence may well have read Scheler, for he read German philosophy easily and was married to an intelligent German woman. He need not have, however, for the two men shared a temperamental affinity in their feeling for what was referred to earlier as the bond of being, which unites man and nature. See Chapter One.
115 *Ibid.*, p. 126.

ing so rapidly that technological innovation could never succeed in liberating man's spiritual energies from the burden of
work as optimists hoped. As modern medicine conquered old
diseases, modern civilization brought new ones in its wake.
Mankind seemed "to be entangling itself in an increasingly
complicated embroilment with nature and with itself and, ever
more deeply in a universe of means [which it would be less
and less able to control] for spiritual ends."[116] Man was becoming the tool of his own machinery. His handiwork was
gradually becoming his master.

The future looked bleak indeed. Society was becoming a
"human mass ever more preoccupied with bending its mental
powers to the organized satisfaction of its relatively lowest
needs."[117] Scheler even formulated this trend into a law of
social evolution: "Every quantitative increase in the pleasure of
the masses or in the alleviation of their rawest forms of distress,
is attended by an eternally irreversible reduction toward
mediocrity of the emotions of happiness and grief."[118] In the
coming years both the quantity and the quality of the forms
of pleasure would decline. The individual's personal freedom
to determine his own course of action would also decrease as
the area of human freedom became ever more restricted, and
there would be an increase of automatic and inexorable collective forces.[119]

Scheler was to remain pessimistic about the level of culture
and the freedom of the cultured individual in the era of adjustment (*Ausgleich*)[120] until his death. As long as he retained
a belief in the redemption of man through the intervention of
God in history, however, he could not abandon all hope. No
trend of historical development was inevitable or irreversible.
It could be reversed, its course altered, through God's redemp-
tive action in history.

116 *On the Eternal in Man,* p. 245.
117 *Ibid.*   118 *Ibid.*
119 *Ibid.*, p. 246.
120 See Chapter Seven.

The philosophy of history we have been analyzing was a product of Scheler's Catholic period. His pessimism regarding the future found its theological foundation in the traditional Christian doctrine of original sin. For Scheler the fall of man was not simply a past event that occurred at the advent of human history; the fall was an ever present metaphysical reality affecting every moment of human time and existence.[121] A world left to itself would constantly decrease in positive value. The proceses of decay and death gnawed relentlessly at the whole of creation. If the world were not continually raised up by redemption, if higher powers did not freely condescend to raise it ever anew, it would fall into nothingness. "Constant danger of death and the possibility of rebirth dependent on redemption, constant sinking to his knees for weakness, walking only by virtue of a power descending in compassion to raise him ever anew" composed the picture of man in history that came to Scheler's mind as he viewed world history *sub specie aeternitatis*. "No *laisser-aller* but only ever-renewed positive *deeds* of redemption on the part of God . . . [could] bring the world drama to a positively meaningful and valuable conclusion."[122]

If "the vital law of withering and death" alleviated only by divine intervention held for history as a whole, and if there were no real "progress" in history as Scheler asserted, what meaning was there in the cosmic drama? Was history no more than a tale told by an idiot? Although Scheler denied that the meaning of history lay in some future goal, he did not deny history any meaning at all.

For Scheler the meaning of history was inexorably intertwined with his conception of the goal of human existence. He believed that the ultimate goal of human life was for the individual to become "like God." "Become perfect, like your Father in heaven," was the commandment of the gospel which Scheler quoted in this connection. Yet men, as individuals,

---

[121] *On the Eternal in Man*, p. 237 ff.
[122] *Ibid.*, p. 237.

could only become more perfect if they were inspired by great models and leaders, Scheler said.[123] Therefore, the goal of history was the production of such models and leaders who could lead lesser men toward perfection.

Although the *ultimate* goal of history might be "the divinization of man,"[124] the *immediate* objective of history, the means whereby the long range goal might be achieved, was the production of an elite of leaders to guide and inspire the masses.[125] Here Scheler's political theory of the "law of elites" coincided with his philosophy of history. His old "teacher," Nietzsche, had viewed history in a similar way. From Nietzsche, Scheler had learned that the meaning of history lay not in its ultimate end, but rather in its highest specimens.[126] Scheler incorporated this Nietzschean view into his Christian framework by insisting that the "divinization of man" could only take place through the instrumentality of an elite. He agreed with Nietzsche that man could best perceive the meaning of history by regarding its highest specimens. To Scheler the heroes, sages, and saints, as models, could show what every man should strive to become. Their perfect *being* could inspire men to "become what we really are."[127]

123 *Nachlass Schriften*, p. 270 ff.
124 *Ibid.*, p. 273.   125 *Ibid.*, p. 272.
126 See Friedrich Nietzsche, *The Use and Abuse of History* tr. Adrian Collins, The Library of Liberal Arts (2nd. rev. ed. Indianapolis and New York, 1957), p. 13.
127 *Nachlass Schriften*, p. 270.

5

From Philosophy to Sociology

BETWEEN 1921 and 1924, Max Scheler's social and political ideas underwent a serious change. The reorientation of Scheler's viewpoint can be seen most clearly in his quest for a common ground of discourse among the conflicting religions and political ideologies in the Weimar Republic. In 1919, Scheler had believed that the resolution of these ideological conflicts could only be found in the religious sphere, namely in a conversion of the hearts of men to the truth of the Roman Catholic faith. If all Germans could be brought to share the same religion, then brotherly love and mutual understanding would replace the discord of ideological conflict and class struggle. By 1924, Scheler had lost faith in what he had believed to be the community building powers of the Catholic religion. He had concluded that if there were to be a lasting resolution of the political and ideological disunity of modern Germany, this resolution could only be achieved by men who had clear scientific knowledge of the sociological basis of ideological differences. Modern society was too diversified to produce charismatic religious leaders who could win the allegiance of men from every social strata. The sociologist, not the saint, had the panacea for social and political disunity. The free-floating intellectual, Scheler intimated, being above particular party affiliations, could learn to analyze the social basis of every party ideology. Recognizing the partial truth of each viewpoint, he could teach the political leaders of Germany to overcome their own ideological prejudices and to develop more flexible practical programs based on the conditions of the time rather than on abstract ideological principles. Such was Scheler's position in 1924, when he published his pioneer work on the sociology of knowledge, establishing this discipline as an important field within German sociology for the next decade.

The abrupt reorientation of Scheler's social and political ideas and research interests in the early 1920's cannot be understood without reference to developments in his personal life and their repercussions on his professional career. Scheler's disenchantment with Catholicism as a unifying ideology for modern Germany coincided with his personal alienation from the Roman Church which refused to recognize the validity of his third marriage. At the same time, once Scheler had lost faith in the truth of the Catholic world-view, he became aware of what he called "the partial truth" of every world view and the limitations of every individual perspective. Scheler arrived at this conclusion at a time when the Weimar Republic appeared to him to be threatened by the unresolved conflict of rival ideologies: Fascism, Conservatism, Liberalism, Catholicism, Democratic Socialism, and Communism. Scheler's desire to construct a framework within which the partial truths of every ideology could be integrated derived from the necessities of his personal life as well as from what he experienced to be the requirements of his historical environment. For this reason, our analysis of Scheler's sociology of knowledge is preceded by this chapter on his life and the intellectual and social milieu in Weimar Germany.

MAX SCHELER had moved to Cologne where he be-
came a professor of sociology and philosophy at the university
in 1919, as the reader will recall.[1] Scheler's academic post in
Cologne brought him into contact with many scholars in the
Rhineland, and he soon became close friends with a specialist
on French culture, Ernst Robert Curtius, at the University of
Bonn. Through Curtius, who circulated in Bonn high society,
Scheler became a regular guest of a wealthy Jewess, Louisa
Koppel, who periodically invited painters, poets, and musicians
to discuss problems of modern aesthetics at her home.[2] At one
such gathering Scheler met a lovely dark-haired girl, Maria
Scheu, who fascinated him with her combination of voluptuous-
ness and intellectual brilliance. For her part, Maria was completely taken with the highly sophisticated philosopher-sociol-
ogist whose magical eloquence enlivened and inspired many a
discussion in Louisa Koppel's living room. She soon enrolled in
his seminar in Cologne.[3] Maerit was quick to sense the danger

[1] Information on Scheler's life in Cologne is drawn from interviews
with several of his Cologne colleagues, especially the late Paul Honigsheim,
Heinz Heimsoeth, Helmuth Plessner, Robert Grosche, and Heinrich Lütz-
ler, as well as from the accounts given by his second wife, Maerit Furtwaengler; his widow, Maria Scheler; and his old friend, Dietrich von
Hildebrand. We have also been able to determine a good deal about
Scheler's comings and goings during the last decade of his life from his
letters to Maerit Furtwaengler, which clearly indicate the inner turmoil
and unhappiness of his last years. A good description of Cologne in the
1920's may be found in the memoirs of Karl Anton Rohan, *Heimat
Europa* (Düsseldorf and Cologne, 1954), p. 175 ff.

[2] Louisa Koppel, who now lives in Zurich, described her Cologne salon
to us and said that Scheler held forth there as one of her most scintillating
guests. She also indicated that on one occasion, shortly after they had met,
Scheler and Maria flirted with each other so openly right in front of
Maerit that it was embarrassing to the other guests; Maerit fled in tears,
and Louisa scolded Scheler for his thoughtlessness. "Now your charm
saves you," she claims to have said, "but once you are dead and your
charm is gone, people will speak ill of you and the shabby way you
have treated your wife."

[3] Information drawn from an interview with Maria Scheler in Munich,
1962.

to her marriage from her husband's new infatuation, but she was unable to regain his attentions.[4]

Scheler's liaison with Maria Scheu put a severe strain on his marriage, and at the same time it brought him into conflict with the university authorities, who had hired him to teach ethics and metaphysics to Catholic seminarians as well as sociology to business and law students at the Cologne Research Institute for the Social Sciences.[5] Soon Scheler began to recognize that unless he could break off his relationship with his mistress, his marriage, his professional status as a Catholic philosopher, and his membership in the Roman Catholic Church would be destroyed.[6] As in the case of his first love affair with Amelie von Dewitz, when Scheler had to choose between obedience to the moral imperatives of his religion and sexual gratification, he was unable to sacrifice "vital values" to "spiritual values," although he recognized and loudly proclaimed that the latter were higher on the absolute value scale.[7]

Scheler began to seek religious counsel from Father Robert Grosche,[8] and even visited his old friend Dietrich von Hildebrand in Munich, to discuss his moral dilemma. Walking with von Hildebrand in the English Gardens in Munich in the autumn of 1919, Scheler indicated his awareness that a crisis was at hand.

You know, I seem to myself like a naughty child who runs again and again to a precipice and whom God, in His infinite mercy, brings back each time just before he falls into the abyss. And still I run away from God's mercy time and again. But I have a terrible premonition that some day God's patience will be exhausted, and He will not draw me back but let me fall.[9]

4 Oral testimony of Maerit Furtwaengler.

5 Scheler's problems with the university administration began in 1921, but became much more serious after his divorce in 1924. See especially his letters to Maerit shortly after the divorce in May, 1924.

6 Letter to Maerit, January 11, 1921.

7 See Chapter One.

8 Oral testimony of Father Robert Grosche, who is still a professor of religion at the University of Cologne. For a time he was Scheler's confessor and spiritual director.

9 See Dietrich von Hildebrand, "Max Schelers Stellung zur katholischen Gedankenwelt," in *Die Menschheit am Scheideweg, Gesammelte*

For some time Scheler was caught between the two women. Gradually, during the course of 1922, he concluded that he could not be happy without the young, vivacious Maria Scheu. As she threatened to leave him unless he divorced Maerit Furtwaengler and married her, Scheler was forced into deciding between the two women. He chose Maria Scheu, but not without much inner turmoil that left an indelible mark on his life thereafter.

In a letter written to Maerit Furtwaengler from Berlin on March 13, 1923, Scheler indicated that he had gradually assuaged his inner suffering by throwing himself into his work. In preparing a lecture on the meaning of suffering, which was presented at Berdyaev's Russian Academy in Berlin, Scheler found that his thinking had become much clearer about everything.[10] The suffering and tension of the last year and his inability to find a feasible solution had almost completely obliterated his ego. Half of him lived for Maerit; the other half for Maria. He felt that he had no energy left for himself. Yet, somehow, he rejoiced and found a sense of inner peace as a result of this enforced liberation from selfhood. He felt that he had matured, and through all the suffering, arrived at an inner self-knowledge that had formerly been lacking. He wrote the wife whom he was about to leave that she was tied to him by an invisible band, and that the two of them still shared a common purpose: to help each other to become better, and to bear this life so that it might blossom and bear fruit.

Toward the end of March, 1923, Maerit left Max Scheler with the understanding that after the divorce she would marry a man selected for her by Scheler, and that he would then be

---

Aufsätze, (Regensburg n.d.), p. 622. Von Hildebrand personally described his conversation with Scheler to us in an interview in Munich, in 1962. He recalled that at the time Scheler was terribly distraught but seemed absolutely helpless to take himself in hand.

10 This information comes from an unpublished letter from Scheler to Maerit Furtwaengler, dated March 13, 1923, which is quoted in my unpublished doctoral dissertation, "Max Scheler: Philosopher, Sociologist, and Critic of German Culture" (University of California at Berkeley, 1965), p. 366.

free to marry Maria Scheu.[11] However, the prospective groom soon sensed that Maerit was only going to marry him because she loved Max Scheler. When he realized that she did not really love *him*, but was only marrying him for Scheler's sake, the man withdrew his offer of marriage.[12] Thus Maerit, having given Max Scheler his freedom, was left alone. Maerit then moved from Cologne to Freiburg at Breisgau where she worked for several years as secretary to Scheler's friend, the economist, Professor Goetz Briefs.

Because he felt guilty about having abandoned her, and because he apparently still loved her, Scheler continued to correspond with Maerit until his death. In these letters, Scheler assured Maerit that he loved no one as dearly as he loved her, that he missed her terribly, and that he longed for the good old days when she had been united with him in body as well as spirit. How much of these outpourings must be interpreted as an attempt to overcome his guilty conscience for having deserted Maerit? How much can be attributed to Scheler's sincere love for her, which he may only have recognized when it was too late, after he had pushed her away from him forever? It is difficult to know. If he had been content with his third wife, he probably would not have written the second as often as he did. But given his restless soul, one wonders whether Scheler could ever have been faithful to any one woman over a long period of time.

Scheler seems to have divorced and remarried in 1923–1924 largely because he could not bring himself to give up Maria. Several times during the year between his separation from Maerit and his marriage to Maria, Scheler wrote his estranged wife that he was still trying desperately to escape the match.[13] On his wedding night, April 16, 1924, he sent Maerit a letter which, considering the occasion, was quite re-

11 This account of Scheler's separation and divorce is based on the autobiographical sketch that Maerit wrote for us in 1962.

12 This story was confirmed by Tony Förster, a friend of Max Scheler's who now lives in Cologne.

13 See, for example, the letters to Maerit of December 22, 1923 and January 10 and 16, 1924.

markable. He wrote that all day he had thought only of her, and that he looked forward to seeing her again as soon as he could get back from his honeymoon![14] He did arrange a secret meeting shortly after his return to Cologne, and continued to see her up to the time of his death.

After his marriage to Maria, Scheler encountered difficulties with his colleagues and superiors who refused to condone his behavior.[15] The couple received an occasional dinner invitation among the wealthy commercial set in Cologne who were willing enough to have a well-known professor to show off in their drawing rooms, but Scheler's table manners were abominable, and his moods were unpredictable. In the midst of light after-dinner chatter, he might plunge into a deep theological problem or make some shocking remark that would ruffle the feathers of the *bien pensant* hostess or disturb her guests.[16]

Scheler was in his element in the semi-bohemian world on the fringes of the university, the world of artists, writers, and other "creative" people whom he considered to be like himself. He got on well with such off-beat academics as Werner Sombart and Ernst Robert Curtius, but he found the average professor too "narrow" and "stuffy." Because he was unable to present himself well to the people who controlled university appointments, and because of the scandal of his prewar career, memories of which were reawakened by the new scandal caused by his second divorce, Scheler was unable to advance as rapidly as he or his new wife wished.

He decided that he must leave Cologne, where his marriage had provoked nasty gossip among the citizenry. Although he despised bourgeois morality, Cologne reminded him of

---

[14] Letter to Maerit, April 16, 1924.

[15] Oral testimony of Louisa Koppel. Scheler visited Louisa to tell her his troubles. She was such a close friend that at his marriage to Maria, Louisa served as his sole witness at the civil ceremony which was conducted in a dreary hotel room, rented for the occasion.

[16] See the description of Scheler in the memoirs of his Cologne colleague, Hans Driesch, *Lebenserinnerungen. Aufzeichnungen eines Forschers und Denkers in entscheidender Zeit* (Basel, 1951), p. 165.

Maerit, and his conscience troubled him. On top of this, the clergy forbade Catholic students, and especially Catholic seminarians to attend his philosophy lectures and seminars. In turn, Scheler began to lash out at the Church for stifling free thought and metaphysical speculation by its "crude dogmatism."[17]

As the years passed, his attacks on Roman Catholicism became increasingly vehement. Probably the Church drew his ire because he found appointments in such anti-Catholic centers as the University of Berlin closed to him because of his reputation as a Catholic philosopher. Even after his death this reputation clung to him, although he had tried to prove that he was no longer a Catholic.[18]

From his letters to Maerit, it appears that Scheler became increasingly restless in his later years. He still hoped to find the perfect woman, the combination of what he considered the four feminine types: mother, lover, nun, and prostitute.[19] As domestic disharmony in his third marriage increased, he began to write more frequently to Maerit. Because their anniversary was Christmas Eve, Scheler thought of Maerit particularly during the holidays. As his first Christmas with his third wife approached, Scheler recalled his many happy memories of Christmas with Maerit. He had begun to associate the holiday almost more with her than with the birth of the Christ-child. He wrote that for him there was no Christmas Eve without Maerit. He was repelled by the superficial jollity of his neighbors, and he missed the loving-looks and laughter and the feeling of oneness

[17] Scheler, *Die Wissensformen und die Gesellschaft* (Leipzig, 1926), p. 433. Compare Scheler's embittered attack on clerical dogmatism in his speech at the German Sociological Congress in 1924: "Wissenschaft und soziale Struktur" in *Verhandlungen des Vierten Deutschen Soziologentages am 29. und 30. September 1925 in Heidelberg* (Tübingen, 1925), pp. 132–133.

[18] His letters in 1924 indicate that Scheler was considered by the philosophy faculty at the University of Berlin for the post left vacant by Ernst Troeltsch's death in February, 1923. After several interviews, Scheler was turned down because several members of the faculty were convinced that he was still too much of a Roman Catholic despite his attempts to convince them to the contrary.

[19] Oral testimony of Tony Förster and Louisa Koppel. Confirmed by Maerit and Dietrich von Hildebrand.

with God he had shared with her at Christmastime in previous years.

Physically separated from Maerit — although he insisted that spiritually they were still united — Scheler recognized a profound contradiction between his inner and outer worlds. In a moment of amazing self-awareness he explained this contradiction as the symbolic expression of his own divided nature that had brought him to this impasse. Ruminating on the tragedy of his situation, Max Scheler concluded that the whole thing had probably been arranged by fate — not an external fate, of course, but the kind of fate that is rooted in the marrow of one's bones, in one's character. His feelings of love and sympathy for her and his chagrin at the suffering he had caused her, had opened his eyes to his own mediocrity and selfishness, he wrote Maerit, not without a touch of self-pity.[20]

The turmoil and confusion of Scheler's personal life in 1923 and 1924 was intensified rather than ameliorated by Germany's condition. The country seemed doomed to economic and political collapse under the pressures of inflation, war debts, and active opposition from radical parties on both the Right and the Left in the early twenties. Scheler felt that the economic and social confusion and the political instability of the Republic grew out of the lack of a common sense of purpose among the German people. Before his divorce he had sought solidarity in Catholicism; he now became convinced that only a sociology of knowledge that incorporated all viewpoints and *Weltanschauungen* into a total system could awaken the spirit of community in the German people. To understand why he was so concerned with overcoming the ideological divisions in Weimar Germany, we must briefly consider the general crisis in German intellectual and cultural life in the 1920's.

[20] Letter to Maerit Furtwaengler, December 20, 1924.

2

W I T H T H E collapse of the Bismarckian Empire in 1918, the old certainties of nineteenth-century German idealism, historicism, and positivism were badly shaken if not dissolved. As the Prussian Minister of Education, C. H. Becker, noted in 1924, Kant seemed to have little to say either to the young or the old in the postwar world.[21] Many Germans looked upon the military defeat as the result of a moral decline they believed had already begun in the previous century. Ernst Troeltsch voiced their mood when he commented, upon hearing of the collapse, that "the external catastrophe . . . [was] only the delayed consequence of our inner weakening since the death of Hegel."[22] Like many another disenchanted liberal, Troeltsch despaired at what he considered to be the "gradual withering of belief in the power of the spirit to mold history."[23] The nineteenth-century German burgher had generally upheld this belief in contrast to the Marxian materialism of the masses. But now the war seemed to have disproved any belief in progress and in the gradual triumph of spirit over nature in history.[24]

With the old idealist world view in doubt, middle-class Germans looked around them in search of a new philosophy of life, and found not simply one, or two, but innumerable philosophies competing for their allegiance. Both Catholicism and socialism had become respectable partners in the Weimar coalition. But beyond these and the traditional German idealism and historicism lay a whole panoply of new sects from the George *Kreis* to anthroposophy and psychoanalysis. Bewildered

[21] C. H. Becker, *Kant und die Bildungskrise der Gegenwart* (Leipzig, 1924), p. 13.
[22] Ernst Troeltsch, "Die Revolution in der Wissenschaft," *Gesammelte Aufsätze zur Geitesgeschichte und Religionssoziologie,* ed. Hans Baron (Tübingen, 1925), p. 653.
[23] *Ibid.*   [24] *Ibid.,* p. 654.

by all these doctrines, the burgher did not know where to turn.[25]

"Look into your own heart," urged the popular philosophers of the day. "There you'll discover the various tendencies stirring within you. Follow your strongest inclination." Looking into himself, often for the first time, the German burgher was aghast. He discovered to his horror, not simply one or two, but a whole host of conflicting drives and impulses. The inner world offered no more security than the external one, so fraught with political and ideological conflict. Here were all these drives, but which was really the primary one? Freud said *libido.* Nietzsche and Adler insisted that it was the *will to power.* On the other hand, Jung proclaimed that behind all these lay the *collective unconscious.* Man should let *archetypal images* encountered in his dreams be his guide. The existentialists, Barth, Kierkegaard, Jaspers, and Heidegger, told him that *anxiety* was the fundamental principle, but the Marxists said this view was nonsense; the productive forces in society determined his very willing and thinking. Faced with this plethora of interpretations of the chaos inside and outside him, the burgher often chose the one that seemed the most inclusive, *Lebensphilosophie,* the cult of the *life force* itself as the ultimate source and goal of history and human existence.[26]

Philosophically, *Lebensphilosophie* represented a revolt against German idealism, especially in its Kantian form, in that it reunited the world of being and the world of values which Kant had separated.[27] The philosopher should not attempt to

[25] A good account of the confusion in postwar Germany may be found in Ernst Troeltsch, *Spektator-Briefe, Aufsätze über die deutsche Revolution und die Weltpolitik 1918–1922,* ed. Hans Baron (Tübingen, 1924). See also Helmut Kuhn, "Das geistige Gesicht der Weimarer Zeit," *Zeitschrift für Politik,* Neue Folge (1961), VIII, p. 5 ff.

[26] Kuhn, *op. cit.,* p. 6. See also Georg Lukács, *Die Zerstörung der Vernunft* (Berlin, 1954), especially chapter four, "Die Lebensphilosophie im imperialistischen Deutschland." Lukács places Scheler in the camp of *Lebensphilosophie,* which is not quite accurate, but he rightly points to the anti-rationalistic tendencies in Scheler's phenomenology (p. 387).

[27] Philipp Lersch, *Lebensphilosophie der Gegenwart,* vol. 4 in the series Philosophische Forschungsberichte, (Berlin, 1932), p. 1. See also Rudolph Weingartner, *Experience and Culture: The Philosophy of Georg*

conceptualize life, taught the new doctrine, but rather he should grasp life itself through an act of intuition.[28] The basic ideas of *Lebensphilosophie*, the cult of life and of intuition, had been expounded before 1914 by Nietzsche, Dilthey, and Bergson.[29] In the 1920's these ideas spread through the general educated public, disillusioned with idealism.

Sociologically, *Lebensphilosophie* represented a revolt against the mechanization (Rathenau) and rationalization (Weber) of life that had been taking place in Germany before the war. Through appeals to the irrational basis of life, these latter-day romantics hoped to triumph over the disconnectedness of experience in mass society. In every sphere of intellectual activity in Weimar Germany, people decried the thought and art of the prewar era as decadent and symptomatic of a civilization that had lost its contacts with life. Germany was overrun in the twenties by a legion who sought to rediscover the primordial ties of allegiance that had been lost by the overly intellectualized culture of the nineteenth century.[30]

As early as 1921 Ernst Troeltsch recognized the irrationalist movement as a "conservative revolution," parallel in many ways to the romantic revolt against the Enlightenment in the first decades of the nineteenth century.[31] Although the intellectual revolutionaries of the twenties claimed that they were the spiritual counterpart of the political revolution of 1919, actually they held essentially anti-democratic aristocratic ideals based on Nietzsche, George, and Langbehn. "They see their social ideal in a far different place than in modern mass democracy," noted Troeltsch. "They seek it in Plato's *politeia* or in an imaginary Middle Ages."[32] Troeltsch saw an affinity between

Simmel (Middletown, Conn., 1960), Chapter One, for an account of the transition from neo-Kantianism to *Lebensphilosophie* in the intellectual development of Georg Simmel.

28 Lersch, *op. cit.*, p. 2.

29 *Ibid.* Compare Max Scheler's essay, "Versuche einer Philosophie des Lebens. Nietzsche – Dilthey – Bergson," *Vom Umsturz der Werte*, p. 311 ff.

30 René König, "Zur Soziologie der zwanziger Jahre," in *Die Zeit ohne Eigenschaften, Ein Bilanz der zwanziger Jahre,* ed. Leonhard Reinisch (Stuttgart, 1961), p. 95.

31 Troeltsch, "Die Revolution in der Wissenschaft," p. 655.

32 *Ibid.*

the twentieth-century romantic movement and the one of the previous century in that both manifested the same struggle between aesthetic-pagan anti-Christian elements, on the one hand, and Catholicizing elements which sought for order through fixed laws and norms, on the other. Both rejected the Enlightenment belief that progress would result from the application of reason to the social order, and both turned to religion as the alternative.

What was Scheler's reaction to the anti-rationalist tendencies in Weimar Germany? Whereas before and during the war he had attacked the Western scientific tradition, now Scheler firmly repudiated the *Lebensphilosophie* of the conservative revolution. In a discussion of the controversy stirred up by Max Weber's speech, "The Vocation of Science,"[33] Scheler sided with Weber against his youthful critics. They were foolish to think that science could be "revolutionized by *Lebensphilosophie*," Scheler said.[34] He agreed with Weber that science must remain "value-neutral." A man engaged in any kind of scientific research should not allow himself to be influenced by modes and fashions of the day. He must serve one god — the truth — Scheler insisted.[35] If modern youth needed spiritual guidance and direction, they should seek them not from the scientist, but from the philosopher and the religious leader, from the sage and the saint.[36]

In the second edition of *The Nature of Sympathy*, published in 1922, Scheler admitted that in his prewar critique of bourgeois society he had gone too far in his repudiation of rationalism.[37] Upon reconsideration he had come to recognize the value of prudence and moderation, he said. His earlier attack on science and humanitarianism applied only to the particular conditions of late nineteenth-century European society

33 Max Weber, "The Vocation of Science" (1919) in *From Max Weber: Essays in Sociology*, tr. and ed. C. Wright Mills and Hans Gerth (New York, 1958), p. 129 ff.
34 "Weltanschauungslehre, Soziologie und Weltanschauungssetzung" (1922). Reprinted in *Schriften zur Soziologie*, p. 13.
35 *Ibid.*, p. 15.   36 *Ibid.*, p. 20.
37 *The Nature of Sympathy*, pp. 99–100.

which had been corrupted by materialism and *ressentiment*. In the postwar world, where murky ideologies and mass movements seemed to be threatening the very foundations of Western culture, the guiding light of reason must not be disparaged or snuffed out.[38]

How can one explain this significant shift in Scheler's stance? Perhaps, like other members of his generation who were disillusioned by the failure of German imperialism and militarism and the humiliating defeat that the *Griff nach der Weltmacht* brought in its wake, Scheler had become sadder but wiser. Like Friedrich Meinecke and Thomas Mann, Scheler became a *Vernunftrepublikaner*[39] and a spokesman of rationalism and moderation as he saw his own mistakes being repeated by the next generation.

Writing of the German youth movement that he had praised so highly both before and immediately after the war, Scheler became concerned with the movement's "dangerous tendency to encourage anti-rationalism and unquestioning obedience to their leaders (*Führer*)."[40] Scheler admired the youth movement's rejection of bourgeois materialism and its concern with fostering an aristocratic style of life, but he now criticized its dilletantism and lamented that it could never really become effective in fostering a new type of man and a new society as long as it lacked a well thought out program that was shared by all of its members. Looking at the movement in 1923, he found that it simply reproduced in miniature all the ideological divisions of German society. Every party and every religious group had its own special youth movement. The movement must free itself from these ideological ties and unite on its own platform, Scheler said.[41]

---

38 *Ibid.*, p. 100.

39 The term *Vernunftrepublikaner*, coined by Friedrich Meinecke to characterize his own attitude to the Weimar Republic, expressed the attitude of a handful of intellectuals of the older generation in the twenties. See W. Bussmann, "Politische Ideologien zwischen Monarchie und Republik," *Historische Zeitschrift*, CXC (1960); and Klemens von Klemperer, *Germany's New Conservatism, Its History and Dilemma in the Twentieth Century* (Princeton, 1957), p. 93 ff.

40 *Schriften zur Soziologie*, p. 396.

41 *Ibid.*, pp. 394–395.

The most serious charge Scheler leveled at the youth movement, however, was that of escapism. He bitterly complained of its tendencies to flee from the responsibilities of rebuilding Germany after the war.[42] Youth seemed to lack the courage and sense of responsibility to work to improve the present order. They lacked what Freud called the "reality principle." Scheler admitted that occasional retreat and withdrawal into the self to rediscover one's inspiration was both admirable and necessary. But he complained that the youth seemed to have no inclination to go from the cave of contemplation back to the world of social reality that was so much in need of their rejuvenating spirit. If the youth did not fill the vacuum of leadership the war had left, it would be filled for them by a new caesar, as Spengler had predicted. Scheler warned particularly of the growing political apathy among the Germans which made him doubt whether the "democracy cast upon us by fate" would be able to survive the attacks coming upon it from the radical parties of the Right and the Left.[43]

In 1925, fearing the extremism of the radical parties, the youth groups and the lower-middle-class proletarianized by the inflation, Scheler spoke out for moderation and restraint. "I am not, and am not known as, a man who bluntly desires enlightenment, and even less as a partisan of what positivism calls 'progress,' "[44] Scheler admitted, but facing the disorder and irrationalism of modern mass democracy, he became frightened. Only a democracy led by a cultured elite could provide a lasting haven for philosophy and science, he said.

To Scheler, "democracy" in Germany seemed to have brought nothing but "the horrible degradation of life to mass psychology, the gradual transformation of a democracy of liberal ideas into a sullen democracy of masses, interests, and sentimentality." Deploring the "revolt of the masses," Scheler worked for the development of "new truly cultured elites" who

---

[42] *Ibid.*, p. 392.

[43] *Ibid.*, p. 393. Scheler expressed a similar concern about the dangers of the new caesarism in his unpublished *Spenglerkritik* (1923).

[44] "The Forms of Knowledge and Culture" (1925) in *Philosophical Perspectives*, tr. Oscar Haac (Boston, 1958), p. 13.

would "forcefully resist this trend.[45] Unless the masses restrained themselves and *served* "spirit and culture," they would have to be held in check by "an enlightened dictatorship" which would pay no attention to the "anticultural masses and its leaders, but would rule them with the whip, the saber, and sugarplums."[46]

In reaction to the anti-intellectual tendencies in Weimar Germany, Scheler became a spokesman of the liberal values he had formerly denounced as bourgeois. The danger to true culture no longer came from the materialism and utilitarianism of the petty bourgeoisie which Scheler had excoriated for their slave-revolt in morality before the war. The threat to the established order — and to the culture built upon it — now came from the radical Right and Left. Therefore, in the mid-twenties, Scheler bitterly criticized Marxism and fascism. Furthermore, now that he had broken with traditional Christianity, he also scorned Catholic theology which he said belonged in the *Gemeinschaft* society of the Middle Ages and had no place in a modern democracy. Finally, Scheler warned of the dangerous tendency among his contemporaries to follow false prophets and egocentric medicine men who promised to restore the Germans' lost world power and heroic folk-spirit.

Before the war, Scheler had joined the chorus of the conservative revolutionaries who denounced the modern world and wanted to return to a romantically conceived folk community. In the 1920's Scheler turned against these anti-rationalist tendencies in German culture and allied himself with the traditions of the Enlightenment. "The Forms of Knowledge and Culture," Scheler's speech at the Lessing Institute for Adult Education in 1925, symbolized this abrupt reversal in his intellectual career. Henceforth, until his death, Scheler was to speak as an apostle of reason. Like Kant, his great predecessor, he warned that "a man who strives for an outlook founded on philosophy must dare to stand on his own reason."[47]

45 *Ibid.*, p. 17.   46 *Ibid.*
47 *Ibid.*, p. 1.

IN THE previous section we discussed the general crisis of values in Weimar Germany and Scheler's reaction to this crisis. In place of the general cultural philosophy of German idealism, in its various forms, which had more or less dominated German intellectual life throughout the nineteenth century, there now appeared a plethora of conflicting world views: socialism in its many forms, radical revisionist, religious, and conservative; Christianity, including a revived militant social-Catholicism and a neo-Orthodox Protestantism; existentialism; psychoanalysis; anthroposophy; various sects that claimed to represent the wisdom of the East, and a whole panoply of movements that attempted to revive philosophical systems of the past, adding the prefix *neo-* to indicate that they had been "brought up to date."

In such a situation, it is not surprising that a school of thought developed which considered the primary task of philosophy to be cataloguing and describing the various world views which were currently available.[48] The idea that the essence of philosophy was the description and analysis of world views had been elaborated by Wilhelm Dilthey before the end of the nineteenth century. The wide diffusion of his ideas and their popularized variants, such as Spengler's "culture-souls" was a product of the postwar intellectual and moral chaos.[49] Scheler spoke of *Weltanschauungsphilosophie* as the philosophical correlate of parliamentarianism in Germany.[50] In a pluralistic society, Scheler felt that one of the tasks of philosophy must be clarification of the different points of view pre-

[48] See Ernst Troeltsch's discussion of *"Weltanschauungsphilosophie"* in his *Aufsätze zur Geistesgeschichte und Religionssoziologie,* ed. Hans Baron (Tübingen, 1925), p. 653 ff.

[49] Troeltsch, *op. cit.,* p. 657. See also H. Stuart Hughes, *Consciousness and Society* (New York, 1958), pp. 336–367.

[50] "Weltanschauungslehre, Soziologie, und Weltanschauungssetzung," *Schriften zur Soziologie,* p. 26.

sented in the market place of ideas in order to help the voter choose among them.

The main tenets of *Weltanschauungsphilosophie* as it was elaborated by Dilthey and — with variations — by other German thinkers such as Max Weber,[51] Karl Jaspers,[52] Gustav Radbruch,[53] and Karl Mannheim,[54] were. (1) that there were a limited number of *Weltanschauungen* which formed the basis of all philosophies and intellectual systems; (2) that these basic approaches to reality stemmed from the temperament of the thinker and from his *lived-experience,* and that the *philosophy* which any thinker elaborated could only be understood when it was considered as the *expression* (whether conscious or unconscious) of one of the basic *Weltanschauungen;* and (3) that no philosophy was absolutely true, but that every philosophy was true in relation to the lived-experience (*Erlebnis*) of its author. The core of *Weltanschauungsphilosophie,* then, was to systematize philosophical relativism and make it a philosophy in its own right.

Scheler agreed with Dilthey and his followers that every philosophy grew out of the "lived-experience" of its author, and he agreed that there were only a limited number of metaphysical systems which recur in history, but he firmly rejected Dilthey's relativistic conclusions.[55] Scheler attempted to accept the postulate of a plurality of types of *Weltanschauung* and at the same time to maintain his belief in absolute truth by redefining the very concept of *Weltanschauung.* He claimed that the *Weltanschauungen* Dilthey had observed were *artificial constructions* (*Bildungsweltanschauungen*) produced by con-

---

[51] Max Weber, *Gesammelte Aufsätze zur Wissensschaftslehre* (Tübingen, 1922), tr. Edward A. Shils and Henry A. Finch as *Max Weber on the Methodology of the Social Sciences* (Glencoe, 1949); and his *Gesammelte Aufsätze zur Religionssoziologie* (3 vols., Tübingen, 1920–1921).

[52] Karl Jaspers, *Psychologie der Weltanschauungen* (Berlin, 1919).

[53] *Gustav Radbruch,* Rechtsphilosophie (Berlin, 1925).

[54] Karl Mannheim, "On the Interpretation of 'Weltanschauung'" (1921) in *Essays on the Sociology of Knowledge,* tr. and ed. Paul Kecskemeti (London, 1952), pp. 33–83.

[55] *Schriften zur Soziologie,* p. 21.

scious intellectual activity. Scheler pushed the frontier of relativity farther back than Dilthey by asserting that these *Bildungsweltanschauungen* varied according to the "basic cultural mentalities" of the different peoples in the world.[56]

A basic cultural mentality, or as Scheler called it, a "relatively natural *Weltanschauung*," lay behind all the intellectual products (*Bildungsweltanschauungen*) of any nation or sphere of culture. Dilthey's typology of metaphysical systems applied only to the philosophical systems which had been generated within the European cultural sphere. A different typology would have to be worked out to characterize the metaphysical systems of India or Japan. Scheler claimed that the relatively natural *Weltanschauungen* upon which all the intellectual systems of a culture were based were generally considered self-evident by the people whose thought was formed by them. These *Weltanschauungen* were "organic growths" which developed gradually over long time spans. They were scarcely affected by theories, and could only be changed through "race-mixture" and/or cultural interchange.[57]

We have said that Scheler attempted to escape Dilthey's relativism by making a distinction in the concept of *Weltanschauung*, yet all we have seen thus far is that Scheler's analysis of *Weltanschauungen* appears to be far more relativistic than Dilthey's. Scheler avoided Dilthey's relativism by insisting that behind all the relatively natural *Weltanschauungen* lay a constant and unchanging absolutely natural *Weltanschauung* which was beyond historical or sociological determination.[58] Scheler admitted that this absolutely natural *Weltanschauung* was "extremely difficult to untangle from the concrete group mentality and living traditions in which it was historically embodied." Nevertheless, he believed that phenomenology provided the

---

56 *Ibid.*, p. 22.

57 *Die Wissensformen und die Gesellschaft* (2nd ed., Bern, 1960), p. 61. Henceforth this edition will be referred to as *Wissensformen*. On Scheler's theory of *Blutmischung* (blood-mixture) compare *Vom Umsturz der Werte*, p. 356, and *Schriften zur Soziologie*, pp. 15–16.

58 *Schriften zur Soziologie*, p. 15, p. 22 ff.

method whereby the "essence" of human thought could be distilled out of its concrete historically and sociologically determined manifestations.[59]

Dilthey and his followers had abandoned philosophy and become sociologists and historians, devoting themselves to describing the plurality of intellectual systems in the world, but denying that philosophy could provide the norms by which to judge their worth and validity. Scheler, on the other hand, insisted that the tasks of the sociologist-historian and the philosopher were complementary, but that neither could supplant the other. As a sociologist he was a relativist, but as a philosopher he remained a believer in absolute truth.

In his speech, "The Vocation of Science," Max Weber had denied that science had the right to posit *Weltanschauungen*.[60] Weber subsumed philosophy under science. The task of philosophy was simply to analyze and to catalogue the various *Weltanschauungen* in the modern world and in the past. His monumental comparative sociology of religions represented a concrete example of this analysis. Weber compared and contrasted ancient Judaism, and the religious of China and India with Western Protestantism in terms of the influence of their doctrines on the economic and social life of the members of these societies. Here the task of the scientist-philosopher was simply to analyze the ideal contents of these religions (*Weltanschauungen*) and to show that certain *types* of doctrine showed an "elective affinity" for certain types of social structure and vice versa.[61]

Scheler agreed with Weber that *science* was unable to posit (*setzen*) *Weltanschauungen*, but he insisted that *philosophy* had both the right and the power to fulfill this task. Through a metaphysics that could establish norms by which to evaluate *Weltanschauungen*, not only could the philosopher describe the various *Weltanschauungen* in terms of the interrelatedness of their ideal contents; he could also determine their

59 *Ibid.*, p. 15.
60 *From Max Weber: Essays in Sociology*, p. 145 ff.
61 Weber, *Gesammelte Aufsätze zur Religionssoziologie*, I, p. 257 ff.

objective value as knowledge, indicating both their errors and their insights.[62] Scheler cited Hegel's *Phenomenology of the Mind* as an example of such a *Weltanschauung setzende Metaphysik.*

Hegel's *Phenomenology* was cast in the form of a "biography of the world-spirit — a biography in which instead of concrete events one had only the comedies and tragedies of the inner life."[63] Hegel's term *Weltgeist* referred to the self as the *subject* to whom historical events and processes occurred. It was as if the *Weltgeist* lived its life, suffering and enjoying its personal fortunes through these individual historical processes. The *Weltgeist* was God incarnate as man, the divinity in disguise, to whom the events of human life were supposed to happen. The *Phenomenology* portrayed a series of stages or varieties of *consciousness* through which the mind proceeded as it developed from common sense knowledge to philosophical insight. The contradictory phases through which *Geist* had passed in the course of human history were thus not simply described as alternative and irreconcilable *Weltanschauungen;* they were explicitly interrelated as dynamic *stages* in a total process unfolding under the ordinance of time.

Scheler admired the boldness of Hegel's attempt to situate all individual *Weltanschauungen* in a broad historical framework. For Hegel each individual incarnation of *Geist* was part of a unified process, the gradual actualization of the potentiality of *Geist* as it objectified itself in history.[64] After Scheler abandoned his belief in a personal God, he developed a metaphysics quite similar to Hegel's, but with one important difference. Whereas Hegel's *Geist* was all-powerful, the moving force behind history pushing ever forward and creating the conditions for its objectification, Scheler's *Geist* was *impotent*, dependent on the prevailing political, economic, and social structures for its realization. Because the "selection" of what

62 *Schriften zur Soziologie*, pp. 22–23.
63 Josiah Royce, *Lectures on Modern Idealism* (4th ed., New Haven, 1964), p. 150.
64 *Schriften zur Soziologie*, p. 23.

"mind-contents" would be actualized at any place and time in history was determined by what Scheler called the *material factors* (*Realfaktoren*) rather than the "ideal factors," Scheler believed that Hegel's *Phenomenology* gave a misleading picture of the unfolding of *Geist* in time.[65]

In his theory of *Weltanschauungen*, Scheler offered several "corrections" to Hegel's view. First of all, the scope was broadened. Although Hegel had claimed to be describing the evolution of thought itself, actually, like Kant, his "human reason" was a uniquely European phenomenon. Scheler's "phenomenology of the mind" would include other cultural mentalities, and thus be more truly representative of the human mind as a whole. Secondly, although *Geist* was shown to be originally autonomous in the supratemporal realm of absolute essence, Scheler's sociology of knowledge would show how every one of its "incarnations" was shaped by the prevailing material factors at the time. Thus, all historical thought systems would be recognized as conditioned by the social matrix in which they were engendered. Thirdly, Scheler rejected Hegel's dialectical view of intellectual history. Hegel had failed to see that there always had been and always would be a "necessary coexistence" of different metaphysical systems. He had related them to each other as *stages* which were gradually overcome in the evolution of mind. Instead, Scheler found that history revealed not one main stream, but many streams of thought flowing side by side, all of which sprang from various and different human personalities and cultures.

We have said that Scheler got around Dilthey's philosophical relativism by insisting that behind all the relatively natural *Weltanschauungen* produced by different cultures lay an absolutely natural *Weltanschauung* as the very foundation of human rationality. Scheler used the term *functionalization* to refer to the process of splintering of truth from this absolute realm into its concrete cultural manifestations in history.[66]

65 See *Wissensformen*, pp. 21–22 where Scheler contrasts his position with Hegel's on this basis.

66 *Wissensformen* p. 26.

Different societies in their encounters with the objective world have undergone different fundamental experiences, Scheler said. The members of one society were struck by different aspects of reality than were the members of another society. This experience penetrated to their mental structure and in due course dominated it. The very forms of cognition and the concepts used in a society were specified in this process with the result that gradually irreconcilable a priori schemata arose which Scheler called relatively natural *Weltanschauungen.*[67]

There are two aspects of this process of functionalization that must be stressed, because they are fundamentally important to Scheler's entire system. First of all, Scheler insisted that although different peoples *saw* reality differently, their different conceptions of reality could all be true. They were simply viewing the same ultimate reality from a different *perspective.*[68] Their perspectives were socially determined, but, to Scheler, this fact did not impair the truth value of their insights. The conditions of the genesis of thought did not detract from its validity.

Secondly, although Scheler insisted on the plurality of world views as a given fact from which all further analysis must begin, he did not abandon his belief in a supratemporal metaphysical sphere of truth in which the individual incarnations of truth participated. He maintained that if one works back from the particular concrete truths which different human societies hold, one will ultimately come upon the metaphysical truth which lies behind all its particular manifestations: "There are many different truths, but they all spring from the perception of the one ultimate realm of ideas and value orderings."[69] On the one hand, he recognized that the human mind is differently filled and even differently constituted in different times and places. On the other hand, however, he stubbornly insisted that behind all the apparently exclusive universes of validity there lay a realm of eternal ideas which imparted true validity and ultimate unity to all the functionalizations of truth in history. Thus he attempted

[67] *Ibid.*, p. 26.
[69] *Ibid.*, p. 26.

[68] *Ibid.*, pp. 145–152.

to unite the philosophy of absolute validity to which he had been committed from his philosophical career, with the relativistic viewpoint of historicism which he had come to embrace through his sociological studies.[70]

Scheler employed this concept of functionalization in his sociology of knowledge in order to retain the insights into eternal essences offered by phenomenology and at the same time to employ a relativistic approach in sociology. The functionalizations of truth in history were all grounded in the eternal logos which was beyond history. To quote Scheler's own words:

The human mind is not only differently filled in different epochs; it is differently constituted. In this respect there are many different truths. They all spring from the perception of the same ontic realm of ideas and value orderings, however. Hence behind all the apparently exclusive universes of validity there lies the one real dimension that imparts true validity and ultimate unity to all of them. Thus, we give up as wholly relative, as historically and sociologically dependent on the particular standpoints, all orderings of *goods, goals,* and *norms* in human societies, as expressed by ethics, religion, law and art, etc., and retain nothing but the idea of the eternal logos, whose transcendent secrets cannot be explored, in the form of a metaphysical *history,* by any one nation, any one civilization or even all cultural epochs that have emerged so far but only by *all together,* including all future ones — by temporal and spatial cooperation of irreplaceable (because individual) unique cultural entities working together in complete mutual solidarity.[71]

This new position is indicative of the general transformation of Scheler's thought between 1922 and 1924. One recalls from Scheler's biography that this was the period during which he broke with Catholicism and divorced his second wife to marry for a third time. As long as he remained a Catholic, Scheler believed in an absolute hierarchy of values which was rooted in the very constitution of the human heart. The Catholic Church, with its theory of a "natural law engraved in the hearts

---

70 An interesting parallel to Scheler's attempt to maintain an absolute value-theory and (simultaneously) a historical relativism may be seen in Ernst Troeltsch's struggles to overcome historical relativism in his *Der Historismus und seine Probleme* (Tübingen, 1922).

71 *Wissensformen,* p. 26.

of men," had provided an implicit frame of reference for his value theory. Once he had left the Church, however, Scheler found himself alone, believing in an absolute hierarchy of values, while his colleagues were generally relativists. In order to save his value theory, Scheler projected it high into the stratosphere, in which it became identified with a hypostatized *Geist* or *logos.* All particular cultural values and norms now gained their validity from participating in the ideal *logos* which was above (*jenseits*) all historical-social determinations. This hypostatized *logos,* even if occasionally disguised as "only a normative concept," was fundamentally important to Scheler as an intellectual tool. It provided him with an Archimedan point, beyond history and society, in which he could anchor his theory of absolute values, a product of his Catholic period which he did not abandon when he left the Church.

6

The Sociology of Knowledge

MOST GERMAN attempts to explain the interaction of *mind* and *society* have either been idealistic (Hegelian) or materialistic (whether Marxian or Positivist). Scheler's contemporaries, Max Weber[1] and Ernst Troeltsch,[2] attempted to tread a middle road between idealism and materialism by suggesting that religious norms and ideals were independent of social circumstances in their genesis but were generally influenced by their

[1] Max Weber never wrote a formal treatise on the sociology of knowledge, but in his studies of the sociology of religion, of law, and of social control he discussed the social determination of ideas. Weber's sociology of knowledge is drawn out of his various works and analyzed critically in Alexander von Schelting's *Max Webers Wissenschaftslehre* (Tübingen, 1934); and in two general surveys of *Wissenssoziologie* to which I am deeply indebted, Ernst Grünwald, *Das Problem der Soziologie des Wissens* (Vienna and Leipzig, 1934); and Werner Stark, *The Sociology of Knowledge, An Essay in Aid of a Deeper Understanding of the History of Ideas* Glencoe, Illinois, 1958).

[2] Ernst Troeltsch, *The Social Teachings of the Christian Churches*, tr. Olive Wyon, 2 vols., (3rd ed., New York, 1960). Troeltsch was inspired to study the relationship between church and sect forms and Christian social doctrine through his close association with Max Weber at the Univerity of Heidelberg before World War I.

historical environment once men attempted to apply these ideals to any social context. Scheler's sociology of knowledge (*Wissensoziologie*) also represented an attempt to find a middle way between idealism and materialism. His main contribution to the development of the discipline was to expand the realm of investigation from the sociology of religious ideals to include the sociology of metaphysical and scientific thought as well.[3]

Scheler's sociology of knowledge is relevant to a study of his political and social ideas because he hoped that this discipline might become "the foundation of all cultural politics."[4] He claimed that in it "the basic problems of educational reform and development, of leadership and administration can find a unifying forum of discussion and a common ground for their mutual cooperation."[5] Scheler hoped that the conflicts among the Republic's ideological parties might be resolved if Germany's leaders learned to recognize the limitations of their particular perspectives and called upon the specialist at *Weltanschauungsanalysis* to teach them how to overcome the one-sidedness of their class-determined perspectives.

3 See *Versuche zu einer Soziologie des Wissens,* ed. Max Scheler, Schriften des Forschungsinstitutes für Sozialwissenschaften in Köln, vol. II, (Munich and Leipzig, 1924). The volume contained a long theoretical introduction by Scheler entitled "Probleme einer Soziologie des Wissens," and eighteen essays on various aspects of the sociology of knowledge, both theoretical and applied. The contributors were Justus Hashagen, Paul Honigsheim, Wilhelm Jerusalem, Paul L. Landsberg, Paul Lichtenberg, Kuno Mittenzwey, Helmuth Plessner, Max Scheler, Lore Spindler, Walter Johannes Stein, H. L. Stoltenberg, W. Vollrath, and Leopold von Weise. Ferdinand Tönnies promised Scheler an article on the sociological relationship between religion and science, but failed to come through with it. Ernst Troeltsch and Paul Barth had also promised articles, but death took them both in 1923. Scheler's "Probleme einer Soziologie des Wissens" was reprinted almost unchanged, except for the correction of printing errors, in *Die Wissensformen und die Gesellschaft* in 1926. All further citations are made to the second edition of *Wissensformen* (Bern, 1960) unless otherwise indicated.

4 *Versuche,* p. 2.

5 *Ibid.*

1

THE BASIC premise of any sociology of knowledge is that human knowledge is neither solely determined by its object nor by its logical antecedents; it is also socially determined. Karl Marx and Emile Durkheim, the two greatest pioneers of the sociology of knowledge, both insisted on the social character of human thought. Scheler agreed with them that all knowledge is a social product; but he differed with them about the forces that are the primary determinants of thought and the degree of determination to which thought is subject. He distinguished his position from theirs in the following terms:

. . . the sociological character of all knowledge, of all forms of thought, is unquestionable. However, this [sociological determination of thought] refers *only* to the *selection* of objects of knowledge, which is determined by the controlling perspective of social interests (*herrschenden sozialen Interessenperspektive*). Neither the content nor the validity of knowledge is sociologically determined, but the *forms* of the mental processes by means of which knowledge is acquired *are* always and necessarily codetermined sociologically, i.e., by the social structure.[6]

Scheler insisted that they were only "codetermined" sociologically because, according to his theory of mind and society, intellectual systems were also determined by the preceding intellectual history of the society in which they occurred. The content and validity of intellectual systems were impervious to social determination because both content and validity were products of a "supratemporal metaphysical sphere of truth in which the individual incarnations of truth participate."[7]

According to Durkheim, not only the content of knowledge was socially determined, but even such categories of thought as space, time, and causality were social products.[8] Durkheim

6 *Wissensformen*, p. 58.
7 *Ibid.*, p. 29.
8 Emile Durkheim, *The Elementary Forms of the Religious Life*, tr. Joseph Ward Swain, (Glencoe, Ill., 1947), p. 416 ff.

maintained that the genesis of thought categories was a result of the group structure and social relations prevailing in a society. He claimed that the categories changed as the social organization changed. To Durkheim, language was simply a "collective representation" of the way in which society ordered its experience.[9] The function of the categories of thought which were derived from the group structure, Durkheim said, was to "dominate and envelop all other concepts."[10] These categories were founded upon the most general experiences of the group. Even religious ideas, he said, were simply a product of the existing social realities.[11]

Scheler firmly repudiated Durkheim's positivism. Durkheim completely failed to do justice to the actual nature of religious and metaphysical thinking, and therefore he could not properly understand the influence of social forms on religious and metaphysical systems. In the introduction to his book, *The Forms of Knowledge and Society*, Scheler stated that his own sociology of knowledge, unlike Durkheim's, was based on a "solid philosophical foundation."[12] Durkheim's positivistic sociology of knowledge was inadequate, Scheler said, because it rejected "a priori all metaphysical and religious knowledge."[13]

It is significant that Scheler's sociology of knowledge began with a critique of positivism. During the course of the nineteenth century, both historical thought and sociological theory were deeply influenced by positivistic assumptions. Darwin's theory of evolution was combined with Auguste Comte's law of the three stages by such men as Herbert Spencer and John Stuart Mill into a positivistic philosophy of history that explained all historical phenomena in terms of their genesis and development. In Comte's view, religion and philosophy were simply primitive forms of science. Scheler attempted to show that Comte's law was invalid because religion, philosophy, and

9 *Ibid.*, p. 417.   10 *Ibid.*
11 *Ibid.*, p. 420 ff.
12 *Wissensformen*, p. 10.
13 *Ibid.*, p. 58.

science were independent disciplines that corresponded to different human spiritual and intellectual needs. A sociology of knowledge developed out of Scheler's critique as he tried to explain the reasons for Comte's philosophical myopia.

Why had Comte reduced *all* thought to *scientific* thought? And — more importantly — why had the positivistic philosophy of history become so popular in the nineteenth century? Scheler suggested that the father of positivism had simply expressed the prevailing attitude of the modern European bourgeoisie which was oriented to knowledge of control and domination rather than to religious and metaphysical knowledge. The sociology of knowledge could show that different types of society fostered religion, philosophy, or science. Scheler felt that a theory of the relation between knowledge and society must begin with a critique of Comte and Spencer because only the positivists had thus far "brought epistemology into a closer connection with sociological statics and dynamics."[14]

Scheler's concern with the sociology of knowledge reflected his old desire to destroy the prevailing cult of science as the ultimate norm of all true knowledge. Scheler did not reject science as such, for he admitted that it was Western man's most important contribution to the history of civilization.[15] But, he was opposed to the idolatry of science, characteristic of positivism since the time of Auguste Comte, which designated scientific knowledge as the supreme form of human cognition.

According to Comte's law of the three stages, human thought had progressed through the course of history from the theological to the metaphysical stage, and thence to scientific, or true knowledge.[16] Comte considered this trend to be inevitable, and believed that gradually the cult of *Humanity,* served

[14] Scheler, *Schriften zur Soziologie und Weltanschauungslehre* (2nd ed., Bern, 1963), p. 29.
[15] *Ibid.,* p. 17.
[16] For a brief account of Comte's law see Henri de Lubac, S.J., *The Drama of Atheist Humanism* (New York, 1950), p. 79 ff. and also Heinz Mauss, "Bemerkungen zu Comte," *Kölner Zeitschrift für Soziologie,* Vol. 5, no. 4 (1953), p. 513 ff.

by a priesthood of scientists and engineers, would replace the superstitious rituals of religion and the ethereal wisdom of metaphysics. Religion was simply primitive metaphysics, said Comte, and metaphysics was an attempt to understand the nature of reality which must inevitably give way to scientific analysis.

Comte seemed to believe that questions which could not be answered by the scientist, such as the question of human immortality, were meaningless. Scheler attacked him precisely on this ground. The *questions* asked by various disciplines were different, Scheler said.

> The positivistic ideal of knowledge, according to which this evolutionary line is measured [i.e., from religion, through metaphysics, to positive science], rests on restricting the objective of knowledge to prediction (*voir pour prévoir*), and on adopting into the field of consciousness only those aspects of reality which can be controlled.[17]

The positivistic ideal of knowledge was only interested "in quantitatively determinable relations of sensual phenomena." It ignored all questions of "essence, substance, and powers."[18]

Scheler insisted that the positivistic law of the three stages of knowledge was completely erroneous. Religious-theological knowing and thinking, metaphysical knowing and thinking, and positive scientific knowing and thinking were not historical phases in the development of science, argued Scheler. Each of these was — and would always remain — a natural and necessary function of the human mind. No one of these three approaches to reality could replace either of the other two, for each was directed to a different objective. The religious task of understanding the world in terms of personal causality, the metaphysical task of contemplating the essences and eternal ideas which were accidentally realized in the phenomena of the world, and the scientific task of ordering the phenomena of experience into mathematical symbols and classifying the phenomena according to type were tasks of equal importance and

---

17 *Schriften zur Soziologie*, p. 29.
18 *Ibid.*, p. 30.

validity for humanity.[19] Each represented an independent mode of human cognition. Scheler believed that religion, metaphysics, and positive science rested on three entirely different tendencies of the knowing mind, and the proponents of each of these disciplines represented different personality types.[20] The scientist could therefore never replace the sage or the saint.

In particular, Scheler attacked Comte's interpretation of religion as a primitive form of understanding nature through which the social group adapted to its environment. According to Comte, religion would inevitably die out all over the world as it was progressively replaced by science. Scheler claimed that Comte had confused the social function of religion with its essential meaning as a "way of salvation."[21] The religious act was directed to God, not society, as its intended object. Comte confused man's sense of participation in the supraindividual totality of the group with man's love of God and longing for salvation of himself and all things. In short, man's worship was not directed to society, but to God.

According to Scheler, "religion rests upon the irrepressible thrust of the personality towards self-maintenance by the salvation of the essence of the person in a holy, personalistic, world-guiding power." The mental processes characteristic of religion (hope, fear, love, will) arose out of the "recognition of the incompleteness of the world and its orientation towards something thought of as holy and divine."[22] The goal of religion was the salvation of the person and the group. Its personality type was the charismatic leader or holy one, or in the organized institution, the ecclesiastic. Its social form was the church, sect or communion, and its historical orientation was retrospective toward "sacred events" completed in the past.[23]

[19] *Ibid.*, p. 30.
[20] *Ibid.*, p. 31. See also *Wissensformen*, p. 68.
[21] *Schriften zur Soziologie*, p. 31.
[22] *On the Eternal in Man*, p. 136.
[23] *Schriften zur Soziologie*, p. 31. Subsequent studies of the history and phenomenology of religion by Joachim Wach and Mircea Eliade, both influenced by Scheler's *On the Eternal in Man*, have shown that Scheler was correct in rejecting the genetic approach of Comte and his school.

Metaphysics, Scheler insisted, was as fundamental a tendency of the human mind as was religion or science. Metaphysics rested on "ever-renewed *wonder* that something should be rather than not be, that something is, rather than is not at all."[24] The metaphysician begins by asking himself: Why does the world, and myself with it, exist rather than not exist? Thus, for Scheler, as for Plato, philosophy began in wonder. The second evident insight, consequent on the wonder at being, was that "there is an absolute being, upon which all non-absolute beings depend for the reality they have received." Scheler claimed a third evident insight of metaphysics to be that in all beings other than the absolute, there was a distinction between essence and existence. He defined metaphysics as "the intuitive understanding of essences, their connections, and synthesis, and their relation to the absolute being and its essence."[25]

According to Scheler's interpretation of the method of metaphysics, its insights were based on *intuition* rather than on observation and deduction.[26] The goal of metaphysics was the highest development of the personality through wisdom. Its personality type was the wise man; its social form, the school of wisdom; its movement, growth of recurrent types. It was the expression of individual creativity and was not cumulative or progressive. However, once an insight into ultimate being was gained, this insight would remain one of the cherished possessions of mankind.[27]

Positive science rested on the need to control nature and society.[28] The mental processes of positive science were experiment, induction, and deduction. Its goal was a world picture in mathematical symbols concerned with functional relations rather than essences. Its personality type was the researcher-

---

24 *Schriften zur Soziologie*, p. 32. See also *Wissensformen*, p. 185 ff.
25 *On the Eternal in Man*, p. 128 ff.
26 *Schriften zur Soziologie*, p. 32.
27 *Ibid.*, p. 33; and *Wissensformen*, p. 90.
28 *Schriften zur Soziologie*, p. 31; and *Wissensformen*, p. 92 ff.

scholar; its social form, a kind of international scientific republic; and its organizations were learned societies, universities, and research institutes. Its progress was based on the division of labor. Thus, science was impersonal, international, continuous, cumulative, and progressive. It resulted in a devaluation of previous achievements.[29]

Scheler pointed out that Comte and his followers had fallen into the error of believing that religion and metaphysics were oriented to the same problems as positive science. The positivists had been too narrowly European in their orientation, he said, because they had taken the *European* intellectual development of the last three centuries for a universal law of human development. Comte had mistaken the religious and metaphysical decadence of the modern bourgeois era for a universal historical tendency.[30]

Scheler attempted to "unmask" the positivist theory of world history as "only the historical self-projection of the west-European middle class, in which the 'spirit of capitalism' had determined the ideals of knowledge and morality."[31] To Scheler, the positivist view reflected specific class interests. "Positivism was the class philosophy of modern industrial enterprise, bent solely on the expansion of power. . . ." Scheler claimed that as positivism had been born with the industrial bourgeoisie, it would die "with the ousting of that class from the conduct of nations and states."[32]

Clearly, Scheler's old hostility to the bourgeoisie and to what he called the bourgeois spirit of calculation[33] intruded into his critique of the positivist view of world history. His assertion that positivism was a product of the bourgeois mentality could not be proved. Its polemical intent, however, reveals something about Scheler and his age. After the war, the "un-

29 *Ibid.*, p. 31.
30 *Ibid.*, p. 32. See also *On the Eternal in Man*, p. 355; and *Wissensformen*, p. 68.
31 *On the Eternal in Man*, p. 355.
32 *Ibid.*
33 See Chapter Two for Scheler's critique of bourgeois civilization.

masking" of beliefs and assumptions that had been cherished by dominant elements of nineteenth-century society became a general practice among German intellectuals on all sides of the political spectrum.

2

THE THEORETICAL foundation of Scheler's sociology of knowledge was already laid in his phenomenological writings. In his *Ethics* (1916), Scheler explained that the eternal order of values which he had described would be perceived differently by men living in different societies. In his study of the phenomenology of religion, *On the Eternal in Man* (1921), he insisted that men living in different societies were likely to conceive of God in different ways, according to their own social patterns and traditions. In his social psychology, *The Nature of Sympathy* (1922), he attempted to relate types of thought and perception to forms of social interaction. *The Forms of Knowledge and Society* (1926) did more than correlate types of thought with types of society; it also offered an analysis of men's knowledge of one another which linked Scheler's sociology of knowledge with his earlier phenomenology.

According to Scheler, "the social sphere (*soziale Mitwelt*), the sphere of society and history, is given prior to all other spheres of human experience."[34] Every man's knowledge that he is a member of society precedes genetically, and directly influences his own awareness of himself as an individual. Scheler could have found support from Dewey and the American social interactionists, Charles Horton Cooley, George Herbert Mead, and Herbert Blumer when he wrote that "the *essential* character of human consciousness is such that the community is in

34 *Wissensformen*, p. 57.

some sense implicit in every individual, and that man is not only part of society, but that society and the social bond are an essential part of himself; that not only is the 'I' a member of the 'We' but also that the 'We' is a necessary member of the 'I' ".[35] The forms of group life in which man lives condition not only his perception of the world around him, but also affect his own self-image.

A large part of *The Forms of Knowledge and Society* was devoted to an account of the relationships between particular types of thought and particular social structures. Scheler's typology of societal forms, discussed earlier, included: (1) the primitive horde or tribe, (2) the organic community, (3) the atomistic society, and (4) the community of persons bound together in spiritual brotherhood (the Church Universal). Scheler believed that the types of knowledge promoted by the "higher" associational forms *presupposed* prior experience of the simpler, lower forms and the types of knowledge to which they were amenable. A knowledge of the existence and character of mental life in the "community of persons bound together in spiritual brotherhood" presupposed an implicit awareness of the existence of other members of the community which had been acquired in the lower associational forms.

The most basic awareness of the existence of others could only arise in the early stages of infancy because the mental pattern of the infant corresponds to that of the primitive horde.[36] At that time, Scheler believed, "we absorbed unconsciously, by means of true identification and a genuine [living] 'tradition,' certain contents and functions of other minds . . . which we should have been quite unable to acquire at a later stage or in any other psycho-social group structure than that of the horde. . . ."[37]

In his sociology of knowledge, Scheler attempted to ex-

---

35 *Ibid.*, p. 52. Compare *The Nature of Sympathy*, tr. Peter Heath (London, 1954), p. 219 ff.
36 *Sympathy*, p. 219.
37 *Ibid.*

plain "how the deep-lying ontological and epistemological relationships among men are adapted to the cosmic order."[38] He
assumed that the essential structures of society (the horde, the
organic community, etc.) were not arbitrary, but were rooted
in human nature and the cosmic order. Therefore, the "epistemological relations among men" (men's knowledge of one
another) were "adapted to the cosmic order" by virtue of their
social determination.

From what has been said thus far, it is evident that Scheler
accepted Marx's premise that "it is not the consciousness of men
that determines their existence; their social existence determines
their consciousness."[39] However, when we come to Scheler's
explanation of the determinants of the contents and forms of
consciousness, the similarity of Scheler's theory to that of Marx
quickly disappears. Instead of citing one factor, such as the
"relations of production" or the "division of labor in society"
as the determinant of intellectual systems, Scheler elaborated a
complex dualistic schema in which thought was said to be "codetermined simultaneously by both intellectual and material
factors (*Ideal-und Realfaktoren*)."[40]

This attempt to integrate idealistic and Marxist interpretations revealed Scheler's heritage; he insisted on preserving the
"eternal essences" of his phenomenological period. These essences were independent of social determination; they were
ideal factors in that they were supposed to exist according to
their own laws. On the other hand, they could only be realized
when men perceived them, and the perception of the ideal realm
was determined by the "ruling perspective of social interests."

What did Scheler mean by *Realfaktoren?* They included
such drives as the power of blood, the will-to-power, and the
drive for economic profit. Scheler did not believe that all drives

38 *Ibid.*, p. 215.
39 Karl Marx, "Contribution to the Critique of Political Economy," in
Marx and Engels' Basic Writings on Politics and Philosophy, ed. Lewis
Feuer (New York, 1959), p. 43.
40 *Wissensformen,* p. 20. See also the beginning of section one of this
chapter.

were equally active at the same time; in fact, they conformed to a law of historical development according to which each drive was predominant at a different stage in the growth of a civilization. The phases, as Scheler outlined them, are reminiscent of Spengler's pessimistic prognosis of decadence in which societies were said to degenerate from the ties of blood to the artificial ties of the capitalist market place. Scheler cited three phases:

1. A phase in which *blood relationships* of every kind and the institutions that rationally govern them . . . form the *independent* variable of events, and blood relationships determine even the *organizational form* of groups; that is, they determine the *scope* of what can happen from other causes of a real sort, for example political and economic.
2. A phase in which this causal primacy — understood in the same limited sense of the determination of scope — passes over to the factors of *political* power, in the first place to the efficacy of the *state.*
3. A phase in which *economy* receives the causal primacy and the "economic factors" determine real events, though for intellectual history they merely open and close the sluice gates of the spirit.[41]

It was only in the period of "high capitalism" that an epoch had begun which could be referred to as *predominantly* "economic." Marx's analysis applied to the modern period of world history, when the economic drive had replaced the more heroic will-to-power of feudal society, but it was a great error for the social scientist to apply Marx's economic interpretation of history — which applied only to decadent modern society — to earlier epochs of world history.

Thus Scheler did not reject Marx's economic interpretation of history outright. It was partially true of different periods in history, and was particularly accurate in explaining the phenomena of modern European history since the dissolution of feudal society and the rise of capitalism. However, Marx, like Comte, had erred, Scheler said, in interpreting as a universal historical tendency something that was, in fact, a unique

[41]*Wissensformen,* pp. 44–45.

phenomenon of modern industrial society.[42] Just as Comte had projected the decline of metaphysics and religion in modern European civilization into a law of universal history, so, also, Marx had been misled into assuming that the fundamental importance of wealth characteristic of modern industrial society was equally characteristic of all previous historical epochs. Scheler admitted that Marx's analysis applied to "the era of Western European history in which wealth determines power, instead of power, wealth,"[43] but he denied that the economic interpretation of history was adequate to explain the social and intellectual history of other epochs and civilizations besides that of modern Europe.

Marx's main error, and that of all naturalistic theories, thought Scheler, was that he assumed the *independent variable* to be one and the same throughout history. Scheler insisted that there was, in fact, no constant independent variable which determined the social and power relations in all historical epochs and civilizations. However, he did see a definite sequence of primary factors that could be summed up in a law of three phases. In the initial phase, blood ties and associated kinship institutions constituted the independent variable; later, political power; and finally, economic factors.[44] Scheler may well have adopted this law of phases, which he described in terms of organic growth and decline, from Spengler.

If the *actualization* of the *ideas* generated in a society was determined by the *prevailing material conditions*, the *selection* of the objects of knowledge was determined by the *prevailing interest perspective* of the ruling social group. According to Scheler, elements of the absolute world of ideas became active in human history only when some elite, the leaders of a particular society, accepted them as their own. From thence they spread to the imitative masses.[45]

42*Eternal in Man*, p. 384; *Wissensformen*, pp. 46–47.
43 *Wissensformen*, pp. 50–51. Scheler agreed with Spengler that the dominance of wealth over political power in a society was a sign of "decadence."
44 *Ibid.*, p. 51.
45 *Ibid.*, p. 51, pp. 258–259.

The substructural material forces in history created certain possibilities for the development of definite mental superstructures. These possibilities could only become actualities, however, if there were leaders who carried them out. As Scheler put it, the substructural tendencies (*Realfaktoren*) "open and close the sluice gates of the spirit,"[46] but there would have to be aggressive, mentally creative men on hand who would see that the gaps opened up and press through them if a potential cultural idea were to be actualized. Thus, behind Scheler's sociology of knowledge, as behind his philosophy of history, lay the law of minorities, his theory of elites.

Whether or not the members of the elite accepted certain ideas depended both on their general cultural ethos and on their drive structure. According to Scheler, no idea could be effective in history unless it united with "interests, instinctual drives, and collective drives."[47] Scheler actually held that "a doctrine of human drives is a *necessary presupposition* for sociology."[48] This means that he broadened the *Realfaktoren* beyond the socio-economic to include the psycho-biological as well.

In the final analysis Scheler did not ascribe primacy *either* to the socio-economic sphere *or* to the sphere of knowledge. Rather, both were determined by the *drive structure* of the elite, and this drive structure was reflected in the prevailing ethos.[49] Thus, according to Scheler, history was the result of the interaction of two ahistorical spheres: mind, which was absolute but impotent, and instinct, which was powerful but blind. The process of history was the result of the intrusion of the ideal sphere of norms into the undirected organismic world.[50] The actual development of a culture, however, was not determined by ideal factors, but by the constitution of the previously existing real factors. Mind could only play a guiding role, hindering or speeding up the general trend of real factors. Mind, in Scheler's view, had a two-fold function: (1) guidance, holding

46 *Ibid.*, p. 40.   47 *Ibid.*, p. 259.
48 *Ibid.*, p. 18.   49 *Ibid.*, p. 51.
50 *Ibid.*, p. 21.

forth a value or idea; and (2) direction, restraining or releasing the instinctive impulses whose movements realize the idea. The modifiable fatality of the real factors, however, would never determine the meaning or content of the intellectual-cultural sphere, for Scheler insisted that these always remained autonomous, developing according to their own laws.[51] The real factors, then, determined only the *selection* of those ideal factors which would be realized in a particular historical culture.

The social scientist, familiar with the prevailing social, economic, and drive structures in a particular society could explain from these why, out of the total spectrum of thought forms potentially available to the human mind, only certain forms could be actualized in that society.

It is always only the difference between the *real* works and the works that are potentially *possible* according to the laws of meaning, that can be explained by the history of real conditions and events in the progress of the history of mind. The *"fatalité modifiable"* of real history by no means determines, therefore, the positive *intellectual content* of the works of the mind, but it rather hinders, releases, retards, or accelerates the actualization and realization of this intellectual content. To employ a metaphor: it opens and closes in a definite *manner* and *order* the sluice gates of the spirit.[52]

Scheler's view, then, in contrast to that of Marx, was that the material factors in history do not determine the *contents* and meaning of spiritual culture; they merely determine the *realization* (*Auswirkung*) of spiritual potentialities. They limit the range of ideal possibilities that can be realized in any given historical situation.

Scheler had formulated his answer to Marx as early as 1917.[53] Taking an example from the history of architecture, Scheler maintained that no one could ever fully explain the style or unique artistic characteristics of the cathedral of Cologne from the conditions of the medieval economy.[54] Only the fact

---

[51] *Ibid.*, p. 20.   [52] *Ibid.*, p. 40.
[53] See his review of a book by Walther Rathenau, "Von Kommenden Dingen," *Hochland*, XIV, 2 (July, 1917).
[54] *Ibid.*, p. 395.

that it was materially possible to build a cathedral in Cologne at the time when it was conceived was determined by the prevailing economic conditions. These conditions determined the fact that the potentiality to build a cathedral, which lay in the minds of civic leaders, could be realized. Who knows, asks Scheler, perhaps they originally intended to build something else? But the prevailing material conditions made it possible that out of the wide realm of choices that might have existed in the minds of the people, a magnificent cathedral was actually built. At the same time, if there had not been adequate capital, adequate manpower, and an adequate supply of materials, the cathedral of Cologne would have remained nothing but an unfulfilled dream. In short, the material conditions prevailing in the Middle Ages determined what kinds of structures could be built. The *idea* had to be actualized within the limits of the prevailing material conditions. In this way, the material factors determined the realization but not the idea of the cathedral, which developed autonomously.

We have seen that although Scheler insisted on the autonomy of mind, in terms of the content and value of ideas, he agreed with Marx that ideas remain impotent unless they are linked up with interests, drives, or social forces. The power of realization comes not from mind, but from the spontaneous action of a small group of leaders who are then imitated by the masses. Thus, in Scheler's sociology of knowledge men are confronted with a dualistic metaphysics that poses serious problems, as Werner Stark, one of Scheler's more recent critics, has pointed out:

Clearly, if these notions were to be taken seriously — and we must not forget that according to Scheler the gap to be bridged between substructure and superstructure is the whole gulf between physical and metaphysical — a meeting of the two could not be imagined at all. For how could a mindless movement select for itself ideas that would suit it; and how or why should ideas descend from their heavenly abode, incarnate themselves in this world, or mingle with the dross and dirt of these lower spheres? Clearly, for the theory to work at all, it is necessary to assume that the substructural bodies have enough *nous* in them from the very beginning to be able to recognize and appropriate ideas which are congenial or useful to them. But if we assume this, then they alone appear as active; they alone decide upon the realization, and even the elaboration (in human terms) of ideas; they alone work the sluice gates . . . through which ideas can enter this world as the sunbeams enter a house through the chinks in the curtains. But if so, thought is altogether powerless.[55]

In short, in spite of all his Platonic exaltation of ideas, there is a tendency in Scheler's sociology of knowledge to reduce ideas to the level of epiphenomena. We shall return to this theme in the following chapter.

3

THE NOTION of ideology was crucial to Scheler's sociology of knowledge; therefore, a brief discussion of earlier usages of the term may be helpful. Although the actual term *ideology* only appeared in the nineteenth century, the idea of "false knowledge" resulting from extratheoretical factors goes back to Bacon's theory of the idols and was later employed by Condillac, Helvetius, and Holbach, the *philosophes* who insisted that "our ideas are the necessary consequence of the societies in which we live."[56] The first person to use the term *ideology* was Destutt de Tracy who was one of a group of savants in Napoleonic Paris.[57] In his *Elements d'Ideologie*, de Tracy attempted to explain the role of selfish interest in the distortion of thinking and production of false knowledge (ideology). The objective of philosophy, according to de Tracy was to expose the

---

55 Werner Stark, *op. cit.*, p. 264.

56 Hans Barth, *Wahrheit und Ideologie* (Zurich, 1945), p. 62. Besides Barth's book, for the early history of the ideology concept we have used H. J. Lieber, *Philosophie, Soziologie, Gesellschaft: Gesammelte Studien zum Ideologieproblem* (Berlin, 1965); Helmuth Plessner, *Zwischen Philosophie und Gesellschaft* (Bern, 1953); and George Lichtheim's "The Concept of Ideology," *History and Theory*, IV, No. 2 (1965), pp. 164–195.

57 On Destutt de Tracy, see Barth, *Wahrheit und Ideologie*, p. 13 ff.

common ground of human needs and aspirations behind all ideologies, thus providing the lawgiver with a means of promoting the common good.[58] Scheler envisaged a similar social function for his sociology of knowledge. By unmasking prejudice, it could clear the way for "true knowledge."

According to Karl Marx, on the other hand, *all* thought was ideological; every intellectual system reflected the interests and position of a particular class. In "The Communist Manifesto," Marx and Engels insisted that the mental productions in a society were nothing but a mirror image of the substructure of existing property relations.[59] "The history of all past society," Marx asserted dogmatically, consisted in "the development of class antagonisms, that is, in the exploitation of one part of society by the other."[60] The social consciousness of past ages moved within certain common forms, Marx said, because these very forms were a product of the hitherto incessant struggles between the classes. These forms were really no more permanent than the class struggle itself, he said. With the disappearance of class antagonisms and the withering away of the state in the classless society, even the ideas of morality and religion, which men assumed to be permanent, would change. They had to change, Marx insisted, because "man's ideas, views, and conceptions, in a word, man's consciousness, change with every change in the conditions of his material existence, in his social relations, and in his social life."[61]

With the change in the economic foundation, the entire immense superstructure is more or less rapidly transformed. In considering such transformations, the distinction should always be made between the material transformation of the economic conditions of production which can be determined with the precision of natural science, and the legal, political, religious, aesthetic or philosophic — in short, ideological forms in which men become conscious of this conflict and fight it out.[62]

58 Lichtheim, "The Concept of Ideology," p. 167.
59 Karl Marx and Friedrich Engels, "The Communist Manifesto," in *Marx and Engels' Basic Writings*, p. 27.
60 *Ibid.*   61 *Ibid.*, p. 28.
62 *Ibid.*, p. 44.

The leading exponent of Marxist *Ideologiekritik* in Weimar Germany was Georg Lukács, whose book, *History and Class Consciousness* appeared in 1923.[63] The essence of Lukács's views was that thought was not determined by economic interests alone, but by both the social structure and the particular system of production together. The social-historical situation of each class, that is, the relation between each class and the social structure as a whole, determined the specific characteristics of its thinking, Lukács said. He admitted that *perception* was identical for the members of all classes. Only the *products* of their thinking were different. Each class conceptualized the perceptual materials in terms of mental categories that were primarily determined by the social structure. These mental categories, shaped by the social structure, affected the contents of the thought of each class. The structure of the mediated contents of thought was not arbitrary, however. With certain classes at certain periods, it reflected the actual structure and movement of the reality that existed independently of human consciousness. On the other hand, when the thought of a class failed to reflect the structure of reality, this failure, said Lukács, resulted from the concrete position of the class in question.[64] In other words, the truth or falsity of one's conceptual framework (*Weltanschauung*) depended on one's class position in society.

It is important to note here that in Lukács's theory there was no unknowable thing in itself. Reality could be known — and was known — by classes whose position within the system of production made the knowledge of reality valuable to their interests. Furthermore, for Lukács, interests did not themselves determine thought. The determinant was the concrete *position of a class* within the social structure. While the thought of a class might vary within the limits of its concrete position, its basic conceptual framework could not pass beyond the limits set by its sociohistorical situation. Whereas individuals might

63 Georg Lukács, *Geschichte und Klassenbewusstsein* (Berlin, 1923). On Lukács, see Victor Zitta, *Georg Lukács Marxism: Alienation, Dialectics, Revolution — A Study in Utopia and Ideology* (The Hague, 1964).
64 Lukács, *op. cit.*, p. 23 ff.

surmount the limitations of their social perspective, classes could not.[65]

It was essential, Lukács declared, to consider the extent to which the totality of the economics of a given society could be perceived from the viewpoint of a given position in the process of production of that society.

For however necessary it is to pass beyond the entanglement of single individuals in the narrowness and the prejudices of their position in life, yet they cannot cross these boundaries which are determined by the economic structure of the society of their time and their position in that society. Class consciousness, therefore . . . is at the same time, a class-determined *unconsciousness* of the social-historical-economic position of the class. . . . Whatever is false in the world-view of a class, therefore, is not arbitrary; it is the mental expression of the objective economic structure.[66]

In regard to the classes who were capable of ruling society, the important point was the extent to which they could become conscious of the actions which they had to perform in order to achieve and organize power. The degree to which a class became conscious of the political imperatives implied in its social position was of fateful significance for all its practical decisions, Lukács said. This awareness determined whether it was capable of solving the concrete problems presented to it by the historical process.[67] For example:

The bourgeoisie, who originally went into battle against the feudal-absolutistic society armed with the knowledge of economic relationships, were completely incapable of completing their own science, their most genuine class-science, [economics]. Even theoretically they had to run aground on the theory of crisis. It did not help them that the scientific solution lay right before their eyes, for to accept this solution even theoretically means to view society no longer from the class standpoint of the bourgeoisie. Hence the barrier that makes the class-consciousness of the bourgeois a false consciousness is objective; it is a result of their class position. No matter how clearly the bourgeoisie may be able to comprehend the problem of the economic structure and its organization, their consciousness

[65] *Ibid.*, p. 48.
[66] *Ibid.*, p. 63.
[67] *Ibid.*, p. 64.

must darken over at the moment when problems arise whose solution already points beyond capitalism.[68]

Lukács criticized the so-called objectivity of bourgeois science as a limited perspective on reality in words that could have been taken directly out of Scheler's critique of positivism.[69] Scientific laws described a logical world of fixed entities that man's understanding could take piecemeal on its own limited terms. Such an ideology was adequate for the development of physical science, said Lukács, but this ideology blinded man to the realities of his own existence in the social world. It inculcated the illusion that existing social arrangements were governed by immutable laws like those which prevailed in the processes of the physical world and that these social arrangements were beyond the power of man to change.

Lukács used the word *reification*, for the process through which the social order came to be regarded as unchangeable.[70] Because of this process, men forgot that social arrangements were transitory and that they could be changed through human action. Furthermore, by isolating the facts of the empirical world for specialized study, scientists disregarded the organic unity which alone gave meaning to these individual facts. Deeply influenced by Dilthey, Lukács argued that a science based solely on causal explanation was unable to grasp the inner structural unity of any society.

As a Marxist, Lukács also argued that objective science was completely blind to the inner dialectic according to which social reality continually moved forward through history. Lukács attempted to *unmask* the social function of bourgeois science. What qualified an empirically oriented system of thought as the ideology of the bourgeoisie was its instrumental value to the dominant class.[71] Nothing could serve the bourgeoisie better

---

68 *Ibid.*, p. 65.   69 *Ibid.*, p. 198.

70 *Ibid.* On Lukács' conception of "reification," see Maurice Watnik, "Relativism and Class Consciousness: Georg Lukács," in *Revisionism, Essays on the History of Marxist Ideas*, ed. Leopold Labedez (London, 1962), p. 142 ff; Zitta, *Georg Lukács Marxism*, p. 240 ff.; and Peter Berger and Stanley Pullberg, "Reification and the Sociological Critique of Consciousness," *History and Theory*, IV no. 2 (1964), p. 199 ff.

71 Lukács, *Geschichte und Klassenbewusstsein*, p. 199.

than this reified structure of thought based on the limited truth of objective science instead of the total truth of Marxian dialectics. Bourgeois objective science served to divert attention from the fatal weaknesses of the capitalist system by identifying what was in fact merely a passing phase of man's historic evolution with the eternal order of nature. In short, to Lukács, bourgeois science was a product of the false consciousness of the bourgeois class. Lukács equated bourgeois consciousness with false consciousness. The interpretation of reality given by the bourgeois was distorted because of his position in society.[72]

Proletarian thought, on the other hand, in Lukács's eyes, represented the incarnation of historical reason itself.[73] Lukács did not regard the triumph of reason as a foregone conclusion; the outcome would depend on whether the proletariat could appreciate and utilize the opportunities history offered it as a class. Because the condition of the proletariat required a revolutionary break with the existing economic system, it offered the only vantage point from which the social system as a whole and its laws of motion could be observed in their proper perspective. Marxist truth was supposed to transcend the illusions of reification because it looked forward to a rational society without classes as the proper alternative to man's self-alienation under capitalism. Lukács admitted that Marxism was a class ideology just as bourgeois science was, but he claimed that whereas the bourgeoisie falsified (i.e., reified) social reality, the proletariat, which was determined to overthrow the bourgeois order, perceived it more accurately.

Although Scheler did not mention Lukács by name,[74] in *The Forms of Knowledge and Society* he sharply attacked Lukács's belief in the superiority of proletarian science over bourgeois science, insisting that although the bourgeoisie had encouraged the development of modern science, science itself was not bourgeois, but universal. Scheler began by denying Lukács's premise that *all* thought was ideological, i.e. class determined.

---

[72] *Ibid.*, p. 64.   [73] *Ibid.*, p. 83.
[74] It is evident from Scheler's letters that he knew Lukács' work.

If there really was no instance in human thought which allowed one to transcend all class ideologies and interest perspectives, then all possible true knowledge would be an illusion, and all knowledge would only be a function of the deficiencies of the class struggle, as the economic interpretation of history argues.[75]

On the other hand, Scheler was convinced that class position played a role in the selection of the objects of knowledge and conditioned many of the basic attitudes men held. He drew up a table of types of thinking as related to class:[76]

Tendencies of lower class	*Tendencies of upper class*
1] Prospective time consciousness	1] Retrospective time consciousness
2] Emphasis on becoming	2] Emphasis on being
3] Mechanistic conception of the world	3] Teleological conception of the world
4] Philosophical realism	4] Philosophical idealism
5] Materialism	5] Spiritualism
6] Induction	6] Deduction
7] Pragmatism	7] Intellectualism
8] Optimism with regard to the future (the past is the "bad old days")	8] Pessimism regarding the future (the past is the "good old days")
9] Search for contradictions	9] Search for identities and harmonies
10] Emphasis on environment	10] Emphasis on heredity

Scheler was quick to point out that these were only general inclinations. To the person who denied them completely, Scheler answered that it was difficult to be aware of them because they were unconscious.[77] These tendencies were extremely important, however, because they were the preconditions of class prejudice. Scheler explained that the antitheses presented in his table were "living styles of thought and forms of intuition as they actually function."[78] They were "class-determined *propensities*

75 *Wissensformen*, p. 171.
76 *Ibid.*
77 *Ibid.*, p. 172.
78 *Ibid.*

of an *unconscious* sort," propensities which were "rooted solely in the *class position* — quite apart from individuality, vocation, race, nationality, and the accumulation of knowledge at the time."[79]

One of the main objectives of Scheler's sociology of knowledge was to show "what already comes to the member of a class as apparently intuited material (*Anschauungsstoff*), such as the objective forms in which he perceives the world.[80] Once the class-determined propensities of thought were brought into the light of consciousness, the thinker could free himself of them, Scheler believed, thus enabling himself to perceive social reality objectively despite his original class bias. Like psychoanalysis, *Wissenssoziologie* was supposed to free men from psychologically and sociologically conditioned self-deception by a process of making conscious the hidden motives of human behavior and thought.

Scheler refused to accept the Marxist idea that all thought was ideology. True knowledge must be distinguished, he said, from the collective interests common to men by virtue of their belonging to certain stations in life, occupations, classes, and political parties.[81] The prejudices induced by a man's socio-economic position could always be overcome, Scheler optimistically insisted, once the person became aware of them.[82] Ideology, by definition, meant false knowledge, or illusion, to Scheler. Ideologies were nothing but rationalizations of the interests and prejudices of particular social groups. Knowledge, on the other hand, was the objective perception of reality.

Thus, Scheler, having granted the partial truth of Marxism, reasserted his belief in the transcendental character of truth. His approach was wholly undialectical and he retained the pre-Marxian conception of ideology. The ideologies which were sociologically determined by one's interest perspective and class

79 *Ibid.*   80 *Ibid.*
81 *Ibid.*, p. 21.
82 *Ibid.* Compare Scheler's earlier essay, "Die Idole der Selbsterkenntnis" (1911) in *Vom Umsturz der Werte* (Bern, 1955), p. 213 ff, in which he explained how self-deceptions caused by extra-theoretical interests could be overcome and "true" knowledge acquired.

position were systems of illusion, not of truth. Marx had been correct to point out the distorting influence of social position on thought. He had erred, however, in equating these socially induced *predispositions* to prejudice and illusion with (1) the forms of being and becoming of things, and (2) the factually valid forms of thought, intuition, and valuation. Engels and Lukács had projected these propensities to error into absolutely fixed ideologies which were said to characterize and delimit the intellectual perspectives of the members of every social class. Against Marx and his followers, Scheler insisted that "class prejudices, and *even the propensities toward class prejudices, can be overcome,* in principle, by every individual member of a class."[83] Once the sociological origin of these prejudices was made known and explained through the sociology of knowledge, these prejudices could be overcome by every man no matter what his class position might be. With the *philosophes,* Scheler shared the belief that reason and education could conquer ideology and produce "true" knowledge.

4

IN LATER sections of *The Forms of Knowledge and Society,* Scheler attempted to demonstrate the influence of various types of social organization on religious, metaphysical, and scientific thought. His primary concern was to explain why metaphysical thought held such an important place in the Orient and why the West had never really considered metaphysical speculation as important as religion and science. In a sense, Scheler simply reversed Max Weber's famous inquiry into the reasons why science had never developed in the Orient as it had in modern Western European civilization.[84]

Scheler interpreted the predominance of revealed religion

83 *Wissensformen,* p. 172. Italics added.
84 See Max Weber, *The Protestant Ethic and the Spirit of Capitalism,* tr. Talcott Parsons (New York, 1930), p. 3 ff.

over metaphysical speculation in the West as a "product of the bourgeois will to power and domination."[85] Once again, Scheler attacked his old foe, the bourgeoisie. The orientation of the Western peoples toward political, economic, and technological power "made possible the victory of a personal theistic revealed religion over the metaphysical spirit,"[86] which Scheler felt had been stifled in the West. He contrasted the development of bourgeois civilization in the West with the aristocratic culture of the Orient which he claimed had encouraged the growth and development of Buddhist metaphysics.[87] Metaphysical inquiry would never appeal to the masses, Scheler said. The aristocratic social structure of China and India provided a congenial environment for metaphysical investigations. Free from worldly cares, an aristocracy had time for self-development and contemplation.

The Western bourgeoisie had always been hostile to metaphysical speculation, Scheler felt, because their primary concerns were inevitably utilitarian.[88] The bourgeois spirit of calculation had already begun to infiltrate Western religious and metaphysical thought in the high Middle Ages.[89] Scholasticism represented the bourgeois spirit in religious guise! Scheler went even further. He claimed that "the power-oriented bourgeoisie had combined forces with the ecclesiastical hierarchy to drive their common enemy, free metaphysical speculation, from the field."[90] This unholy alliance had resulted in "the victory of the practical Roman spirit of domination over the contemplative, theoretical, inquiring spirit of the East."[91] The Western Church had become more Roman than catholic, as a result.

Scheler's bitterness against what he considered to be the anti-metaphysical spirit of the bourgeoisie was already evident in his critique of bourgeois *ressentiment* before the war.[92] However, his attack on the church and his claim that the church and

---

[85] *Wissensformen*, p. 71.
[86] *Ibid.*
[87] *Ibid.*
[88] *Ibid.*, p. 77.
[89] *Ibid.*, p. 78.
[90] *Ibid.*, p. 81.
[91] *Ibid.*
[92] See Chapter Two.

the bourgeoisie had allied against free metaphysical speculation is a novel theme that only appeared in his work after he ran into the opposition of ecclesiastical authorities at the University of Cologne. After his third marriage, and his break with the Roman Church, Scheler became increasingly vehement in his denunciation of Catholicism, and he substituted his own pantheistic metaphysics for the doctrines of the Roman Church.[93]

To Scheler the Orient, which had a long tradition of metaphysical speculation, now seemed appealing. He hoped that in the future the West might learn techniques of metaphysical investigation from the East.[94] His sociology of religion exposed the reasons for the anti-metaphysical bent of Western religious thought. His sociology of metaphysics indicated how various forms of social organization fostered or discouraged metaphysical speculation. Clearly, Scheler's sociology of knowledge was designed to serve as the prolegomena to his metaphysics.

In contrast to metaphysics, which, according to Scheler was a product of the aristocracy, positive science was the product of two social strata which were originally separate: professional intellectuals on the one hand, and men of practical experience in the crafts and industry, on the other.[95] Modern science and technology, which had spread from the West across the world, had been born of the marriage between the philosopher and the artisan, a marriage that Scheler traced back to the Renaissance.

93 *Wissensformen*, p. 82. Scheler complained that Catholic dogma stifled metaphysical speculation by proclaiming Thomistic metaphysics as the only true system. He now decried "the threat to the individual from the existence of institutions designed for the purpose of salvation whose dogmas are bound to suppress independent thought and to cause rigidity of religious consciousness even among believers." Scheler found the Church's "most dreadful weapon" against metaphysical speculation to be "the prohibition of doubt (*das Verbot schon des Zweifels*) regarding matters of faith and morals as *sinful*."

94 *Ibid.*, p. 187.

95 *Ibid.*, p. 92. Compare Edgar Zilsel, "The Sociological Roots of Modern Science," *American Journal of Sociology*, XLVII (January, 1942), pp. 544–560.

The difference between Greek and modern science lay in the modern mechanical world picture, which was a unique product of the ethos structure of the European bourgeoisie.[96] Modern technology was not merely an application of pure theoretical science only determined by pure logic, mathematics, and observation. The will to dominate and control conditioned the thought and perception, as well as the methods of the observer, from the beginning.[97]

The theory of knowledge can convincingly show that the pure desire for knowledge, the use of logic, mathematics, and observation, would never lead us to a mechanistic explanation of the phenomena of nature and the soul. . . . The forms of thought and perception from whose active functioning this world view arose, are by no means constitutionally inherent in the human mind as such. The Kantian principles of reason [were] . . . simply one mode of thinking [which] the new will to power over nature carved out of all "possible" modes of experiencing the world. It was not "pure reason" or the "absolute spirit" which at the beginning of the modern age sketched out the tremendous program of a comprehensive mechanistic explanation of nature and man . . . but the new will to power over nature and the desire to work upon her on the part of the rising bourgeoisie.[98]

Scheler found that this new will to power had ousted by degrees both the high valuation of the dominion of man over man and nature that had prevailed in feudal society, and the contemplative quest for knowledge of a priestly and monastic society that desired to perceive and mentally mirror the essences and forms of ultimate reality.[99]

96 *Wissensformen*, p. 104.

97 *Ibid.* Compare p. 114 where Scheler quoted Spengler: "Within Baroque philosophy Western natural science stands by itself. No other culture possesses anything like it, and assuredly it must have been from its beginnings, not a 'handmaid of theology,' but the servant of the technical will to power, oriented to that end both mathematically and experimentally—from its very foundations a practical *mechanics*." Oswald Spengler, *The Decline of the West,* tr. Charles Francis Atkinson, 2 vols. (New York, 1950), II, p. 300.

98 *Wissensformen*, pp. 197–198.

99 *Ibid.,* p. 164.

In the medieval period, man's will to power had manifested itself in the desire to rule men, i.e. it had been political in its orientation.[100] The desire for dominion over territories and things had existed only as a means toward dominion over men. The feudal will to power over men was paralleled by the clergy's will to power over the goods of salvation. Together they founded a system of rule that was based on military might and religious tradition, on the saber and the cowl. But when the old ruling groups were replaced by the bourgeoisie, the will to power took on different forms. It was now economic and technical, directed toward a productive transformation of material things.[101] No longer was the domination of men the end; man now became the instrument through which nature could be dominated.

The liberation of labor that resulted from the breakup of the feudal world was "the driving factor for the development of positive science."[102] Human labor could only be fully exploited after every feudal tie was broken that implied the right to protection by one's lord. Scheler considered this process of liberation of labor to be the main tendency of modern society. Spencer (*sic*) had called it the transition from *status* to *contractus*.[103] Nominalism replaced medieval realism on the theoretical level, just as the contract replaced more personal ties on the social level.[104] But nominalism, as such, might have passed and a new metaphysical system might have developed.

Why did no new metaphysical system develop in Europe once nominalism and Protestantism had liberated metaphysics from ecclesiastical restrictions? Scheler answered that metaphysics was not economically productive.[105] The bourgeoisie, which earned its own wealth, was not inclined to support an economically unproductive intellectual and contemplative class as the feudal ruling class had done. Here, the transition from

---

[100] *Ibid.*, p. 165.   [101] *Ibid.*

[102] *Ibid.*

[103] *Ibid.*, p. 163. Actually it was Sir Henry Maine, not Spencer, who described the transition from feudal to modern society in these terms.

[104] *Ibid.*, p. 165.   [105] *Ibid.*, p. 166.

barter to a money economy made the difference. "Where the produce of the soil was immediately consumed, a certain liberality prevailed."[106] This liberality declined with the rise of a money economy because money could be kept indefinitely and could even be increased when it was invested wisely. The new bourgeois elite had a personal interest in increasing its tax revenues from unproductive restricted work forms. It saw no profit to itself from supporting such an economically unproductive estate as the clergy. As a result, the economic basis for a class that could afford to pursue metaphysical contemplative studies became highly restricted.

It was the *economic* unproductiveness of the contemplative strata, not their epistemological poverty, that brought about the collapse of medieval society and metaphysics, and made metaphysics the work of individual solitary thinkers and their schools. The causes were, thus, eminently *political.*[107]

Scheler recognized that the moral pathos of the reformers against the "lazy monks," despite the fact that it was cloaked in religious and moralistic language, represented the economic and political interests of the bourgeoisie.

The liberation of labor worked to the advantage of positive science at the expense of metaphysics. Nominalism and Protestant theology also provided a conducive atmosphere for the development of science. Nominalists and reformers alike had no use for the naïve conceptual realism of medieval metaphysics.[108] In rejecting medieval metaphysics, they eliminated the greatest obstacle to the development of science. Men could set their own goals for controlling nature only when they saw no objective teleogical order in the universe.

Scheler noted a number of similarities between the thought forms and attitudes of the Protestant reformers and the scien-

[106] *Ibid.* Compare Georg Simmel, *Philosophie des Geldes* (Berlin, 1900), p. 92.
[107] *Wissensformen*, p. 167.
[108] *Ibid.,* p. 100.

tists from Galileo to Newton. Both Protestants and scientists shared a nominalistic mode of thought and a general belief that the uniqueness of man lay in his *will* rather than in pure contemplative reason. They also shared a common concern with freedom of inquiry and with certain knowledge. Whereas the scientists were concerned with the *facts* about the external world, the Protestants were concerned with certitude regarding the *facts* of salvation. Finally, they both shared a dualistic view of reality, dividing it into mental and physical (Descartes) or church and world (Luther).[109]

This dualism rejected the medieval marriage of physical-vital-spiritual reality which lay at the heart of what Scheler called the medieval biomorphic metaphysics. The ties between this world and heaven, represented by the Catholic ideas of the communion of saints and of the kingdom of God as partially incarnate in God's church on earth were denied by Luther. The new scientists rejected the medieval ontology which conceived of all reality in terms of its participation in the great chain of being, that is, in terms of hierarchical relations referred to the perfect source of being, God.[110]

These common viewpoints derived from the bourgeois background of both of these movements. Both reflected the lived experience (*Erlebnis*) and value orientation of the rising bourgeois entrepreneurial class.[111] Their drive structure was oriented toward work rather than contemplation. All the psychic energy "wasted in prayer and fasting" that had been organized by a priestly caste whose orientation was toward salvation was now directed to work in this world. Scheler cited Max Weber's account of the role Protestant asceticism played in the accumulation of capital.[112] He also noted that the spirit of self-denial "in the service of scientific truth" characterized the activity of

---

109 *Ibid.*, p. 122.
110 On the medieval view of the Great Chain of Being, see Arthur O. Lovejoy, *The Great Chain of Being, A Study in the History of an Idea* (New York, 1960), chapter three.
111 *Wissensformen*, p. 101.
112 Max Weber, *The Protestant Ethic.*

the scientist once science evolved from its beginnings among amateurs into an organized profession.[113]

The nominalistic philosophy of Duns Scotus and Ockham, and above all, their emphasis on the role of *will* in the life of God as well as man, was sociologically and psychologically conditioned by the transition from *Gemeinschaft* to *Gesellschaft* social relationships which occurred during the Renaissance period.[114] Scheler characterized medieval biomorphic thought as parallel to the social experience of men living in an organic community (*Lebensgemeinschaft*).[115]

In the biomorphic world view, a thing was perceived as *good* to the extent that it *was* (possessed being), and *bad* to the extent that it *was not*, i.e. was deprived of the perfection of being. A thing was *better* in the hierarchy of being to the extent that it possessed its own act of existence (*esse*); *poorer*, to the extent that it was dependent on something else for its existence. God, as pure being in itself, was at the peak of the hierarchy. Seen sociologically, this type of thought, that traced value back to being, was a product of the organic community (*Lebensgemeinschaft*) in which all social forms — church, state, estates, professions, etc. — were interrelated in a hierarchy which paralleled the perceived hierarchy of being.[116] Those who were more autonomous, i.e. the princes and nobility, were higher on the scale; those who depended on others for their very existence (subsistence), such as the serfs, were lower in the hierarchy. This parallel of social forms and thought forms was not accidental, Scheler observed. The social forms of the *Lebensgemeinschaft* had been projected unconsciously into the world order. Scheler found this projection to be but another example of his thesis that social relations determined human thought forms.

113 *Wissensformen*, p. 101.
114 *Ibid.*, p. 117, p. 122.
115 *Ibid.*, p. 122. On the place of the organic community in Scheler's hierarchy of societal forms, see chapter four, section four.
116 Compare Nietzsche's analysis of the parallels between "good and bad" and "higher and lower" in aristocratic societies. *The Genealogy of Morals*, p. 197 ff.

In the new *Gesellschaft* social organization that emerged with the collapse of the feudal order, the vital ties between man and man were broken. *Contractus* supplanted *status* relationships. "The contract theory . . . is assuredly based in origin upon a feeling of estrangement from the social environment with which one has to deal (just as its correlate, the psychological theory of analogy, is)," Scheler commented in an earlier work.[117] In the new society, thought, as a living *function*, emancipated itself from the emotional organic ties of the *Lebensgemeinschaft*. Descartes's *Cogito ergo sum* was symbolic to Scheler of the new situation in which autonomous thought came to be considered the essence of human nature. At the same time, Scheler recognized that the new individualism, rationalism, and idealism, the new distance of man from subhuman nature, and the new direct relation of man to God signified a "tremendous leap forward in human self consciousness." This new *Weltanschauung* expressed the lived experience of a new human type.[118]

According to Scheler, once the medieval *Gemeinschaft* dissolved, the forms of being, considered God-given by the Schoolmen, began to be considered as mere thought forms rather than as ontological forms. Men considered them to be the result of a regular, predictable, dynamic process. The *stability* of the old society, and therefore of the old world image, had dissolved. In its place modern man had put a spatially conceived world, with a timeless dynamic. Reality now appeared to unfold in a vast stream of becoming in time, in which ever new forms came and went.[119] Only at this stage of human social development, when all forms and strata of society were in flux, did modern biological thought become possible. The ideas of studying organic nature in terms of its *evolution*

---

117 *Sympathy*, p. 232.
118 *Wissensformen*, p. 120. Scheler cited Wilhelm Dilthey's analysis of Renaissance man, *Weltanschauung und Analyse des Menschen seit Renaissance und Reformation*, Gesammelte Schriften II (6th ed. Gottingen, 1960).
119 *Ibid.*

and inorganic nature in terms of a united, formal mechanical model now appeared. Here, once again, man's social experience conditioned his understanding of nature.[120]

We have indicated that Scheler considered the modern scientific world view to be a great leap forward in the history of human thought. Nevertheless, he felt it to be one sided. The *value-neutral* approach of modern philosophy and science was based on a specific value orientation — namely the desire to dominate and control nature. Metaphysical and religious knowledge were denied as worthless because they did not help man to control nature, the latter being considered as the sole objective of human thought.

In his critique of nominalism and positivism, Scheler revealed the ulterior motives of his analysis. His main objective was to show the limitations of the scientific world view — to grant it a place, but to oust it from its dominant role in contemporary life and thought. In order to undermine positivism, Scheler attempted to expose the close ties between capitalism, science, and technology, and to show that the scientific world view had prevailed because it had served the interests of the rising bourgeois entrepreneurial elite.

Although the triumph of scientific over religious and metaphysical thought could be explained sociologically, Scheler did not conclude that the scientific world view was false. "If reality did not already possess a formal and mechanistic aspect, no . . . will to power would be able to separate it from the experience of that reality."[121] Thus, once again we see that *only* the *special selection* of the modes of thinking at a given time was determined by social and historical factors — *not* the modes themselves.

Scheler's interest in social psychology, and in the emotional ties of sympathy and empathy between man and man and between man and nature led him to some perceptive observa-

---

[120] *Ibid.*, p. 121.
[121] *Ibid.*, p. 197. Compare Lukács, *Geschichte und Klassenbewusstsein*, p. 199.

tions about the evolution of science. He found that "each new objective realm which science has conquered in her history has had first to be seized by an access of affection; only then could there supervene an age of sober and intellectually more objective research."[122] The new natural science, born during the Italian Renaissance, presupposed a new feeling for nature.

New emotional relations to animal and plant, that is to say to all which in nature, as something animate, is akin to man, are the bridges to a novel intoxication with nature. The extent and nature of the process of sympathetic empathy into, and identification with, nature are vastly different in the different epochs of human history. At the height of the Middle Ages they reach a minimum in extent and intensity. In the Renaissance this inherent potentiality of man's mind and soul breaks forth with hurricane force. . . . It would be an erroneous interpretation of the forces which have overcome the anthropomorphism of the medieval world-view to regard them only, or even primarily, as the outcome of rational thinking. To think — that is precisely what the Schoolmen could do more acutely and methodically than all the generations of modern scientists. Initially, it was rather an orgiastic and ecstatic, emotional surrender to nature, and a new experiential attitude which brought an opening up of the mind towards the world.[123]

This new love of nature which made men attentive to her true character was not like the Christian *agape* that demanded the passive surrender of the lover to the loved one. Instead it resembled the heathen *eros*, with its active desire ot appropriate, to have, and to hold nature. For this reason, domination became the decisive element in the new attitude from which the study of reality was undertaken. Scheler saw this spirit of domination, which had triumphed over the spirit of love, in the Renaissance attitude to power. This new conception of power simultaneously manifested itself in Bodin's doctrine of sovereignty, in Hobbes' and Machiavelli's philosophy, in Calvin's theology, and in the Baconian spirit which wanted to see in order to foresee and to foresee only so far as this promoted man's power over nature. Scheler noted that even Vico betrayed

---

122 *Wissensformen*, pp. 110–111; translation quoted from Stark, *The Sociology of Knowledge*, pp. 114–115.
123 *Ibid.*

this attitude of domination when he wrote that man can only know objects to the extent that he can produce them himself.[124] The new money economy had given a new direction to the will to power, and a new kind of knowledge was ready to serve the bourgeoisie as a weapon in its struggle for emancipation and for power. This quest for power took the form of a struggle for control over nature based on the understanding of its laws. In short, the new sciences were the outcome of the new spirit of enterprise that was no longer willing to accept traditional but unexplained relations of divine origin. All such relations were now considered to be amenable to rational explanation. Scientific knowledge was harnessed immediately to practical ends because the bourgeois scientists began with this objective in mind. Knowledge was pursued for the sake of power.[125] As the new bourgeois naturalistic explanation of the world provided mastery over nature, it served the social function of ministering to the rising group, and hence became predominant.

When Scheler presented some of these ideas to the sociological guild in his talk, "Science and Social Structure," at their annual congress in 1924, his approach was sharply criticized by the other speaker on the program, Max Adler.[126] A neo-Marxist, Adler complained that Scheler's sociology of knowledge was too speculative and *geistesgeschichtlich*. Ultimately, because of his theory of drives, Scheler's conclusions rested more on specious biological assumptions than on hard empirical data. However, in the discussion that followed, numerous voices were raised in Scheler's defense, including those of Alfred Weber and Robert Michels, and Adler came in for his own share of criticism.

[124] *Ibid.*, p. 197. [125] *Ibid.*, pp. 166–167.
[126] Scheler's and Adler's talks, and the subsequent discussion were published in the *Verhandlungen des vierten deutschen Soziologentages am 29. und 30. September 1924 in Heidelberg* (Tübingen, 1925).

5
___

BECAUSE SCHELER'S *Wissenssoziologie* was an amalgam of several diverse intellectual currents, it provides the
historian with a cross section of some of the key intellectual
tendencies in Weimar Germany. Here, as on earlier occasions,
Scheler's mind, so receptive to diverse strains of thought — and
so unconcerned with the incompatibility between these strains
— serves as a microcosm of his intellectual milieu, of the culture
of his epoch.

The significance of the sociology of knowledge in Scheler's
own intellectual development can be summarized briefly: (1)
The volume of studies in the sociology of knowledge that
Scheler edited, and the long theoretical introduction which he
contributed to that work, solidified the sociological direction of
his thought which had been indicated by his critique of Comte
in 1921. The publication of that volume of studies established
Scheler's reputation among German sociologists as one of the
founding fathers of *Wissenssoziologie*. (2) Scheler's sociology
of knowledge represented his attempt to come to grips with all
the intellectual tendencies that he felt threatened the success
of his metaphysical anthropology: positivism, historicism, Marxism, and *Lebensphilosophie*. It also represented the culmination of his earlier interests in the forms of human society and
the effect of these ties on man's perception of the eternal
hierarchy of values. (3) Finally, Scheler found an immediate
practical application for the sociology of knowledge. It could
be used to enable men to overcome the limitations of their
various sociologically conditioned viewpoints. Through what
he called perspectival vision, Scheler hoped that the ruling elite
would be able to select the truth out of every social perspective.
The elite would then be able to integrate all of these truths
into a social program that would win the allegiance of all citizens. *Wissenssoziologie* could thus become another form of social
cement. It would enable the ruling class to hold the society

together and direct it according to their superior vision. The manipulative implications and the social function of *Wissenssoziologie* became more explicit in 1929 when Karl Mannheim published his book, *Ideology and Utopia*.[127]

The function of the sociology of knowledge in Scheler's thought was thus twofold. It could unmask the social roots of all ideologies, thereby freeing the ruling elite from the limitations of any individual viewpoint. And it could prepare the way for Scheler's metaphysical anthropology, to which we now will turn.

[127] Karl Mannheim, *Ideology and Utopia, An Introduction to the Sociology of Knowledge,* tr. Louis Wirth and Edward Shils (New York, 1936).

7

The Metaphysics of Adjustment

THE SUBJECT of this chapter is Scheler's metaphysics and the political philosophy of his last years. It may at first seem odd that these two topics are drawn together in the same chapter, but as will be shown below, Scheler analyzed the world situation in the 1920's in metaphysical terms, and he hoped that the new elite, which he believed was developing in Weimar Germany, would heed his explanation of the metaphysical meaning of his contemporary era. In Scheler's metaphysics, man, situated at the crossroads of existence between spirit and nature, has a metaphysical mission of self-deification whereby he participates in the cocreation of God out of the primal ground of being. According to Scheler, the metaphysical dualism between mind and instinct lay behind all the political and social dislocations of the twentieth century. Awareness of the *metaphysical* basis of the tensions between nations, classes, and generations was a prerequisite to their *practical* solution, he said. Therefore, Scheler devoted himself, during the midtwenties, to lecturing wherever he thought he might reach the developing elite who would lead Germany in the "Age of Adjustment." A few articles, and his lectures at the Lessing Adult Education Institute in Berlin, at Hermann Keyserling's School of Wisdom in Darmstadt, and at the German Institute of Politics in Berlin provide the only clues we have to Scheler's metaphysics of man.[1]

Before considering the general contours of Scheler's metaphysics of man, one may ask why Scheler chose to cast his final system in the form of metaphysical anthropology rather than pure metaphysics. Scheler's *Ethics* contained a detailed discussion of the nature of man as a spiritual entity, and his philosophy of religion included an account of the participation of man in divine knowledge, but the only work of his phenomenological period (1912–1922) that posed the question of the nature of man was a short essay published in 1915.[2] There he already showed a keen interest in the similarities and differences between men and animals and found the difference to lie in man's capacity for *ideation*. In his preface to *Man's Place in Nature* (1927) Scheler explained that:

[1] The broad outlines of Scheler's metaphysics can be reconstructed from the following speeches and articles, most of which appear in *Philosophical Perspectives*, tr. Oscar A. Haac (Boston, Beacon Press, 1958).
    (1) "Bildung und Wissen," Address to the Lessing Institute, Berlin, January 17, 1925.
    (2) "Mensch und Geschichte," *Die Neue Rundschau*, XXXVII, 11 (November, 1926), pp. 449–476.
    (3) "Spinoza. Eine Rede," Speech delivered at Amsterdam to commemorate the 250th anniversary of the death of Spinoza, February, 1927.
    (4) "Die Stellung des Menschen im Kosmos," Lecture at Keyserling's School of Wisdom in Darmstadt, April, 1927. This lecture was printed by the School in their yearbook, *Der Leuchter*, and has since been reprinted several times independently. We have used the English translation by Hans Meyerhoff, *Man's Place in Nature* (Boston, Beacon Press, 1961).
    (5) "Idealismus – Realismus," *Philosophische Anzeiger*, II (1927), 255–324.
    (6) "Der Mensch im Weltalter des Ausgleichs," Address on the anniversary of the Deutsche Hochschule für Politik in Berlin, November 5, 1927.
    (7) "Philosophische Weltanschauung," *Münchener Neuste Nachrichten* (May 5, 1928).
[2] Scheler, "Zur Idee des Menschen." Reprinted in *Vom Umsturz der Werte* pp. 171–196.

The questions "What is man?" and "what is man's place in the nature of things?" have occupied me more deeply than any other philosophical question since the first awakening of my philosophical consciousness. . . . I have had the good fortune to see that most of my earlier philosophical work has culminated in this study.[3]

But this statement only indicates that he had long been concerned with the question of man; it does not explain why this problem more than any other should have been *the* fundamental question for him. The answer, we think, lies in his reaction to the increasing relativism and historicism which had come to characterize Western thought by the early twentieth century.

Over and over, as one studies the writings of Scheler's contemporaries, one finds a feeling of metaphysical *anomie*. Owing to the development of modern thought and society, men had lost any sense of purpose or direction. As Scheler wrote:

. . . man is more of a problem to himself at the present time than ever before in all recorded history. At the very moment when man admits that he knows less than ever about himself, and when he is not frightened by any possible answer to the question [what is man?] there seems to have arisen a new courage of truthfulness — a courage to raise this essential question without any commitment to any tradition, whether theological, philosophical, or scientific, that has prevailed up to now. At the same time he is developing a new kind of self-consciousness and insight into his own nature based on the increasing accumulation of knowledge in the new human sciences.[4]

In former times, to be sure, there was a great discrepancy of opinions and theories as to the nature of man and his relationship to nature. But there always remained a general orientation, a frame of reference to which all individual differences might be referred, which could form the common ground of discussion and the basis for a synthesis. Philosophy, theology, natural and social science took turns at being the guiding discipline. The real crisis came toward the end of the nineteenth century when men ceased to believe in any unifying discipline.

3 *Man's Place in Nature,* p. 3.
4 *Man's Place in Nature,* p. 4.

Nietzsche proclaimed this situation in his parable of the death of God. By 1919, Erich von Kahler's lament, "Today an established authority to which we can appeal no longer exists,"[5] had become a well known refrain. Scheler, looking back from the twentieth-century anarchy, described the situation with mixed feelings: "In approximately ten centuries of history, this is the first in which man finds himself completely and utterly 'problematical,' in which he no longer knows what he is and simultaneously *knows that* he does not have the answer."[6]

The old authorities were dead or dying. But what had come in their wake? As Scheler looked around him in Weimar Germany, he was troubled by "the painful impression which our times make upon me — an impression of puzzling shallowness."

I know of no time in history when the guiding elites were in greater need of true culture and when it was harder to attain. This tragic statement applies to our whole world and epoch, our age of disunity, and of masses which are no longer controllable. . . . One is seriously frightened because not only this or that country, but our entire civilized world is in grave danger of gradually — almost inaudibly — sinking and drowning in the gray shapeless dawn of non-freedom and hollowness which increases daily.[7]

Having abandoned his Catholicism, and never having embraced scientific naturalism or Hegelian idealism, Scheler felt that none of the old idols of Western man could be resurrected to provide guiding ideals in the twentieth century. "*My conviction* leads me to believe that the elite, as a group that must guide the coming adjustment into the right paths, may not give allegiance to *any* organized church."[8] The elite would not base its metaphysical view of the Ultimate exclusively on any one tradition, but would make room for the fullness and variety of insight which the history of religion and metaphysics offered. "Essentially, the elite will derive its picture of God and world,

---

5 Erich von Kahler, *Der Beruf der Wissenschaft* (Berlin, 1920), p. 10.
6 *Philosophical Perspectives*, p. 65.
7 *Ibid.*, p. 13.   8 *Ibid.*, p. 125.

to which its life and deed are committed, from the *spontaneous* forces of its own spirit."[9] A completely new metaphysics of man was the only hope, a metaphysics that recognized the impotence of God and the fundamental importance of creative human personalities in the universe. Religion might still serve as a crude "metaphysics for the masses,"[10] but Scheler's metaphysics of man alone could satisfy the thinking and serve to guide and inspire a new elite.

We deny the basic presupposition of theism: a spiritual, personal God, omnipotent in his spirituality. For us the basic relationship between man and the Ground of Being consists in the fact that this Ground comprehends itself directly in man, who, both as Spirit and as Life, is but a partial mode of the eternal Spirit and Drive. . . . We need but transform the old idea of Spinoza (that the original Being becomes conscious of itself in man in the same act by which man sees himself grounded in this being), so that man's knowledge of being so grounded is the result of active commitment of our own being to the demands of *deitas* and the attempt to fulfill this demand. In and through this fulfillment, man cooperates in the creation of God who emerges from the Ground of Being in a process whereby Spirit and Drive interpenetrate increasingly.[11]

Scheler believed that "a completely metaphysical and religious — and therefore also political and social — integration and reconciliation of classes"[12] could only be possible on the basis of his metaphysics. Why? Because it alone offered a conception of man, nature, and God that included both the light and darkness of reality, both *mind* and the demonic *drive* for existence and life, which (in Scheler's view) pulsated through all being.

The man who is most deeply rooted in the darkness of earth and nature, and of the "*natura naturans*" which produces all natural phenomena, "*natura naturata*," and who simultaneously as a

9 *Ibid.*
10 *Ibid.*, p. 1. "The masses will never be philosophers," Scheler warned, quoting Plato: "philosophy belongs and always has belonged to an *elite* centered around the outstanding personality of a thinker."
11 *Man's Place in Nature*, p. 92.
12 *Philosophical Perspectives*, p. 122.

spiritual person, in his consciousness of self, reaches the utmost heights of the luminous world of ideas, that man is approaching the idea of total man, and therewith, the idea of the substance of the very source of the world, through a constantly growing *interpenetration of Spirit and Drive.* "The person who has had the deepest thoughts, loves what is most alive" (Hölderlin).[13]

1

ALTHOUGH SCHELER never really explained his new metaphysics of *Geist* and *Drang* in detail, one can gather the broad outlines of his position from "Philosopher's Outlook,"[14] the last article he published before his death. He felt that a traditional metaphysics, such as that of Aristotle, which proceeded from concrete objects to the absolute being, was obsolete. Kant was right, Scheler said: "Quite correctly he [Kant] stated that *all* concrete being, of the inner as well as of the outer world, must first be related to *man.*"[15] According to Scheler, "all forms of being depend on *man's* being. The concrete world and its modes of being are not 'being in itself' but only an appropriate counterbalance to the entire spiritual and physical order of man."[16] An adequate knowledge of the *"ultimate source* of all things" could only be derived from a "knowledge of the essence of man explored by 'philosophical anthropology.' "[17] Man, said Scheler, is both a *microcosm* of all the essential aspects of being — physical, vital, spiritual, and personal — and, at the same time, a *microtheos,* a miniature of the "ultimate source of all things."[18] For this reason, Scheler felt that man as *microcosm* and *microtheos* was the key subject for metaphysical inquiry.

Scheler called his metaphysics *Heils-und-Erlösungswissen*

---

13 *Ibid.,* p. 111.   14 *Ibid.,* pp. 1–12.
15 *Ibid.,* p. 10. Compare Martin Heidegger, *Kant and the Problem of Metaphysics,* tr. James Churchill (Bloomington, Indiana, 1962), p. 216. The book is dedicated to Max Scheler.
16 *Philosophical Perspectives,* p. 10.
17 *Ibid.*   18 *Ibid.,* p. 11.

The Metaphysics of Adjustment

(saving knowledge), to distinguish it from *Bildungswissen*[19] (knowledge directed to the cultivation of the person), and *Herrschaftswissen*[20] (knowledge of domination or control of nature).

> *The supreme aim in forming a metaphysical outlook* . . . [was] to conceive and consider absolute being through itself *in such a way* that it corresponds and is appropriate to the *essential* structure of the world . . . [and] to the real *existence* of the world as it appears to us in its resistance to our drives and to all fortuitous circumstances. . . . We obtain *metaphysics* only when we tie *together* the findings of reality-conscious experimental sciences and the results of ontological first philosophy (i.e., the ontology of the nature of the world and the self) and then relate both of these to the conclusions of the disciplines which involve judgment (general theory of values, aesthetics, ethics, philosophy of civilization). This process leads us first to metaphysical problems on the frontiers of the experimental sciences . . . and from there to metaphysics of the absolute.[21]

His metaphysics became a substitute form of religion. Through it, man was able to unite himself with — or rather, recognize himself to be a part of — the ultimate metaphysical principles of the universe, *Geist* and *Drang*, mind and instinct.

Although Scheler's explanation of the relationship between *Geist* and *Drang* is exasperatingly confusing and unclear, the following quotation indicates what Scheler considered to be the "two *fundamental attributes* of ultimate being:"[22]

(1) Ultimate being must contain an infinite, ideating *Spirit* and a *rational power* which causes the essential structures of the world and of man himself to emanate jointly from itself.

(2) Ultimate being must contain an *irrational driving force* which

---

[19] *Ibid.*, p. 5. Scheler defined *Bildungswissen* as "the knowledge of all forms of being and of the essential structure of all that is." It is evident from Scheler's account that *Bildungswissen* meant the knowledge of essences attained through eidetic intuition (*Wesensschau*).

[20] *Ibid.*, p. 4. Scheler defined *Herrschaftswissen* as "knowledge of control," that is, the knowledge attained through experimental science, knowledge of the laws of fortuitous reality in contrast to the essential reality grasped by eidetic intuition.

[21] *Ibid.*, pp. 8–9.   [22] *Ibid.*, p. 8.

posits equally irrational existence and fortuitous circumstance (the images we see), a dynamic, imaginative potency, the common root for centers and fields of force of organic nature and for the *one life* which rhythmically appears in the birth and death of all individuals and species.

An increased understanding of these two attributes of the activity of ultimate being would give meaning to the world.

What was the meaning Scheler derived from his intuition into the fundamental structure of ultimate being? Scheler believed that through man's understanding of the world basis, the blind *élan vital* which pulsed through all being was gradually becoming spiritualized. On the other hand, "the infinite spirit, which originally was powerless and could not formulate ideas," was gradually acquiring power and strength. The ultimate goal of being in time was "the gradual inter-penetration of Spirit and Drive" through the instrumentality of human thought and action.[23]

In Scheler's new system, the omnipotent personal God of Christianity became the impersonal Absolute Spirit of German idealism.[24] According to Scheler, however, the Absolute Spirit was pure potentiality, totally dependent on man for its realization in the world. In fact, the Absolute Spirit was little more than a reification of the realm of absolute values that Scheler had to anchor somewhere once he had abandoned his original belief in a personal God as the ultimate guarantor of value.

To understand Scheler's metaphysics at this point, it is necessary to recall one of Scheler's earliest postulates, the distinction between essence and existence,[25] that is, between value and being. Following Kant and Eucken, Scheler maintained that "value precedes and is independent of being." What

23 *Ibid.*, p. 9, and p. 111.

24 On the idea of the Absolute Spirit in German idealistic philosophy, see Nicolai Hartmann, *Die Philosophie des deutschen Idealismus* (2 vols., Tübingen, 1921–1924); and a more elementary account by Josiah Royce, *Lectures on Modern Idealism* (New Haven, 1919).

25 This distinction lay at the core of Scheler's phenomenology. In contrast to common sense and science which provided man with knowledge of fortuitous reality, phenomenology was supposed to give man knowledge of essences.

he meant by this was that the ideal is *teleologically prior* to the real. The *good* exists in the world of the mind, or to use Scheler's terminology, "in the realm of essences" beyond the physical world of man's experience. According to Scheler's teleological idealism, man has the responsibility to attempt to shape his physical and social world, the world of nature, in such a way as to bring it into conformity with the world of transcendental ideals.

Now if the *ideal* were separated from the *real ab initio*, as Scheler insisted, what guarantee was there that the two could ever be united? As long as he believed in a personal God, Scheler insisted that the two were united in the mind of God. Once he had abandoned this belief in a personal God, however, the only link could be the transcendental ego of the human person. Man, as a composite of spirit and matter, of mind and instinctual drives, could infuse spirit into the world of matter by shaping it according to his ideals. In itself, the world of essences, the ideal realm, remained pure potentiality. That is, in itself, it remained impotent unless actualized by man.

Situated at the crossroads between the world of existence (nature) and that of essence (spirit), man had a unique metaphysical destiny. It was his task to spiritualize the world. At the same time, man was the realizer of God, that is, of the Absolute. Without man, the Absolute would remain pure potency. "The Ground of Being," that is, the Absolute, "comprehends and realizes itself in man who, both as spirit and as life, is a partial mode of the eternal Spirit and, at the same time, of Drive" (instinct).[26] The Absolute could only become conscious of itself at the time when man recognized himself as grounded in the Absolute. In these last years, Scheler claimed that "man cooperates in the creation of God in a process whereby Spirit and Drive interpenetrate increasingly."[27] in fact, "the birth of man and the birth of God" became for Scheler "reciprocally dependent."[28] The Primal Ground of Being would remain pure potentiality if it were not for man in whom it

[26] *Man's Place in Nature*, p. 92.
[27] *Ibid.*, p. 93.   [28] *Ibid.*

could become conscious of itself and through whom it could become actualized in history.

"The only access to God," Scheler now proclaimed, was "not theoretical contemplation which tended to represent God as a concrete being, but personal and active *commitment* of man to God and to progressive self-realization,"[29] i.e., self-deification. Scheler's metaphysics explained man's metaphysical destiny as *collaborator* in the two attributes of the *eternal act*, i.e., "its spiritual power to create ideas" and "it's momentous force which we can feel present in our own drives."[30] Man was thus *not* the imitator of a world of ideas which was already present in God before the creation, as traditional Western Christian metaphysics claimed. Instead, according to Scheler, man was the "cocreator, cofounder and coexecutor of a stream of ideas which *develop* throughout world history with man."[31] Man became "the only locus in which and through which original being grasps and recognizes itself, but man is also the being in whose free *decision* God can *realize* and sanctify his pure essence."[32] Scheler felt that the most divine attribute of man was his ability to make *decisions*, for in his decisions man became the collaborator of God, helping the divinity to realize itself in the course of world history.

Needless to say, Scheler had no illusions that this "sophisticated doctrine" could ever become the guiding *Weltanschauung* of the masses. "Most men require the consolation of belief in an all-powerful God who cares for them. Only the intellectual elite can admit that we must care for God by creating him out of the Primal Ground in history."[33] Such was the doctrine that Scheler offered the new elite which he hoped to foster in his last years. He knew that many would feel a wistful longing for the consolations of their abandoned personal God, but he assured them that, if they faced life courage-

---

29 *Philosophical Perspectives*, p. 11.
30 *Ibid.*, p. 12.   31 *Ibid.*
32 *Ibid.*
33 *Man's Place in Nature*, p. 94.

ously, they would find new strength in being conscious of their significant role in the "creation of God" and in the embodiment of absolute values in history.[34]

Man, for Scheler, was the microcosm through which the ultimate metaphysical basis of the world could be understood. Furthermore, in understanding himself, man enabled God to come into being in time, to move from potency to act, from substance to function.[35] Anthropology replaced metaphysics and theology as the guide to ultimate realities. Scheler's philosophy of man became a metaphysics of the dialectical interplay between mind and life, the coordinates of the ground of being of which man was supposed to be "the purest and supreme finite representation."[36]

We have found that in Scheler's sociology of knowledge, mind was said to be impotent. If ideas were to have any historical significance, they would have to be adopted by some elite who, being inspired by these ideas, carried them out of the realm of the ideal into historical actuality. In contrast to Hegel, Scheler denied the so-called cunning of reason. By itself, reason was impotent. Mind could inhibit instinctual drives, however, and thereby seduce psychic energy into working for the attainment of spiritual goals set by the ego:

Spirit has its own nature and autonomy, but lacks an original energy of its own. The negative acts of inhibition, which originate in the spiritual act of willing, provide energy for the spirit, which, to begin with, is impotent and consists only of a group of pure "intentions." They do not produce the spirit itself. . . . [Spirit] cannot generate or cancel the instinctual energy; it cannot enlarge or diminish it. It can only call upon the energy complexes which will then act through the organism in order to accomplish what the spirit "wills." . . . Subject to its own ideas and values, the spiritual "will" withdraws from the opposing vital impulses the *images* necessary for action. At the same time it lures the drives with a bait of appropriate images in order to coordinate the vital impulses so that they will execute the project set by the spirit.[37]

34 *Ibid.*
36 *Ibid.*, p. 55.

35 *Ibid.*, p. 62.
37 *Ibid.*, pp. 57–62.

Scheler's theory of civilization being built upon energy derived from instinctual forces recalls the theories of Schopenhauer, Nietzsche, and Freud. Scheler differed from them in that whereas they derived mind itself from repressed energy, he insisted on the independent existence of mind. It acquired *power*; but not *existence* from repressed libido. The crucial weaknesses in Schopenhauer's and Freud's negative theories of repression were that they could neither explain *what* it is in man that denies the will to live, nor the *purpose* of repression, sublimation, and negation of the will to live.[38] According to Scheler's theory of sublimation, mind was not generated from repression; it already existed, and was autonomous. He agreed with Freud, however, that the mind repressed libido in order to use the energy it thereby acquired for its own purposes.

Like Freud, Scheler believed that gradually, through the course of history, reason was gaining on instinct.[39] But this gain was the case "only by virtue of the fact that ideas and values tend to become appropriated by the great instinctual tendencies in social groups and by the common interests that link them."[40] The power the mind acquired through sublimation of instinctual energy was extremely limited, however. Mind could not *prevent* the inevitable triumph of instinctual drive; it could only *delay* it. At the same time, even this minor power of regulating and directing instinctual energy was something. Scheler spoke of it as "a process of gaining power and activity for the spirit . . . a process of making the spirit come to life."[41]

It should now be clear that Scheler considered man to

---

38 *Ibid.,* p. 62.

39 *Ibid.,* p. 68. Compare Freud's words in *The Future of an Illusion* (1927), quoted in H. Stuart Hughes, *Consciousness and Society: The Reorientation of European Social Thought, 1890–1930* (New York, 1958), p. 152: "We may insist as much as we like that the human intellect is weak in comparison with human instincts, and be right in doing so. But nevertheless there is something peculiar about this weakness. The voice of the intellect is a soft one, but it does not rest until it has gained a hearing."

40 *Man's Place in Nature,* p. 68.

41 *Ibid.,* p. 62.

be a citizen of two worlds. Biologically he was part of nature; spiritually he was part of mind. This dualistic view of man has haunted Western philosophy since the time of Plato. From the metaphysical point of view, Scheler saw in the spiritual (*geistig*) acts of man "a manifestation of the very essence of the Ultimate Source of things."[42] Man was not simply a dead-end road of nature, as he appeared to be from the biological point of view. As a spiritual being, he was a manifestation of the divine spirit itself, and he was capable of deifying himself through collaboration with the divine source of things:

Man is the being, intrinsically *lofty* and *noble,* raised above all of physical life and its values, even above all of nature, the being in which the psyche has *freed* itself from *subservience* to life and has purified itself into "spirit," a spirit in whose service "life" enters in an objective as well as in a subjective, psychic sense. We have here an ever new and growing process of "becoming man."[43]

Yet this process of transmutation of nature into *Geist,* or rather of bringing nature into the service of *Geist* — the task of man according to the whole tradition of German idealism since Kant — had not been, and probably never would be fully completed. The dualism between *Geist* and *Leben* was rooted in the ultimate nature of reality itself, said Scheler. Whereas Kant had preserved God above this process of eternal becoming, with Hegel, God — now called "the Absolute *Geist*" — and nature were joined in a dialectical process of becoming. Scheler's view paralleled Hegel's, with the one exception that *Geist,* according to Scheler, was impotent. Man became the creature in which "Fundamental Essence" (Hegel's Absolute *Geist*) began "to know and grasp itself, to understand and save itself."[44] Through the active energy of all his drives and blood he fed the *Geist* that originally was impotent. Without man, the divinity could not attain its own purpose. The whole of human history was now given a purpose in Scheler's eyes. It was the process

42 *Philosophical Perspectives,* p. 25.
43 *Ibid.,* pp. 29–30. Italics in original.
44 *Ibid.*

by which man became God, or rather, through which man enabled God to become Himself in man. All civilization, culture, history, state, church, and society existed for the sake of man's spiritual development *in Deo*.[45] "The process of becoming man is both a self-deification and a collaboration in realizing the idea of divinity which is essentially present in the substrata of the life force."[46]

Scheler further elaborated his idea of an evolving God in *Man's Place in Nature*:

This train of thought obviously cannot stop short of the highest form of Being—the worldground. Even the Being which is its own cause (*causa sui*) and upon which everything depends cannot, in so far as the attribute of spirit applies to it, possess any original power of energy. Instead, it is the other attribute — the *natura naturans* in the highest Being, the all-powerful drive charged with infinite images — which must account for reality and for the contingent qualities of this reality which are never determined unequivocable by the essential laws and ideas. If we call the spiritual attributes of the highest Ground of Being *deitas*, then we cannot impute any positive, creative power to what we call Spirit or Godhead in this highest ground. Thus, the idea of a creation *ex nihilo* is untenable. If there is in the highest Ground of Being this tension between spirit and drive, then the relationship of this Being to the world must be different.[47]

Man thus meant something in the development of God himself. His history was interwoven in the growth of God. Scheler had joined the tradition of such German mystics as Meister Eckhardt who assumed a kind of interplay between the timeless, growing, being of divinity and of the world as history. Man, the microcosm, became not only the culmination of nature in which the latter was spiritualized, but the incarnation of divinity. So conceived, man became the mirror of the absolute.

45 *Ibid.*, p. 31.   46 *Ibid.*, p. 30
47 *Man's Place in Nature*, p. 70.

S C H E L E R expounded his new philosophy of the impotent
God in several public lectures and articles before his sudden
death in 1928. The German educated public was fascinated by
Scheler; his public lectures were packed. The Lessing Cultural
Institute in Berlin asked him to speak at their anniversary
celebrations in January, 1925. His speech on this occasion, "The
Forms of Knowledge and Culture," presented his theory of the
cultivated man and was designed to counteract the specializing
tendencies of German education, which seemed to him to be
moving in the direction of vocational training.

This same theme recurs in his speech on Spinoza in Amsterdam, where he was asked to speak at the commemoration
of the 250th anniversary of the philosopher's death in February,
1927. The previous year, Scheler caused a sensation at Keyserling's School of Wisdom in Darmstadt, when he explained
his philosophical anthropology and his conception of man's
unique place in the cosmos. He spoke for four hours, uninterrupted. It was almost as if he knew unconsciously that he would
never live to write down his new system, that this would be his
one and only chance to present it to the world. He concluded
his speech with the following words:

I have heard it said that it is not possible for man to endure the idea
of an unfinished God, or a God in the process of becoming. My
answer is that metaphysics is not an insurance policy for those who
are weak and in need of protection. It is something for strong and
courageous minds. Thus it is understandable that man reaches the
consciousness that he is an ally and co-worker of God only in the
process of his own development and growing self-knowledge. The
need for safety and protection by an omnipotent being beyond man
and the world, and identical with goodness and wisdom, is too
great not to have broken through all barriers of sense and intelligence during the times of man's immaturity. This relationship is
childlike and weak. It has detached man from God and it is expressed in the objectifying and evasive relations of contemplation,

worship, and prayer. In place of this relationship, I put the elementary act of a personal commitment to the deity, the self-identification of man with the active spiritual movement of the deity.[48]

The Nietzschean side of Scheler's heritage had triumphed at last over the Catholic. Scheler was now a Zarathustra, preaching the religion of the *Übermensch*, which he called instead, the total man. This new human type would be born out of the social dislocations taking place in the postwar world, the age of adjustment (*Ausgleich*). Recognition of the fact that man is the cocreator of the universe and even of God would provide consolation enough to the strong of heart. They could find support in knowing that they were participants in the "total process of realizing values in world history insofar as this process had moved forward toward the making of a 'God' "[49]

Scheler's lecture left the audience spellbound. After a long fearsome silence, they broke into loud applause and stamped their feet as only a crowd of enthusiastic Germans can do. Scheler walked out of the hall flanked by Count Hermann Keyserling and Carl Jung, as the audience stood in respect and admiration, inspired by his last words.

It is, perhaps, significant that Max Scheler chose to present the main outlines of his metaphysical anthropology at Keyserling's School of Wisdom in Darmstadt.[50] Like Scheler, Keyserling combined an interest in the natural sciences with his metaphysical concerns. As a young man he had forced himself to study experimental science to counteract his undisciplined mind:

The pigeon-holing of thoughts, which the scientist can hardly dispense with, was altogether alien to me; because of my nervous weakness I was unable until my thirty-second year, when I took up Indian Yogi exercises, to concentrate uninterruptedly on any subject

48 *Man's Place in Nature,* p. 94.
49 *Ibid.,* p. 95.
50 Count Hermann Keyserling, *The World in the Making,* tr. Maurice Samuel (New York, 1927) contains a long autobiographical section entitled, "My Life and My Work, as I See Them," from which the information here given has been drawn.

for any length of time; in my essential construction the element of fantasy so far overbore the impulse to exact research that, *for this very reason*, I gladly submitted, during my student years, to the discipline of the science of experimental chemistry and crystallographic measurement.[51]

The School, founded in 1920 by Keyserling, was subsidized by Grand Duke Ludwig of Hessen, whose castle still dominated the little town of Darmstadt, although he had voluntarily abdicated the throne in 1918. Keyserling had become famous in Germany before the war for his *Travel Diaries* and other writings that offered the reader a pseudomystical synthetic philosophy which combined the best from East and West. The *Travel Diaries* contain the Count's reflections on a voyage around the world, but the external journey seems to have served primarily as a catalyst to a journey within himself. In these self-reflections Keyserling found himself and discovered the vocation which he attempted to fulfill in his School after the war.

The objective of the School, according to its founder, was "to turn the particular, such as it presents itself, into a symbol of the universal,"[52] in other words to disclose the metaphysical meaning of all forms of human experience. Like Scheler, Keyserling attempted to make a virtue out of the manichean dualism of his personality. A man of mixed background — he was a Balt, with both Slavic and Germanic blood — Keyserling believed that he combined in his own personality what he considered to be the tendencies of East and West: contemplation and vital action. He agreed with Scheler that man in the modern world had become too intellectualized, and that as a result mind had become almost impotent in the face of the instinctual drives which completely dominated the mass man. The School of Wisdom was to become, Keyserling hoped, "a strategic headquarters" for the reorientation of modern man's vital impulses. "It undertakes, by means of the proper psychological methods, to assimilate the impulse of life-renewal on the basis of the spirit which I stand for into the broad body

[51] *Ibid.*, p. 32.   [52] *Ibid.*, p. 67.

of historical reality,"[53] Keyserling said, describing the objectives of the School in his autobiography.

Keyserling had a rather grandiose conception of himself and his mission. He spoke of himself as a "statesman and field marshal" who could turn metaphysical wisdom to practical account:

I must be a *Realpolitiker* before all; my purpose being to thrust the world one stage further ahead, my first thought must be to set things in motion. . . . It is indeed in the tension between the two poles of my being, translated into a special rhythm, that the Alpha and Omega of my practical effectiveness is to be found. Since these two poles are literally in complete opposition, there exists between them an extreme tension, so that the resulting rhythm must be extraordinarily vigorous. This is the whole secret of my stimulating energy. It is not because of originality in the presentation of truths which I alone have perceived, but because certain truths, most of them immemorial and all of them known as such to many others, have found in me a long-range transmission apparatus, that I am able to help others on their way.[54]

Apparently the tensions of this self-styled savior and genius did not serve their cosmic purpose as well as Keyserling hoped, for shortly after he wrote these words he voluntarily entered a psychiatric clinic and emerged two years later shorn of some of some of his delusions of grandeur, the hypertensions of his nature, as he put it, now having been "converted into normal tensions."[55] Whereas the School had originally been almost completely identified with the personality of its founder, after his psychoanalysis, Keyserling began to invite other speakers so that the School might become a more perfect instrument of expression for the spiritual tendencies of the age.

By the end of 1922, sessions at the School of Wisdom had assumed the form they would have when Scheler spoke there four years later. Keyserling now described his own function at the School as being that of "an orchestral conductor of the spirit."[56] He would draw together the fundamental themes of the age as expressed by such men as Leo Frobenius, Rabin-

53 *Ibid.*
55 *Ibid.*

54 *Ibid.*, p. 68.
56 *Ibid.*, p. 71.

dranath Tagore, Thomas Mann, Carl Jung, Leo Baeck, and Max Scheler; and through the synthetic powers of his own genius, blend them into orchestral form, thereby imparting to all of the individual themes a new and richer meaning.[57] The object of the orchestration process was to disclose a higher harmony behind seemingly discordant points of view. Like Scheler, Keyserling opposed relativism, and instead adopted a kind of perspectivism which he called complementarism or "absolutism on a higher plane."[58] At Darmstadt every individual was encouraged to listen not in a reflective or critical mood, but "so adjusted that the partial perceptions of truth shall be able to coalesce within him into a higher unity."[59] Keyserling promised that if one approached the lectures and discussions with the proper frame of mind, a higher synthesis would take place within one, and one would depart transformed, having learned to view reality spiritually and with deeper insight.

> I see my significance [Keyserling wrote, summing up his hopes for the future] in the demonstration of *the extent to which the qualities, which almost all people accept in themselves as final and fixed by fate, can be transmuted by the use of force and insight* — proving that to this extent, man can become the master of his own fate . . . and that, therefore, world-ascendency . . . and the state beyond world history . . . are not Utopian aims but thoroughly realizable.[60]

Keyserling seems to have believed that a new epoch in history was currently dawning and that he and the people who attended his school could — once they understood the metaphysical meaning of the new age — help to "set in motion an upward shift of the level of all humanity.[61]

Scheler felt a great personal amity for Keyserling, and in-

---

57 *Ibid.* I have selected these names at random to give a cross section of the contributors to the School's journal, *Der Leuchter*, and the summaries of each year's activities printed in the School's semi-annual publication, *Der Weg zur Vollendung*. The publisher of these journals and all of Keyserling's works written after the war was Otto Reichl, who was a wealthy personal friend of Keyserling's in Darmstadt. Reichl published the first edition of Scheler's "Die Stellung des Menschen im Kosmos" in *Der Leuchter*, in 1927.

58 Keyserling, *op. cit.*, p. 73.

59 *Ibid.*

60 *Ibid.*, p. 77.   61 *Ibid.*

deed, spoke of him and his "great mission" in his letters to Maerit Furtwaengler.[62] To Scheler, the School probably seemed to be an excellent place to present his metaphysical ideas because people were attracted there who were interested in a pseudoreligious metaphysics that would give a sense of meaning to their lives. Furthermore, although Keyserling seemed to be a bit too taken with himself,[63] he stood for a number of ideals quite similar to Scheler's.

Both men agreed that the multiplicity of *Weltanschauungen* in the modern world had to be reconciled in some form of higher synthesis. Both also agreed that a redistribution of modern man's vital energies was then taking place and that the task of the philosopher was to guide and direct those changes so that they could be brought into the service of spirit, which, by itself, was impotent. Finally, both men feared and deplored the revolt of the masses, and believed that the unruly forces in society must be controlled in the same way that vital energy had to be if the higher synthesis of vital action and spiritual contemplation were to be achieved.

Keyserling spoke of their present era as materialistic and anti-religious, "the age of the chauffeur":

The determinant mass-type of this age is the chauffeur. His born type of leader is the Bolshevist or Fascist. Only the living opposition within the cultural elite can develop upwards into carriers of a new meaning which the chauffeur world can point to as its own. All over the world there is emerging an involuntary union of those who, conscious of the meaninglessness of the world of today are striving for the creation of new meaning. But, by themselves, the section of mankind who represents the deeper side of life is today an impotent minority.[64]

He felt that only one thing could be done to counteract the revolt of the mass man: a new human type must be created from within the cultivated classes. This new man would be "the

[62] Unpublished letters to Maerit Furtwaengler, November, 1926, and February–March, 1927. Scheler's friendship with Keyserling was stimulated by his attraction to the Count's lovely wife. He seems to have visited the Keyserling home several times in 1926–1927.

[63] Letter to Maerit Furtwaengler, November 2, 1926.

[64] Keyserling, *op. cit.*, p. 265.

embodiment and carrier of a meaning capable of animating all life." Keyserling failed to specify how this new man was to be produced, i.e., through selective breeding or merely through education. He simply stated that the new man would have to be "as psychologically conscious as he is metaphysically, as apt for *Realpolitik* as for the apprehension of meaning," integrating within himself the whole breadth and depth of mankind.[65]

Similarly, Scheler placed his hopes for the future in the burgeoning of a new elite. And he, too, conceived of a new man as a bridge between East and West and a synthesizer of all the social and intellectual tendencies of the age. The new man would reconcile in himself and "encompass the different kinds of thought, moral codes, and religious modes of life prevailing in the upper and lower classes."[66] Scheler's new man "would know how to take into account the sources of deception, the effect of his belonging to a class and his participation in the mythos of national history."[67] By combining the sociology of knowledge with a knowledge of the metaphysical tendencies of the age, he would be able to "see realities with sober clarity and discern possible ways of bridging the contradictions they entail."[68]

3

JUST AS Scheler had once willingly fabricated various ideologies to rationalize German nationalism and militarism, so now — in the mid-twenties — he contributed an ideology that rationalized the status quo.[69] During the war, Scheler had

---

[65] *Ibid.*, p. 267.

[66] "Man in the Era of Adjustment," *Philosophical Perspectives*, p. 121.

[67] *Ibid.* [68] *Ibid.*

[69] On Scheler's political views during his last years, see the essay by his last assistant in Cologne, Dr. Herbert Russel, "Max Scheler und die Probleme der deutschen Politik," *Hochland*, XXVII (1930), pp. 47–60; and Paul Honigsheim, "Max Scheler als Sozialphilosoph," *Kölner Vierteljahrsheft für Soziologie und Sozialwissenschaften*, VIII, No. 3 (1929), pp. 14–25.

been an ardent nationalist and had glorified spiritual militarism as Germany's world-historical mission.[70] In the twenties, however, when the defeated German nation was allowed to have nothing but a token army, Scheler denounced Germany's earlier aggressive militarism and praised the instrumental militarism (*Zweckmilitarismus*) that he had scorned when Germany was stronger.[71] Formerly Scheler had defended a spiritual cosmopolitanism and a continental European federation which would be led by the Central Powers;[72] now Scheler spoke of a worldwide redistribution and adjustment of various forces — instinctual, sexual, economic, social, and religious, as well as political. Speaking to the men and women whom he expected to be the leaders of the new Germany in the days ahead, Scheler expounded his philosophy of "Man in the Era of Adjustment"[73] in words strikingly similar to those in Karl Mannheim's book, *Man and Society in the Age of Social Reconstruction* (1935).[74] In the mood of reawakened confidence that came with the economic and political stabilization provided by the Dawes Plan and the Locarno Pact, the admission of Germany to the League of Nations, and Stresemann's Policy of Fulfillment,[75] Scheler once again expressed the mood of the hour with an inspiring ideology.

In October, 1926, Scheler received a letter from the ex-

[70] See Chapter Three, Section three.

[71] See Scheler's speech at the Reichswehrministerium in Berlin, January, 1927, published posthumously as *Die Idee des Friedens und der Pazifismus* (Berlin, 1931).

[72] The Reconstruction of European Culture" (1918). Reprinted in *On the Eternal in Man*, pp. 406–448.

[73] See Scheler's convocation address at the Deutsche Hochschule für Politik, November, 1927, "Man in the Era of Adjustment," reprinted in *Philosophical Perspectives*, pp. 94–126.

[74] Karl Mannheim, *Man and Society in the Age of Social Reconstruction*, tr. Edward Shils (London, 1940).

[75] On the impact of foreign affairs on the Weimar Republic in the "Locarno Era," see Ludwig Zimmern, *Deutsche Aussenpolitik in der Ära der Weimarer Republik* (Göttingen, 1958), p. 247 ff.; and Werner Conze, "Deutschlands politische Sonderstellung in der zwanziger Jahren," in *Die Zeit ohne Eigenschaften, eine Bilanz der zwanziger Jahre*, ed. Leonhard Reinisch (Stuttgart, 1961), p. 32 ff.

Reichschancellor, Dr. Joseph Wirth, who was concerned about the instability of the Republic and asked Scheler to speak out and to help make it more appealing to the German people.[76] Scheler jumped at the opportunity to serve as a publicist for the nation once again and left immediately for Berlin. Through Dr. Wirth he met Otto Gessler, the Minister of the Army, and his first lecture in Berlin was soon arranged.[77] He was to speak to an assembly of officers at the Reichswehr Ministry in January, 1927.

The lecture was announced in advance, and the hall where Scheler spoke was completely filled. Scheler reported in a letter describing his tremendous success with the army that ten generals, including General Heye, Chief of the General Staff, sat in the first row. In introducing Scheler, Gessler said that for army reform in the present just as in the time of the Wars of Liberation, philosophy and military leadership must work together, and that Scheler was the one German philosopher who had already proved that he was the man for this task.[78] Scheler then came to the rostrum, eyes flashing. He spoke for two and one-half hours, uninterrupted except for occasional clapping from the audience. The main idea of his speech was that the hope of lasting peace for the whole world in the near future was an idle dream, but permanent peace in Europe was a real possibility. Germans, as good Europeans, should attempt to make peace a probability.[79] How could this be done? To begin

76 The letter from Wirth has been lost, but Scheler spoke of it in a letter to Maerit Furtwaengler on October 19, 1926.

77 Otto Gessler, *Reichswehr Politik in der Weimarer Zeit,* ed. Kurt Sendtner (Stuttgart, 1958), p. 413 ff.

78 Gessler does not record the words he spoke in his memoirs, but Scheler, who was very flattered to be compared to Fichte and Hegel quoted the words in a letter to Maerit Furtwaengler in which he summarized his speech point by point and noted the reactions he felt these points had provoked.

79 This account of Scheler's speech and its reception is based on a report by Howard Becker, who heard the lecture at the Hochschule and also made a point of speaking with several army officers who had heard the speech at the Reichswehrministerium to determine the military audience's reaction to Scheler's talk. See Howard Becker, "Befuddled Germany: A Glimpse of Max Scheler," *American Sociological Review,* VIII (April, 1943), pp. 207–211.

with, Scheler lit into the romantically minded militarists among the Stahlhelm and the Nazis who insisted that war was necessary to the cultivation of heroic virtues and to the preservation of national unity. Reversing himself completely from his former stance, Scheler now maintained that pacifism could be as heroic as militarism. The abolition of war need not lead to moral and cultural decay, to the sloth of luxury and the base commercialism he had denounced in 1914. On the contrary, it was the peace *after* war which led to cultural degeneracy. The antidote to the current decadence was not to draft men into the army and fill them with dreams of military greatness, but instead, to teach them social responsibility by requiring them to devote a year or two of their lives to the service of the community at large in a kind of domestic peace corps.

One might suppose that these words ruffled the army officer corps to whom Scheler presented this speech, but they loved it. Scheler sharply distinguished his present position from the strongly militaristic one he had taken during the war, admitting his radical departure from the beliefs he had once held and propagated.[80] He had learned from the war that the pernicious doctrines of Schiller, Treitschke, and Hegel must be abandoned forever. He even attacked the militarism he had admired during the war as the ideology of the Prussian officer caste: "This kaiser was first war-lord, and he played, as he thought, a high hand. But we all know, do we not, that he was only a pawn of the junkers? . . . Their support, however, gave him courage to act without the knowledge of his ministers . . . and the German people had to pay the piper!"[81]

We have said that although Scheler attacked aggressive nationalistic militarism and the Prussian military ethos, the officer corps loved his speech and approvingly interrupted him often with clapping and stamping of feet. How could this be? Their enthusiasm is difficult to understand, but it may be par-

---

[80] *Ibid.*, p. 209.   [81] *Ibid.*, p. 210.

tially accounted for by the remainder of Scheler's speech in which he announced that although the Germans should avoid chauvinistic militarism, instrumental militarism was necessary for their self-preservation. He protested the restrictions on armament imposed on Germany by the Allies:

We dare not go too far in the direction of pacifism until other nations which now have the power to make Germany the cockpit of Europe and which have already made her the Cinderella of Western civilization show more desire for lasting peace on an even-handed basis. Do not forget that the lie of sole guilt for the war still stands, that we have been compelled to destroy our pitifully weak defenses in the East, that French troops still trample the West, and that we are expected to pay the war-debts of Europe. . . . Until we get justice instead of empty promises *we must unalterably oppose all forms of pacifism* which regard the ultimate goal of lasting peace as attainable *now.* . . . We must, in this day in which we live, learn to be *instrumental militarists;* we must — this audience must — build an army large enough to maintain our national independence in the *full* sense of the word. It must be an army *realistic* enough to regard itself as only a means [to the maintenance of peace] and to cast off the folly of war for war's sake; it must be *idealistic* enough to see as the final goal of our instrumental militarism a new and better Germany, a united Europe, and a world *some day* at peace — lasting peace![82]

General Heye informed Scheler afterward, through Gessler, that he and most of his comrades found Scheler's ideology exceptionally well thought out. They believed that it might well form the basis of Germany's future military arrangements — at least this belief is what Scheler reported in a letter to Maerit, his ex-wife. Scheler was so pleased that he decided to have the speech printed. General Heye promised to have the General Staff buy several thousand copies and to make it required reading for officers in training.[83]

The speech was such a success that Scheler was asked to repeat it at the Deutsche Hochschüle für Politik for the benefit

[82] *Ibid.,* p. 210. Compare *Die Idee des Friedens,* pp. 61–62.
[83] See Scheler's letter to Maerit Furtwaengler, January 13, 1927.

of a civilian audience. This Institute of Political Studies had been founded by Dr. Ernst Jäckh,[84] who stated its objectives when it first opened in 1920: "Our task must be to become the crystalization point for the intellectual and spiritual rebuilding of Germany — and through [the building of] a new Germany, also a new Europe, in such a way that those who fell in the war will not have died in vain."[85] During the next thirteen years, the Hochschule established itself as the training ground for the young men who hoped to become the leaders of German democracy. Many of Germany's best young political minds were assembled on its staff, including Arnold Bergsträsser, Moritz Julius Bonn, Arnold Brecht, Goetz Briefs, Willy Hass, Theodor Heuss, Hajo Holborn, Sigmund Neumann, Martin Spahn and, a Swiss, Arnold Wolfers. If Scheler wished to reach the new elite that was developing in Germany, surely here was the place. Jäckh asked him to give the convocation address in November, 1927 and to offer a series of public lectures on "Morals and Politics,"[86] during the winter semester. The lectures have not been published, but Scheler's convocation address, "Man in the Era of Adjustment" gives some indication of the fare he offered at the Hochschule.

The convocation address reveals Scheler's conception of the role of the elite in the postwar world. He called the twentieth century the *Era of Adjustment* (*Ausgleich*), and explained that for the developing new elite to be effective in this changing world, it must be aware of the direction and inner meaning of the social changes that were going on.[87] To the untrained eye, the twentieth-century world might appear purely chaotic. The

[84] For the history of the Hochschule, see Ernst Jäckh and Otto Suhr, *Geschichte der deutschen Hochschule für Politik,* Schriftenreihe der deutschen Hochschule für Politik; (Berlin, 1952). See also the memoirs of Ernst Jäckh, *Weltstaat, Erlebtes und Erstrebtes* (Stuttgart, 1960).

[85] Jäckh and Suhr, *Geschichte,* p. 5.

[86] The manuscript of these lectures is in the hands of Maria Scheler, Scheler's widow and the editor of his complete works. She declined to show them to us, however, claiming that she plans to publish them soon.

[87] "Man in the Era of Adjustment," p. 95.

uninitiated would not be able to decipher the hidden meaning of the process of equalization or balancing that was taking place, but Scheler thought that his sociology of knowledge and his metaphysical anthropology gave him the necessary insight to guide the developing elite.

The Hochschule seemed to be filled with Germany's future leaders. Scheler warned the young men of the need for elites, even in a democracy.[88] If those who believed in democracy did not produce a governing elite, the fascists would. Democracy, more ruthlessly than any other form of government, had *magnified* the old historical contrasts between population, groups, confessions, and parties in Germany, but democracy was not responsible for these contrasts. By revealing them, it simply outlined the *problems* that the elite must solve. European democracy was now facing a difficult crisis. The coalition governments were inevitably weak and were constantly being upset and reshuffled. Germany experienced a kind of stalemate, what Bonn described as "a kind of permanent balance of power"[89] which protected the minority's interests, but prevented the majority from carrying out their policies. As Bonn explained:

Organized permanent interests, not arguments and sentiments are the decisive factors in [our] elections. There often is a permanent deadlock, a continual wrangle between the opposed economic groups with the result that neither the capitalists nor the socialists are able to impose their will on their opponents; *the nation is paralyzed.*[90]

This state of affairs had produced the clamor for a dictator. While the world seemed to be going to pieces, these two rival social systems squandered precious time and energy fighting with each other. "Nothing happens," Bonn complained, "for the parliament is supported by loyal bureaucrats who have learned only how to forestall action, not to bring it about."[91]

[88] *Ibid.*
[89] Moritz Julius Bonn, *The Crisis of European Democracy* (New York, 1925), p. 84.
[90] *Ibid.*, p. 82. [91] *Ibid.*, p. 85.

Scheler was exasperated with the continual haggling among the parties and their reluctance to sacrifice even the slightest ideological principle in a compromise of any kind. He saw the handwriting on the wall and warned against the tendencies toward dictatorship on the right and on the left:

> Democracy will be able to survive only if it can, so to speak, seize the weapons from its opponents and produce and tolerate a well-chosen, mobile, effective elite which provides the nation with a unity of culture (*Bildung*) and power. Whether we Germans succeed in this task or not will determine not only the fate of our national culture and the dignity of our human form, but the very historical destiny of our state.[92]

Democracy in Germany was facing a severe crisis that was doomed to become ever more severe. A new elite was going to take over. The question was: who would make up this new elite, democrats, fascists, or communists?[93] Scheler, the *Vernunftrepublikaner*, hoped that democracy would survive because he felt that democracy, despite its disadvantages, guaranteed the most intellectual and cultural freedom.[94]

Just as in his letters to Maerit during the last years of his life Scheler increasingly spoke of *fate* and acceptance of one's fate, so now he viewed the political and social scene with similar fatalism and pessimism. The adjustment of political and economic tensions in Europe was a fate imposed by the results of war; Scheler viewed the war as a catastrophe that had set in motion a world revolution which was changing the power structure of the whole world. Nationalism, the idea of the absolutely sovereign nation state, would have to retreat in the coming era; federalism was bound to develop in its place. Germany could not have any more colonies, but that was fine, because colonies were becoming a thing of the past anyway. A dedicated Europeanism, in contrast to nationalism was the order of day. Scheler said: "Europeanism is our destiny, even if it is not our choice."[95]

92 *Philosophical Perspectives*, p. 95.
93 *Ibid.*, p. 14 and p. 94.   94 *Ibid.*, p. 96.
95 *Ibid.*, p. 119.

The social dislocations caused by the war and the inflation that followed had brought new classes into existence and had driven others — such as the grand bourgeoisie — out of their former role as the backbone of the nation. The group that lost most in the inflation was the growing class of employees (*Angestellten*) which had continually become more bureaucratic. The group that was on the rise was that of the magnates of finance and the energizing industries. Scheler did not refer to the Jews, surprisingly enough, in his account of the social transformations of the Weimar era.

Scheler hoped that the great social transformations taking place would encourage a feeling of *solidarity* that would cut across national frontiers in Europe. Formerly, Scheler had idealized national solidarity and deplored international alliances, particularly ties based on economic interests held in common. Now the ever-changing Scheler, thoroughly chastened by his earlier follies, began to speak of the international ties between members of the same classes that could help act as a bulwark of peace! Having recently participated in a meeting of Prince Anton Rohan's League for Cultural Cooperation in Frankfurt, Scheler found that:

I was considerably surprised, in spite of my close acquaintance with this movement over several years, that the tendencies there expressed resembled closely the spirit and politics of the "Holy Alliance." If they were somewhat less "holy," they were so much the more impelled by a *growing fear*, shared by the grand bourgeoisie in Europe that their power as a class would be endangered by any future war between nations. We can in the future, count on the growth of pacifism in the capitalistic upper bourgeoisie. Europeanism, advanced by both the lower and the upper classes, is indeed our destiny, not our choice. Here again it is our task to guide the adjustment politically and economically into the proper channels and forms.[96]

[96] *Ibid.*, p. 119. Compare the similar remarks in *Die Idee des Friedens*, pp. 57–59, where Scheler also spoke of the class solidarity of the grand bourgeoisie all over Europe and how this class solidarity might serve as a bulwark of peace.

4
___

I F T H E developing new elite were to act effectively, Scheler said, it would need to understand the political, social, and intellectual tendencies of the twentieth century *and* the general direction in which world history was moving. He therefore outlined this direction as he conceived it. In 1916 he had spoken of the war as the beginning of the common history of humanity, the first world-historical event in which all mankind had been directly involved. He had called the war a world revolution, in which the colonial peoples were throwing off their bonds and coming into their own. Now, in 1927, Scheler proclaimed that this world revolution had not ended in 1918 with the signing of the armistice; it had continued and was still going on within the framework of a tenuous peace. For this reason, Scheler doubted that there could be a lasting *world* peace for some time to come. The only reasonable hope men might cherish was that future wars within the European culture sphere might be avoided. In particular, Germans should work to ease tensions between England and Russia, because should war break out between these two, Germany would not only be engulfed, she would be torn by civil war, the capitalists supporting England, and the socialists and communists siding with the Soviet Union.[97]

In his novel, *The Magic Mountain*, Thomas Mann placed Germany, symbolized by Hans Castorp, midway between East and West, between what he called the Asiatic and the European principles. To Mann these two principles — Asiatic force, superstition, sloth, and darkest reaction; and European justice, freedom, knowledge, and progress — were in perpetual conflict for possession of the world. Hans Castorp was unable to choose between them; both principles were aspects of the German soul. He was like "the lonely boatsman on the Holstein lake, looking

[97] *Philosophical Perspectives*, p. 118. Compare Scheler's remarks on the Soviet Union in his earlier work, *On the Eternal in Man*, p. 430ff, and Scheler's remarks on Russia in *Wissensformen*, p. 186 ff.

with dazzled eyes from the glassy daylight of the Western shore to the mist and moonbeams that wrapped the Eastern heavens."[98] Mann himself hoped that the Germans might create a synthesis of the two principles. The Russian sense of solidarity and brotherhood should be fused with Western individualism to produce a kind of aristo-democracy, a society of free, creative, unregimented personalities, imbued with a keen sense of social responsibility and a spirit of cooperation.[99] When he became disillusioned with Germany after 1933, Mann looked to America as the land that might succeed in creating a society at once free and socially conscious.

Interestingly, Scheler's conception of Germany's mediating role between East and West corresponds to Mann's in many respects, even to the point of his vision of America as the potential promised land. Already toward the end of the war, Scheler had insisted that the Germans could learn more from Russia than from the West which was overly individualistic. German culture was similar to Russian, in that it had arisen entirely from below.[100] Scheler's meaning here is obscure. He must have completely ignored the importation of Western culture into Russia since the eighteenth century. His knowledge of Russian culture was drawn largely from Dostoevsky and Leontiev who stressed its native popular roots. At any rate, Scheler believed that "rich fruit" could be derived from the complementary blending of Germanic individualism and the Slavonic sense of community.[101] The result would produce a combination of the intellectual and the mystical, discipline and generosity, active Christianity and contemplative devotion. After the war, Scheler hoped that Germany's economic and military aid to the Soviet Republic would create close ties between the two new governments and result in mutual cultural interpenetration (*Kulturdurchdringung*) between East and West. Germany as a Western nation could offer Russia science, technology, and

98 Quoted in Andre von Gronicka, "Thomas Mann and Russia," in *The Stature of Thomas Mann*, ed. Charles Nieder (New York, 1947), p. 323.

99 *Ibid.*, p. 324.

100 *Eternal in Man*, p. 431.

101 *Ibid.*, p. 432.

economic aid. At the same time, being "more receptive to Eastern spirituality" than most other Western nations, Germany could learn spiritual techniques of contemplation and the sense of solidarity and community from Russia which she could then introduce to the Western peoples by her example. This whole process would be thrown away by an Anglo-Russian war. Germany would be forced to choose between East and West when her real vocation was to create a fusion of the two. Therefore, Germany, who was gradually overcoming her pariah position among the Western nations through Stresemann's Policy of Fulfillment should attempt to act as peacemaker and cultural transmitter (*Vermittler*) between Russia and the West.[102]

But what of Scheler's interest in America? Scheler anticipated a probable war between the United States and Japan because of their rivalry in the Pacific, but he hoped that this war might be averted through interpenetration of Eastern (especially Chinese) culture into the United States. What America, and all the West for that matter, could learn from the Orient was "the politics of the hunter," i.e., the art of waiting and of passive resistance.[103] The increasing mixture of blood and races in America, and the gradual suppression of the Anglo-Saxon predominance in American life, the growth of socialism and communism in America, and the rebellion of youth against America's Puritanical traditions — all these things — coupled with the influence of Chinese culture through immigration, Scheler hoped would lead to the development of a new elite. This new American elite would combine the arts of control over nature (technology) developed in the West, with the arts of self-control and meditation perfected in the East. As a result, the American character would lose the "stiffness and stuffiness" it had acquired from England, its original mother, and replace these traits with a warmer, more generous, and at the same time more contemplative spirit.[104]

102 *Wissensformen*, p. 187.
103 *Philosophical Perspectives*, p. 119.
104 *Wissensformen*, p. 188.

Scheler's rather fantastic accounts of the "meeting of East and West" in Germany and America indicate what he conceived to be the tendencies of the age of adjustment on the international and intercultural level. What interested him even more, however, was the tendency toward adjustment which he believed to be taking place in man as such. The intercultural adjustment was but a symbol and symptom of the inner adjustment that must go on in every man all over the world as mankind moved toward a universal world civilization. Scheler characterized this world-historical tendency in glowing terms:

If I had to inscribe a name on the gate of the incipient era . . . only one would seem appropriate to me, that of *"adjustment"*; adjustment of almost all characteristic and specifically *natural* traits, physical and psychic, which distinguish the social groups into which we can divide humanity, and at the same time, a tremendous *increase* in *spiritual* individual, and relatively individual, e.g. national differences; adjustment of *racial* tensions; adjustment between mentalities, conceptions of self, world, and God, in the great *cultural groupings* especially in Asia and Europe; adjustment between the specifically *male* and *female* ways of thinking in their rule over human society; adjustment between *capitalism* and *socialism* and, thereby, of class arguments and class conditions and rights between upper and lower *classes;* adjustment in the share of political power of so-called *civilized, half-civilized,* and *primitive peoples;* adjustment also between relatively primitive and highly civilized mentalities; relative adjustment between youth and old-age in the evaluation of their mental attitudes; adjustment between *technical knowledge* and *cultural growth,* between physical and spiritual work, adjustment between the spheres of national economic interests and contributions in the realm of civilization.[105]

According to Scheler, this tendency toward adjustment would lead to an "ever increasing differentiation of the spiritual individuality of man."[106] This meant that men everywhere would become more truly themselves; each man would be more able to fulfill his spiritual vocation in a world civilization that consisted of a proper balance between *spirit* and *life* which had

[105] *Philosophical Perspectives,* p. 102.
[106] *Ibid.,* p. 116.

formerly been functionalized in different cultures in a one-sided fashion.

In the age of adjustment, the era of "total man,"[107] the various differences between the overly rationalized and mechanized West and the overly spiritualized East would be reconciled in a new synthesis in which each man, everywhere, would be able to fulfill his full potentiality. The total potentiality of mankind, which had hitherto been functionalized into different cultures, would be united into one world civilization. Like Spengler, who had proclaimed a universal historical law of cultural growth and decline as man's fate, Scheler insisted that "this adjustment is not something we 'choose'; it is inescapable *fate*. Whoever resists, whoever wishes to cultivate some so-called 'characteristic,' 'specific' ideal of man, one already concretely formed in history, will work in thin air."[108]

In these years when he was working out his metaphysics of man, Scheler came to view history as the progressive self-revelation of the human spirit. Looking back across the centuries, Scheler believed that he could see "the whole portrait of manifold humanity drawn and painted . . . presenting the *idea* of man in temporal form."[109] History presented a panorama of diverse images that revealed "the human form in its ever-changing aspects."[110] This approach to history was essentially suprahistorical. Looking for the eternal forms, the essence of man and his works *behind* history, Scheler was really considering history as a work of art, a masterpiece created by the spirit of man.

Just as in his metaphysics Scheler had drawn heavily upon the tradition of German idealism from Kant to Hegel, so in his philosophy of history Scheler depended on the traditions of German historicism from Herder to Burckhardt. With Burckhardt, Scheler believed that the manifold potentialities of human nature had never been — and could never be — actu-

---

107 *Ibid.*, p. 102. 108 *Ibid.*, p. 103.
109 *On the Eternal in Man*, p. 201.
110 *Ibid.*

alized by any one civilization. Thus, if one wished to contemplate the spirit of man in its full breadth, one would have to consider the whole of human history. Even then one's view would necessarily remain inadequate, as the transformations of man in the *future* would have to be included to round out the picture.

Nevertheless, Scheler believed that the general trend of human history was clear. Gradually, through fits and starts, man was moving toward a cosmopolitan world civilization in which the accomplishments of each culture would become accessible to all.[111] In its formal structure, world history did not consist in a rhythmic unfolding of a plurality of elements, races, or cultures each of which was doomed to inevitable extinction after it had played out its role on the stage of history, Scheler said. The error in this view, held by Spengler, was that it ignored the possibility of cultural interchange and diffusion, the possibility of cultural renewal through repentance and rebirth. Scheler also rejected the Marxist and positivist interpretations of history as progressing according to a unilinear evolution. Instead, he compared the structure of history to a river system in which a great number of rivers continued their particular courses for centuries. Nourished by innumerable tributaries, these rivers "finally tend to converge and to unite in one great stream."[112]

Scheler's philosophy of history might best be summed up with a quotation from *The Nature of Sympathy* (1922):

In the total enterprise of human knowledge, no one people can altogether take the place of another. Only long term and simultaneous *cooperation on a world-wide scale* between the individual yet complementary portions of humanity can bring into play the total capacity for knowledge inherent in mankind at large, without distinction of time or place. We must, therefore, dismiss the simplified view of evolution as an upward march of the world process directed toward the undisputed sovereignty of the civilized male, and even of the civilized male European. The phases of evolution are never

111 *Ibid.*, p. 245.
112 *Philosophical Perspectives*, p. 105.

merely stepping stones, for each has a unique character and *value of its own.* Evolution is never simply a progress; it always involves decay as well.[113]

Here Scheler broached a theme that became increasingly important to him in his last years: the idea that European man must no longer consider his own culture the norm of civilization against which all other cultures could be judged. The excessively active, bustling European could learn much from the so-called backward peoples, if he would but listen and observe them. Western Faustian man was exhausted from his exertions; he needed a "rest cure in the profundities, the sense of eternity, in the repose and dignity of the Asiatic spirit."[114] And his contact with the East would do him good in another way. It would force him to reappraise the whole Western cultural tradition against what the East had to offer and to reassess what the West held in common with Asia. Out of this reappraisal there would gradually emerge an awareness in the West, Scheler hoped, that Europe now needed the inspiration of the contemplative peoples of the East in order to make further contributions to the developing total culture of mankind.[115]

5

S C H E L E R's lectures in Berlin in 1927 seem to have been more popular with the older generation than with the young men and women on the extreme right and left, or even with dedicated young democratic liberals like Arnold Bergsträsser and Sigmund Neumann. The latter felt that Scheler spoke as a man who had been disenchanted with his earlier ideals, and had come around — as did so many of his generation — to republican democracy only because he felt that there was no other reasonable alternative. Scheler, like the other elders could

113 *Sympathy,* p. 32.
114 *On the Eternal in Man,* p. 429.
115 *Ibid.,* p. 430.

not really provide sound direction for the future, for his whole way of looking at politics and society had been formed in the Wilhelmian epoch and was ill-adapted to the new social situations and mass democracy that had developed in Germany after the war.[116]

A young pacifist who was not only anti-militarist but also anti-nationalist, Wolf Zucker, probably reflected the mood of many of the idealistic youth who wanted something more inspiring to guide them than Scheler's rationalizations for his own capitulation before the ruling forces in Germany. Zucker described Scheler as the most interesting lecturer at the Hochschule in 1927 — most interesting because Scheler was "the *feuilleton* professor who conjured metaphysical meaning out of everyday events." "You want mysticism? We have all kinds; just name your poison,"[117] Zucker parodied Scheler.

Scheler's technique is to mystify his audience with paradoxes and contradictions, and then to release the tension by reassuring them that the greatest wisdom comes not from the intellect, but from intuition. His metaphysical gnosis offers the answer to every problem. Scheler's system has a place for everything; it is *extremely* tolerant. And why squabble over petty issues when the whole system seems so lovely? Whatever happens in the real world . . . the assassination of a dictator, or the failure of such a plot . . . either can be explained by Scheler's sociology and metaphysics. His philosophy is adapted to account for any situation; like the barber's stool, as one of Shakespeare's fools says, it's designed for any ass.[118]

Scheler's metaphysics, in which mind and instinct were said to be forever striving against each other, seems to have been a projection on an abstract level of the conflict that Scheler experienced both in his own life and in postwar German society. As noted in the previous chapter, the Weimar Republic was torn by deep and seemingly irreconcileable political and ideological divisions. Throughout his life, Scheler sought to smother the roaring class struggle that threatened to destroy

---

[116] Oral testimony of Arnold Bergsträsser and the late Sigmund Neumann.
[117] Wolf Zucker, "Max Scheler in Berlin," *Die Weltbühne,* XXIII (February, 1927), p. 276.
[118] *Ibid.,* p. 277.

the cultural values he cherished. Now at the end of his life, Scheler became extremely pessimistic. In his letters to Maerit during these years, the theme of fate and the need to accept one's destiny recurred periodically. Being unable to find a satisfactory solution to his personal life, Scheler spoke of fate and resignation. On the other hand, in his public utterances, he spoke of man's freedom to make *decisions,* a power which man derived from his participation in divinity.

We have repeatedly seen in this study that Max Scheler considered the main problem of modern Germany to be the lack of a common sense of values or purpose among its citizens. Before, during, and after the war, Scheler preached a philosophy of solidarity through which the political and ideological divisions of Germany might be overcome. The contents of his philosophy changed as Scheler moved from nationalism to Catholicism to pantheism, but in all cases the function of these religious-metaphysical systems remained constant. He saw in each of them a form of social cement. Once he became disillusioned with the unifying power of Germany's national mission and with the "community building powers of the Catholic Church," he abandoned these for his own private religion of the impotent evolving God. The latter also provided a unifying principle, as can be seen from Scheler's statement:

A completely *metaphysical and religious* and, therefore, also political and social *integration and reconciliation of classes* will be possible only on the basis of a metaphysics, a conception of self, world, and God, which comprises light and darkness, the spirit and the fate determining demonic drive for existence and life.[119]

Scheler had become increasingly pessimistic about the power of mind to shape reality, and therefore, of the power of any ideological or religious system to provide unity. In a world torn by the strife among conflicting classes, the power of reason seemed nil indeed. Scheler projected this struggle between reason and blind will (or pure instinct) into a metaphysical system which postulated an eternal struggle between these two

119 *Philosophical Perspectives,* p. 122.

elements that could never be wholly overcome. The unifying principle now became being itself. The *Weltgrund*, to use Heidegger's term, was conceived to be *above* both poles of the contrast, and in it alone, *through human action, Geist* and *Leben* were reconciled.

This resolution of strife in the harmony of the *Weltgrund* became Scheler's answer to the problem of evil. He now abjured all organized religion and the traditional idea of a personal God. "The Christian idea of a purely spiritual, creative God, of the fall of man, and of the hereditary, irremediably sinful constitution of man," like the classical idea of man held by the Greeks and the idealist conceptions of man and God — all these, according to Scheler, were exclusively *ideologies of the upper class.*[120] The lower class would retain its purely materialistic conception of man and its economic and social interpretation of religion as long as the upper class retained its idea of the spontaneous power of *Geist* or God.

This ideological impasse might only be broken by a new conception of the relationship between man and God that recognized their mutual interdependence. The new elite would discover this.

My conviction leads me to believe that the elite, as a group that must guide the coming adjustment into the right paths, may not give allegiance to any organized church. . . . It will not base its metaphysical views as exclusively on the tradition of Luther, Kant, and German idealism as have the elites of the recent German past, nor will it base itself exclusively on any other tradition.[121]

This new elite would derive its picture of God and the world "from the spontaneous forces of its own spirit, from its own *Erlebnis.*" From this position it would try to decide which elements of traditional church dogma and ideas of justice were or were not relevant to the conceptions it had acquired "in its own debate with reality."

If an elite that would not be hostile to democracy were

[120] *Ibid.*   [121] *Ibid.*, p. 123.

to arise — and Scheler pinned his hopes on the advent of such an elite — where would it come from? It would emerge from "the gradual amalgamation of 'cultural groups' which have formed around leading personalities."[122] Scheler was no more specific. His bare statement leaves a wide room of margin, to say the least. He was firmly convinced that such elites were in the early stages of development in Weimar Germany. The question was: would they mature in time? "It may be years yet, perhaps decades, before this growing elite, which today is still too *critical* of our culture, will be prepared for reality and life . . . and be able to replace the present interim leadership in Germany."[123] If the elite arrived before it was too late, it would be able to prevent the destruction of the Republic and instill in it "ideals of *arete* [virtue] and a *live spiritual content*"[124] so that it would capture the imagination and the whole-hearted allegiance of the German people. And if the elite did not arise in time? Scheler did not say, but we know the answer only too well.

6

WHAT MADE Scheler postulate a "becoming God" in his last years when, as late as 1921, he had dismissed pantheism as "utter nonsense" and a "contradiction in terms?"[125] The answer lies in his own restless psyche. He spoke of *himself* in his last years when he described man as "the eternal Faust, the creature always seeking and desiring (*bestia cupidissima rerum novarum*), never at peace with his environment, always anxious to break through the barriers of his life here and now, always striving to transcend his environment, including his own state

---

[122] *Ibid.*, p. 94.   [123] *Ibid.*, p. 96.
[124] *Ibid.*
[125] A large section of the book, *On the Eternal in Man,* which contains Scheler's philosophy of religion, is devoted to a critique of pantheism.

of being."[126] In his metaphysics, intellect and instinct, the divine and the demonic, are forever struggling against each other, and their battleground is the human soul. Avidity for new things became the mainspring of man's spiritual life; the desire to be oneself gave way to the desire to become the embodiment of the ever-changing Absolute. The Catholic Nietzsche withdrew into the mists of Schellingian pantheism.

Letters to Maerit during these years indicate Scheler's growing sense of isolation. He felt completely alone, buried in ice, he wrote.[127] Maerit now appeared increasingly attractive. She was the love of his life, he wrote her, the only woman who had ever really understood him.[128] On Holy Thursday, 1926, he wrote Maerit in Rome asking her to participate in the profundities of the paschal liturgy for him.[129] At religious holidays such as Christmas and Easter, he missed the deep feeling of oneness with the universe that the liturgical celebrations at Maria Laach and Beuron, centers of the liturgical renewal then underway in the church, had meant to him. But he could not bring himself to return as he had done during the war. His feet were now set in another direction. He was engrossed in a metaphysical anthropology which explained the process of man's own self-deification. Catholicism provided an adequate religion for the masses, but "the masses will never be philosophers," he wrote.[130] For the spiritual and intellectual elite, only a profound, challenging philosophy of man's participation in the creation of God would suffice.

Scheler now began to consider life and history as almost totally *fated*. There seemed to be so little real choice; destiny ruled men's lives. But acceptance of one's fate, resignation before the implacable will of the gods had its own consolations. He regretted ever having gone to Cologne, regretted having

---

126 *Man's Place in Nature*, p. 55.
127 Letter of May 10, 1926, from Max Scheler to Maerit Furtwaengler. Parts of this letter are quoted in Oesterreicher, *op. cit.*, p. 196.
128 *Ibid.*   129 *Ibid.*, p. 197.
130 *Philosophical Perspectives*, p. 1.

given up Maerit, and assured her that his years with her in Munich and Berlin were the happiest of his life.[131] He recalled the words of Goethe: "For every man there comes a time when he is driven out of the paradise of warm feelings," claiming that since he had left Maerit his paradise was gone and his heart was broken. Since then he had led a dark, nomadic existence, searching and struggling. Now at last he had become resigned, and found that he could even rejoice that his former feelings of a false security had vanished. In their place he had discovered his own heroic attitude toward life, grounded in his brave, realistic metaphysics, which alone enabled him to keep going on in spite of his poor health and his depressions.[132]

One wonders whether Scheler was thinking of his own life when he wrote that " 'destiny' is the series, the host of happenings which, though we have in no way sought, anticipated, expected, or chosen them, are yet felt in a quite peculiar way to be *characteristic of us*, once they have happened."[133] He recognized that, taken together, the events of a life that seemed accidental when they happened, represented "a single pervasive theme running throughout a career, whose total pattern bears the individual stamp of the person to whom the career belongs."[134]

Inspired by his reading of Miguel de Unamuno's *The Tragic Sense of Life*, a book that he felt he might have written himself, Scheler found that there was an amazing unity of style in the way things happened to him. Perhaps everything had been absolutely necessary after all. He found a certain consolation in this recognition of necessity as he became bitterly aware of his inability to alter his situation. But the consolation of fate was fleeting. More often he felt frustration at his helplessness.

---

[131] Letter of December 21, 1927 from Max Scheler to Maerit Furtwaengler, quoted in my unpublished doctoral dissertation, "Max Scheler: Philosopher, Sociologist, and Critic of German Culture" (University of California at Berkeley, 1965), pp. 563–564.

[132] Letter of July 29, 1927 from Max Scheler to Maerit Furtwaengler, *Ibid.*

[133] *Sympathy*, p. 197.

[134] *Ibid.*

As his father had been dominated by his mother, Scheler found himself increasingly dominated by his wife. He complained to Maerit that he was losing self-respect as he found himself unable to stand up to his wife's stronger personality.[135]

Not only was his third wife a burden to him, and his second one a thorn in his conscience, but the first one now began to trouble him again. Amelie von Dewitz had raised Scheler's son, Wolf (born circa 1900), but the boy had grown up to be a petty criminal. Unable to do anything with her son, Frau von Dewitz had delivered Wolf to Scheler shortly before he divorced Maerit to marry Maria.[136] Maria had no patience with the boy, and Scheler was constantly bailing Wolf out of trouble in Cologne. When Scheler found out that his son was being kept by a prostitute, he contacted the girl and tried to break up the liaison, but she was determined to marry the boy. The prostitute was about eight years older than Wolf, and Scheler envisioned the old pattern that he had been through himself with the boy's mother. In desperation he offered his son a handsome stipend if he would go abroad for awhile and try to forget the girl, but Wolf had his father's stubbornness. He refused. Finally Scheler sent him to a chauffeuring school in the south of Germany hoping that he would learn an honest trade. Wolf ran away from the school and continued to plague his father with debts and problems. The boy eventually became a Brownshirt and was killed in a street fight.[137]

By 1927 Max Scheler had become internationally famous. He may have had a difficult time obtaining a good position in another German university, but he made up for this as best he could be giving public lectures in France,[138] Austria, the Nether-

---

[135] Letter of July 29, 1927 from Max Scheler to Maerit Furtwaengler.

[136] Oral testimony of Maerit Furtwaengler.

[137] My information about Scheler's problems with his son is drawn from references to Wolf in his letters to Maerit Furtwaengler.

[138] See Ernst Robert Curtius, *Französischer Geist im neuen Europa* (Berlin, 1925), p. 339 ff, in which he describes his experiences with Scheler at the international *Entretiens d'Été* at Pontigny, France, in 1924, where Scheler caused a sensation with his lectures (in German) on the contemporary significance of St. Augustine and Meister Eckhardt, introducing his phenomenology and metaphysics in France at the same time.

lands, and Switzerland, and by traveling widely in Germany. He even received offers to lecture in Japan, India, China, the United States, and the Soviet Union. However, he had become ill with a heart condition by this time and was unable to sail across the oceans to the Orient or to America. He was sorry not to be able to go, particularly because he wanted to see America, which he had heard much about from Emil Ludwig. He wrote Maerit that he had learned from Ludwig how one must live in order to live long – which appeared to be the goal of most Americans.[139] Ludwig had assured him that he was undoubtedly the best-known German philosopher in America. The idea of recuperating among these delightfully primitive people who seemed so full of exuberance and *joi de vivre* tempted him sorely. He almost went to the international philosophical convention in New York where he was scheduled to give the main lecture at one of the four general sessions, but his doctor advised against the trip so he went to see Maerit in Bavaria instead.[140]

Scheler had received an invitation to give a series of lectures in the Soviet Union, and he planned to go to Russia during the Christmas season in 1927 and to stay for several weeks.[141] Lunacharsky and Trotsky's sister, Mme. Karsavina, sent him an official invitation from the Soviet government. His hopes were high about the trip. He planned to give six lectures on God and the state, and six on his ontology and epistemology, as well as several on his anthropology. He never went, and the reasons are unclear, but presumably his health prevented him from making the trip. He was delighted to be internationally known, even if he was not able to travel to the far corners of the earth, and he wrote to Maerit, wondering who would have thought that her little Max would ever become so famous?[142]

Despite his worldly success, in his last years Scheler was bitterly unhappy and alone. He wrote Maerit that the only

---

[139] Letter of August 5, 1927 from Max Scheler to Maerit Furtwaengler.
[140] *Ibid.*
[141] Letter of March 10, 1927 from Max Scheler to Maerit Furtwaengler.
[142] Letter of August 5, 1927 from Max Scheler to Maerit Furtwaengler.

thing that kept him going was his work.[143] In his isolation he turned to his old friend Nietzsche as a kindred spirit. Invited by Frau Förster-Nietzsche to give a lecture on Nietzsche's idea of man to the Nietzsche Society in Weimar, Scheler made the pilgrimage to Sils Maria in the beautiful Swiss canton of Engadin. There, walking through the hills and valleys where Nietzsche had written so many of his works, Scheler found a temporary sense of peace. But the more he thought about Nietzsche's ideas, the more agitated his mind became. He found he could not possibly compress all he had to say into one lecture. It would have to be a lecture series at least; in fact, he would write a book on Nietzsche. Now that he had abandoned the *mythos* of Catholic doctrine, he felt that he understood Nietzsche fully at last.[144] He strolled out to the little Chasté peninsula that reaches into the lake at Sils. There he discovered Nietzsche's lovely poem "Mitternachtslied" engraved on a stone. He read it, and reread it, and was glad to be there alone.

Perhaps the best portrait of Max Scheler during these last years is the one painted by Otto Dix that now hangs in the Philosophy Faculty's room at the University of Cologne. Dix captured Scheler's penetrating glance, coming from the eyes that seemed to leap right out of his face. Scheler knew that the portrait was not flattering, but he admitted that there was much truth in it. Aside from the Dix portrait, these words of Ludwig Curtius present a perceptive characterization of Scheler as he was at the end of his life, burdened with guilt, frustrated, worried, and alone.

In the summer of 1927, in the late afternoon, as I worked on my lecture for the following day, the doorbell rang. I opened the door and found a man standing outside who was not really old but who was rapidly aging and looked very run down. I didn't recognize him until he spoke. "You don't remember me," he said in a disappointed tone, "I'm Scheler." I fell back amazed and a real feeling of awe overcame me. I had known him since my Munich days [before the war] and had seen him now and again since, but I had always kept

[143] Letter of February 16, 1928 from Max Scheler to Maerit Furtwaengler.
[144] Letter of April 23, 1927 from Max Scheler to Maerit Furtwaengler.

my distance because I did not want to follow his metaphysical journeys always in a different direction, always presented with the same enthusiasm and pathos. But now at this meeting, somehow things were different. Just looking at him I was deeply moved. In his fallen beardless face despite a balding scalp and toothless mouth, there still shone that thoughtful brow, and from his lovely innocent blue eyes a stream of goodness — and yet helplessness — poured forth. . . .

The dogmatic confidence with which he always defended the various intellectual positions he held in the course of his checkered career sprang partly from a consciousness of his intellectual superiority over his opponents; but it sprang even more from his love of truth in which every theoretical change grew out of his own direct, personal, practical moral experience. "The mind undermines" (*Der Geist ein Wühler*) stood written on his brow. Even at the end, when his face was a ruin, it glowed with an invincible spiritual brilliance.[145]

In his last semester at the University of Cologne, the winter of 1927, Scheler's heart grew weaker and his powers began to fail him. Almost as if to spite fate, he turned to the subject of vital energy and the theory of instincts in his lectures, describing in detail the physiological changes that take place in the male and female genitals during orgasm. He succeeded in shocking his mixed audience, if that was his intention.[146] But as he ranted on about blood and instinct, his old students began to sense that he was no longer the same man. He chain-smoked, his hands shook, and he was unsteady on his feet. The wellsprings of inspiration, the source of his *charisma*, dried up inside him. "It was tragic to watch him die before our very eyes," one of his students recalled to me.[147] "I came out of the lecture hall and said to my neighbor, '*Scheler stirbt!*' Others picked up the cry, and it rustled down the corridor like death itself stalking Max Scheler out of the lecture hall to his grave."[148] In

[145] Ludwig Curtius, *Deutsche und antike Welt, Lebenserinnerungen* (Stuttgart, 1950), p. 375.
[146] This story was told to me by Professor Gerhard Masur, who attended some of Scheler's lectures in 1927.
[147] The student was Elizabeth Sugg-Bellini. She now practices psychology in Munich, where she told me of Scheler's last lectures at Cologne.
[148] *Ibid.*

January, at the end of the semester, Scheler was too worn out to carry on his examinations. He fled to Ascona to recuperate, hoping to be well in time to take up his new position in Frankfurt in the spring.[149]

The cure in Ascona did Scheler good, and he moved to Frankfurt in mid-April, 1928. He had been given a professorship in philosophy and sociology and expected to receive a good salary despite the fact that he would no longer be the director of a sociological institute as he had been in Cologne.[150] Ernst Cassirer, who was also interested in philosophical anthropology, was scheduled to come to Frankfurt for the spring, and Scheler looked forward to comparing notes with him.

Frankfurt appealed to Scheler for other reasons as well.[151] The faculty there included some of the brightest young men in the social sciences as well as many of Scheler's old friends and acquaintances. Among the younger men, Scheler anticipated assistance in his research on the sociology of knowledge from Karl Mannheim and Theodore Adorno. He also looked forward to discussing the sociology of religion with Gottfried Salomon, who had been Ernst Troeltsch's assistant in Berlin. Richard Wilhelm and Rudolf Otto sponsored an Oriental Institute that interested Scheler enormously. There he hoped to learn more about the Eastern methods of meditation and self-control that had fascinated him for many years. All in all, Frankfurt was a stimulating cosmopolitan city, with an exciting Jewish intellectual community and excellent theatre and music, and it was on the main line between Bonn and Heidelberg, with universities that Scheler liked to visit. Darmstadt, where Count Keyserling had his School of Wisdom, was also nearby.

One other consideration may also have entered Scheler's mind when he accepted the appointment at Frankfurt. He would be less than an hour's train ride from Maerit. Soon after

[149] Letter of January 25, 1928 from Max Scheler to Maerit Furtwaengler.
[150] Letter of January 26, 1928 from Max Scheler to Maerit Furtwaengler.
[151] Scheler described his anticipations of professional contacts at Frankfurt in several letters to Maerit Furtwaengler.

he settled in Frankfurt, he made the short journey down to Heidelberg. He loved the old university town and walked through the ruined castle and the wild gardens with Maerit. As they walked — little knowing that this was to be almost their last time together — they talked about their good old days before the war, in Munich and Berlin, when they were penniless but happy.[152] The one blight on their marriage had been Maerit's inability to produce a child. Scheler told her how sad he was about the way Wolf had turned out. But it was too late now. Such was fate. At least, from now on Maerit would be nearby; he would come to see her often. He promised.

Max Scheler took the train back to Frankfurt that night. Maerit came to visit him the following weekend. He was feeling fine. He left her at her hotel and went back to the home of Professor Gelb, an old friend with whom he was staying until his wife and his furniture arrived from Cologne. During the night he suffered a severe stroke and was taken to the hospital. The attack occurred on May 13, 1928.[153] By the nineteenth he seemed to be doing well again. He asked Maria for a glass of beer. She went to get it. While she was out, a nurse came in with a thermometer. Thinking it was Maria with the beer, Scheler sat up quickly, excited. The sudden movement was too much for his weak heart. He fell back; his hands dropped to his sides. He was dead within a few minutes. His brain was bottled for science.[154]

Max Scheler was given a Roman Catholic burial in Cologne despite the fact that he had left the Church. His pregnant widow was not present, but the ever faithful Maerit was there

152 Oral testimony of Maerit Furtwaengler.

153 *Ibid.*

154 Professor Kurt Goldstein collected famous brains, keeping them on display in bottles in his laboratory. Maria had not given Goldstein permission to bottle Scheler's brain, so when a friend who had seen Scheler's brain in a bottle in Goldstein's office told Maria, she wrote Goldstein to return it to her at once. She received it in the mail within a week, packed in a cigar box. She had the brain buried beside Scheler's body in Cologne.

to the end.[155] At Scheler's grave, Ernst Robert Curtius, his old friend, spoke a word of farewell:

The concept of the person is given a fundamental role in Scheler's philosophy, and the philosophical act is defined as a personal act of rising, in which the whole man lovingly opens himself to the whole of being. . . . Sympathy was to Scheler a key to the cosmos, and he saw in love the movement toward a higher value. . . . He knew that the essence of another man is ineffable, that it can never be exhausted in concepts, that it steps forward in its purity and completeness only when seen in love. These basic theses of his metaphysics were certainties of the heart before they were truths of his thought. What he demonstrated as philosopher, he lived as man, and applying to him his own philosophical insights, we may say that what is innermost, deepest, and truest in his nature steps forward in its purity and completeness only when seen in love. . . .

It was only a few weeks ago that I last met Max Scheler, when, in a small circle of friends, he spoke of his ideal of man's activity. He called that life the highest and best which . . . devotes itself to the tasks of this world, and yet is not totally absorbed in them, but inwardly abides in the quiet of contemplation, *in der Stille der Gottesanschauung.* To the few people who heard him then for whom this conversation was their last impression of his earthly existence, these words will remain a testament.[156]

[155] A few months later Maria gave birth to a boy who she named after her deceased husband. Apparently disinclined to follow in his father's footsteps, Max Scheler, Jr. has made a name for himself as a professional photographer in the *Bundesrepublik.*

[156] Oesterreicher, *op. cit.,* p. 197.

8

Conclusion

THE STORY of Max Scheler's intellectual and personal life is one of a series of failures. It is the tragic story of an extremely intelligent and sensitive man who failed to fulfill his intellectual potential in his roles as a philosopher, sociologist, and critic of German culture in the twentieth century. The reasons for his professional failure derive from the conditions of his personal life. As a man, Scheler lacked the strength of character and self-discipline that might have enabled him to marshal his unusual talents for the achievement of his chosen objectives.

Over and over again during the course of his lifetime, Scheler's professional career as a teacher and scholar was disrupted by the chaos of his erotic life. His early career was vitiated by his involvement with an older woman, Amelie von Dewitz, who became his mistress and eventually his wife, but who ruined him professionally in Jena and again in Munich. In his later years, once again, erotic involvements threw Scheler's professional life into chaos. He had gained a wide following among German Catholics during World War I, and had been appointed to teach Catholic moral philosophy at the University of Cologne after the war. His divorce and remarriage caused his break with the Church, which put him in an awkward position at the university. Before the final rupture, when the Archbishop of Cologne warned Scheler that he had a responsibility to live a chaste circumspect life if he wished to continue teaching Catholic ethics at the university, Scheler replied: "I only point the way; a sign doesn't have to go where it points."[1] Scheler's failure resulted from the gap between theory and practice in his life. In a relativistic age, he taught a theory of absolute values; yet he not only failed to live by the values he taught, but freely adapted his philosophical theories to the endless changes in his personal life.

Scheler's *intellectual* career was equally disordered, even when considered in the context of the general disorder of the times in which he lived. In the preceding pages we have traced the many and various changes in his professional and personal life with the hope of throwing some light on the development of his political and social ideas. We have seen that his quest for community led him to probe the social structure of modern Germany in search of what he called community building powers. We found that this concern with community remained constant regardless of his changing ideological allegiances. At various times in his checkered career, Scheler thought that social cohesion in a pluralistic society might be provided by the army, the church, the youth movement, and even the proletariat. Scheler had a good sense of the political realities of Wilhelmian and Weimar Germany, for although he spoke in grandiose metaphysical terms, he always managed to switch parties in time to be speaking for the group that was on top.

How can we explain Scheler's seeming lack of intellectual integrity? And, more importantly, how can we explain the fact

[1] The story of Scheler and the Archbishop is reported in an anonymously published article, "Wann sagt man 'Voilà un homme'?," in *Die Neue Zeitung*, CXV (May 18, 1953), p. 2.

that his many ideological changes were so blithely accepted by a good portion of the educated German public who considered him to be one of the great thinkers of the modern period? The two questions are interrelated; Scheler's philosophical and political opportunism resulted from his desire to express in metaphysical terms the intellectual and political tendencies of his age. What Scheler lacked in consistency he had in immediacy, and herein lay his appeal. No matter what the events of the day, Scheler could always conjure up a metaphysical meaning for them. He thereby dignified the German drive for world power with a halo of idealism and moral fervor. As an ideologist, he gave German autocracy and militaristic imperialism a *raison d'être*.

In conclusion, we may ask what were Scheler's contributions to modern thought, and what was his historical significance in twentieth-century Germany? A list of Scheler's intellectual achievements is impressive; he contributed to the development of ethics and value theory, social psychology, sociology of knowledge, and philosophical anthropology. The most notable men who came under his influence were Ernst Cassirer,[2] Alois Dempf,[3] Martin Heidegger,[4] Paul Landsberg,[5] Ortega Y Gasset,[6] Karl Mannheim,[7] Alfred von Martin,[8] Gabriel Marcel,[9]

---

[2] Ernst Cassirer, *An Essay on Man, An Introduction to a Philosophy of Human Culture* (New York, 1954), pp. 48–49.

[3] Alois Dempf, *Theoretische Anthropologie* (Bern, 1950).

[4] Martin Heidegger, *Kant and the Problem of Metaphysics*, tr. James S. Church (Bloomington, Ind., 1962), preface, and pp. 215–220. See also the many references to Scheler in Heidegger's *Being and Time*, tr. John Macquarrie and Edward Robinson (London, 1962), 47–48 and *passim*.

[5] Paul Ludwig Landsberg, *Einführung in die philosophische Anthropologie* (Frankfurt, 1934).

[6] Ortega Y Gasset, *The Modern Theme*, tr. James Cleugh (New York, 1961), p. 60 ff.

[7] Karl Mannheim, *Ideology and Utopia, An Introduction to the Sociology of Knowledge*, tr. Louis Wirth and Edward Shils (New York, 1936). See also Mannheim's *Essays on the Sociology of Knowledge*, ed. Paul Keckesmeti (London, 1952), pp. 154–179 and *passim*.

[8] Alfred von Martin, *The Sociology of the Renaissance*, tr. W. L. Lütkins (New York, 1963), pp. 22–24; and *Ordnung und Freiheit* (Frankfurt am Main, 1956), *passim*.

[9] Gabriel Marcel, *Etre et Avoir* (Paris, 1935), pp. 303–304.

Jacques Maritain,[10] Helmuth Plessner,[11] Joachim Wach,[12] and Peter Wust.[13] On the other hand, although he was an innovator and catalyst in many fields, he failed to criticize and verify his hypotheses through careful research procedures. He relied almost entirely on his intuition, and as a result, much of his thought was arbitrary and often self-contradictory. His lack of self-discipline prevented him from making a greater and more lasting contribution in the fields that interested him.

As to Scheler's historical significance, our study has revealed him as a mirror of many intellectual and political tendencies in early twentieth-century Germany. His prewar critique of positivism and of bourgeois civilization brought him close to the camp of the conservative revolutionaries who denounced the materialism and social atomism of modern society and longed to recreate the imagined group solidarity of the Middle Ages. Scheler's unique contribution to the conservative revolution was to unite Nietzschean vitalistic and aristocratic ideas with Catholic corporatist ideas of hierarchy and group solidarity. Scheler's wartime writings cloaked the German drive for world power in metaphysical terms, glorifying militarism as the primary attribute of the German spirit. In the latter part of the war, and in the postwar period Scheler became a spokesman of Catholic political and social ideas. Faced with the threat of the proletarianization of culture after the revolution, Scheler spoke out in defense of the bourgeois culture he had excoriated before the war. At this time he also became a supporter of the Republic, and warned the German people of the dangers of the extremist movements that were beginning to threaten the life of the Republic.

10 Jacques Maritain, *De Bergson à Saint Thomas* (Paris, 1944), pp. 128–129.

11 Helmuth Plessner, "Die Aufgabe der philosophischen Anthropologie," in *Zwischen Philosophie und Gesellschaft* (Bern, 1953).

12 Joachim Wach, *The Comparative Study of Religions*, ed. Joseph Kitagawa (New York, 1958), p. 24 and p. 64 ff.

13 Peter Wust, *Dialektik des Geistes* (Augsburg, 1928); and "Max Schelers Lehre vom Menschen," *Das Neue Reich*, XI (1928–1929), p. 102 ff.

One of the most obvious characteristics of Weimar Germany was the plurality of world views and the lack of a common ground of discourse among them. Scheler developed his sociology of knowledge as an intended antidote to this situation. The sociology of knowledge was supposed to help the members of coalition governments to overcome their party prejudices by showing them the social roots of their ideologies. Freed from ideological prejudices, these men would be able to plan and organize society on the basis of an objective understanding of the real problems of the day. Furthermore, Scheler believed that the sociology of knowledge might form the basis of cultural integration all over the world in the twentieth century, which he called the era of adjustment.

Finally, in his last years, Scheler developed his philosophical anthropology in order to counteract the tendencies toward irrationalistic *Lebensphilosophie* and the cult of instinct and vitalism in Weimar Germany. According to Scheler, man was not only an instinctual animal but also a spiritual being. Man's cosmic task was to spiritualize nature, not to subordinate his spirit to it as such vitalists as Spengler and Klages claimed.

At the end of his life, Scheler became a spokesman for the liberalism and bourgeois culture that he had formerly condemned. He warned of the dangers of irrationalism and fascism, but failed to propose an adequate alternative. One cannot really be sure of how Scheler would have responded to the triumph of National Socialism in 1933, but if the opportunism that characterized most of his life is any indication, one can well suppose that he would have greeted the triumph of the will, cloaking it with a metaphysical meaning despite his proclaimed hostility to fascism.[14]

Despite his repeated failures, however, Max Scheler was a remarkable and historically significant figure in twentieth-century Germany. His life and thought reflect the turmoil of the

[14] For a perceptive critique of Scheler's social theory, indicating the respect in which it prefigured Nazi conceptions, see V. J. McGill, "Scheler's Theory of Sympathy and Love," *Philosophy and Phenomenological Research*, II (1942), pp. 273–291.

age and society in which he lived. In a highly intuitive manner, he put his finger on one of the key problems of our age: the lack of leadership and of a sense of community that results from rapid social change. In the end, he discovered the dangers of anti-rationalism, but only after he had spent most of his life fabricating various ideologies which undermined the liberalism he finally embraced.

Bibliography

Unpublished Materials

1. Scheler's *Nachlass* in Maria Scheler's home in Munich.
2. Scheler's letters to Maerit Furtwaengler at her home in Heidelberg.
3. Maerit Furtwaengler's autobiography.
4. Peter Wust's letters to Tony Föster at her home in Cologne.
5. Oral interviews with Scheler's friends and relatives, and with some of his former colleagues and students.
6. Ernst Robert Curtius, "Speech at Max Scheler's Funeral," made available through the courtesy of Maerit Furtwaengler.

Books by Max Scheler

NOTE: The books are listed chronologically. Whenever possible I have used the volumes in Scheler's collected works edited by Maria Scheler, published in Bern by the Francke Verlag, 1954 ff. (cited as *G.W.*)

SCHELER, MAX. *Beiträge zur Feststellung der Beziehungen zwischen den logischen und ethischen Prinzipien.* (Dissertation) Jena, Vopelius, 1899.

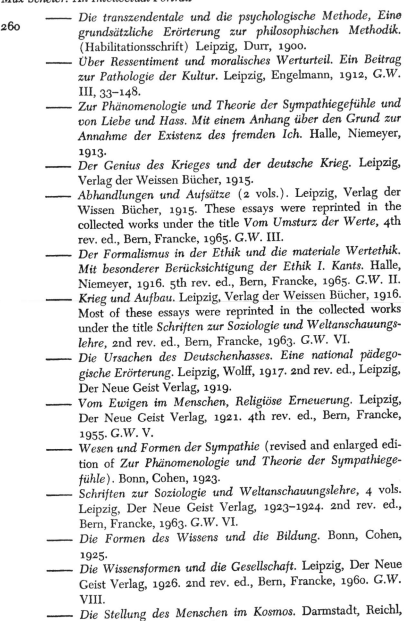

—— *Die transzendentale und die psychologische Methode, Eine grundsätzliche Erörterung zur philosophischen Methodik.* (Habilitationsschrift) Leipzig, Durr, 1900.

—— *Über Ressentiment und moralisches Werturteil. Ein Beitrag zur Pathologie der Kultur.* Leipzig, Engelmann, 1912, G.W. III, 33–148.

—— *Zur Phänomenologie und Theorie der Sympathiegefühle und von Liebe und Hass. Mit einem Anhang über den Grund zur Annahme der Existenz des fremden Ich.* Halle, Niemeyer, 1913.

—— *Der Genius des Krieges und der deutsche Krieg.* Leipzig, Verlag der Weissen Bücher, 1915.

—— *Abhandlungen und Aufsätze* (2 vols.). Leipzig, Verlag der Wissen Bücher, 1915. These essays were reprinted in the collected works under the title *Vom Umsturz der Werte,* 4th rev. ed., Bern, Francke, 1965. G.W. III.

—— *Der Formalismus in der Ethik und die materiale Wertethik. Mit besonderer Berücksichtigung der Ethik I. Kants.* Halle, Niemeyer, 1916. 5th rev. ed., Bern, Francke, 1965. G.W. II.

—— *Krieg und Aufbau.* Leipzig, Verlag der Weissen Bücher, 1916. Most of these essays were reprinted in the collected works under the title *Schriften zur Soziologie und Weltanschauungslehre,* 2nd rev. ed., Bern, Francke, 1963. G.W. VI.

—— *Die Ursachen des Deutschenhasses. Eine national pädegogische Erörterung.* Leipzig, Wolff, 1917. 2nd rev. ed., Leipzig, Der Neue Geist Verlag, 1919.

—— *Vom Ewigen im Menschen, Religiöse Erneuerung.* Leipzig, Der Neue Geist Verlag, 1921. 4th rev. ed., Bern, Francke, 1955. G.W. V.

—— *Wesen und Formen der Sympathie* (revised and enlarged edition of *Zur Phänomenologie und Theorie der Sympathiegefühle*). Bonn, Cohen, 1923.

—— *Schriften zur Soziologie und Weltanschauungslehre,* 4 vols. Leipzig, Der Neue Geist Verlag, 1923–1924. 2nd rev. ed., Bern, Francke, 1963. G.W. VI.

—— *Die Formen des Wissens und die Bildung.* Bonn, Cohen, 1925.

—— *Die Wissensformen und die Gesellschaft.* Leipzig, Der Neue Geist Verlag, 1926. 2nd rev. ed., Bern, Francke, 1960. G.W. VIII.

—— *Die Stellung des Menschen im Kosmos.* Darmstadt, Reichl, 1928. 6th ed., Bern, Francke, 1962.

Articles and Speeches by Max Scheler

SCHELER, MAX. "Arbeit und Ethik," Zeitschrift für Philosophie und philosophische Kritik, CXIV, No. 2 (1899), 161–200.

—— "Kultur und Religion," Allgemeine Zeitung (October, 1903), 233–236.

—— "I. Kant und die moderne Kultur. Ein Gedenkblatt," Allgemeine Zietung, No. 35, (February, 1904), 273–280.

—— "Über Selbsttäuschungen," Zeitschrift für Pathopsychologie, I, No. 1 (1912), 87–163. G.W. III, 213–293.

—— "Über Ressentiment und moralisches Werturteil. Ein Beitrag zur Pathologie der Kultur," Zeitschrift für Pathopsychologie, I, Nos. 2–3 (1912), 268–368. G.W. III, 33–148.

—— "Der Formalismus in der Ethik und die materiale Wertethik, Mit besonderer Berücksichtigung der Ethik I. Kants," Part I, Jahrbuch für Philosophie und phänomenologische Forschung, I (1913), 405–565. Part II, Jahrbuch, II (1916), 21–478.

—— "Frauenbewegung und Fruchtbarkeit," Der Panther, II (1913), 16–23. G.W. III, 197–213.

—— "Zur Funktion des geschlechtlichen Schamgefühls," Geschlecht und Gesellschaft, VIII (1913), 121–131 and 177–190. G.W. X, 65–154.

—— "Zur Psychologie der sogenannten Rentenhysterie und der rechte Kampf gegen das Übel," Archiv für Sozialwissenschaft und Sozialpolitik, XXXVII (September, 1913), 521–534. G.W. III, 293–311.

—— "Versuche einer Philosophie des Lebens," Die Weissen Blätter, I (November, 1913), 203–233. G.W. III, 311–341.

—— [under the pseudonym: Ulrich Hegendorf] "Zur Rehabilitierung der Tugend," Die Weissen Blätter, I (December, 1913), 360–378. G.W. III, 13–33.

—— "Der Bourgeois," Die Weissen Blätter, I (February, 1914), 581–602. G.W. III, 343–362.

—— "Über das Tragische," Die Weissen Blätter, I (April, 1914), 758–776. G.W. III, 149–171.

—— "Die Zukunft des Kapitalismus," Die Weissen Blätter, I (May, 1914), 933–948. G.W. III, 382–399.

—— "Der Bourgeois und die religiösen Mächte," Die Weissen Blätter, I (July, 1914), 1171–1191. G.W. III, 362–382.

—— "Ethik. Ein Forschungsbericht," Jahrbücher der Philosophie, II (1914), 81–118.

—— "Der Genius des Krieges," Die Neue Rundschau, XXV (October, 1914), 1327–1352.

—— "Völker, Vaterländer und Fürsten," *Die Neue Rundschau,* XXV (October, 1914), 1387–1394.

—— "Europa und der Krieg," *Die Weissen Blätter,* II (January, February, March, 1915), 124–127, 244–249 and 376–380.

—— "Krieg und Tod," *Zeit Echo,* II (February, 1915), 101–104.

—— "Zur Psychologie der Nationen," *Die Neue Rundschau,* XXVI (July, 1915), 999–1001. *G.W.* VI, 353–356.

—— "Das Nationale in der Philosophie Frankreichs," *Der Neue Merkur,* II, No. 8 (August, 1915), 513–530. *G.W.* VI, 351–352.

—— "Liebe und Erkenntnis," *Die Weissen Blätter,* II, No. 8 (August, 1915), 991–1016. *G.W.* VI, 77–99.

—— Über östliches und westliches Christentum," *Die Weissen Blätter,* II (October, 1915), 1263–1281. *G.W.* VI, 99–115.

—— "Soziologische Neuorientierung und die Aufgabe der deutschen Katholiken nach dem Kriege," *Hochland,* XIII: 1 and 2 (October, 1915–March, 1916), Pt. 1, 385–406, 682–700 and Pt. 2, 188–204 and 257–294.

—— "1789 und 1914," *Archiv für Sozialwissenschaft und Sozialpolitik,* XLII (September, 1916), 586–605.

—— "Die christliche Gemeinschaftsidee und die gegenwärtige Welt," *Hochland,* XIV: 1 (October, 1916), 641–672. *G.W.* V, 355–403.

—— "Zur Apologetik der Reue," *Summa* I (January, 1917), 53–83. *G.W.* V, 27–60.

—— "Die christliche Persönlichkeit," *Summa* I (January, 1917), 144–146.

—— "Die deutsche Wissenschaft," *Summa* I (January, 1917), 151–153. *G.W.* VI, 356–358.

—— "Vom Wesen der Philosophie," *Summa* I: 2 (April, 1917), 40–70. *G.W.* V, 61–100.

—— "Von Kommenden Dingen," *Hochland,* XIV: 2 (July, 1917), 385–411.

—— "Zur Idee des Menschen," *Summa* II: 1 (January, 1918). *G.W.* III, 171–197.

—— "Recht, Staat und Gesellschaft," *Hochland,* XV: 1 (November, 1917), 129–141.

—— "Vom kulturellen Wiederaufbau Europas," *Hochland,* XV: 1 (February–March, 1918), 497–510 and 663–681. *G.W.* V, 403–451.

—— "Deutschlands Sendung und der katholische Gedanke," *Schriften des katholische Frauendienstes* (Berlin, Germania, 1918).

—— "Zur religiösen Erneuerung," *Hochland,* XVI: 1 (October, 1918), 5–21. *G.W. V.*

—— "Gedanken des Verstehens" (from *Die Ursachen des Deutschenhasses*), *Westdeutsche Wochenschrift,* I (1918), 97.

—— "Innere Widersprüche der deutschen Universitäten," *Westdeutsche Wochenschrift,* I (1919), 493–495; 511; 524–527; 539–541 and 551–553.

—— "Politik und Kultur auf dem Boden der neuen Ordnung," in *Der Geist der neuen Volksgemeinschaft,* published by the Zentrale für Heimatsdienst (Berlin, Fischer, 1919), 30–51.

—— "Von zwei deutschen Krankheiten," *Der Leuchter, Jahrbuch der Schule der Weisheit,* VI (1919), 161–190. *G.W.* VI, 204–220.

—— "Prophetischer oder marxistischer Sozialismus," *Hochland,* XVII: 1 (January, 1919), 71–84. *G.W.* VI, 259–272.

—— "Wert und Würde der christlichen Arbeit," *Jahrbuch der deutschen Katholiken* (1920), 75–89. *G.W.* VI, 273–290.

—— "Der Friede unter den Konfessionen," *Hochland,* XVIII: 1 (November, 1920–January, 1921), 140–147 and 464–486. *G.W.* VI, 227–258.

—— "Die positivistische Geschichtsphilosophie und die Aufgaben einer Soziologie der Erkenntnis," *Kölner Vierteljahrsheft für Soziologie und Sozialwissenschaften,* I, No. 1 (January, 1921), 22–31. *G.W.* VI, 27–35.

—— "Zu W. Jerusalems Bemerkungen," *Kölner Vierteljahrsheft für Soziologie und Sozialwissenschaften,* I, No. 3 (April, 1921), 35–39. *G.W.* VI, 327–330.

—— "Universität und Volkshochschule," in *Zur Soziologie des Volksbildungswesens,* Leopold von Wiese, ed. (Schriften des Forschungsinstitutes der Sozialwissenschaften in Köln, Vol. I) Munich, Duncker and Humbolt, 1921, 153–191. *G.W.* VIII.

—— "Vom Verrat der Freude," *Erstes Almanach des Volksverbandes der Bücherfreunde* Berlin, Wegweiser Verlag, 1922, 70–76.

—— *Walther Rathenau. Eine Würdigung zu seinem Gedächtnis.* (Speech given by Max Scheler July 16, 1922 at the memorial ceremony for Walther Rathenau held at the University of Cologne.) Cologne, Marcan Block Verlag, 1922. *G.W.* VI, 361–376.

—— "Die deutsche Philosophie der Gegenwart," in *Deutsches Leben der Gegenwart,* ed. Philipp Witkop, Berlin, Verlag der Bücherfreunde, 1922, 127–224.

—— "Weltanschauungslehre, Soziologie und Weltanschauungssetzung," *Kölner Vierteljahrsheft für Soziologie und Sozialwissenschaften*, II, No. 1 (January, 1922), 18–33. *G.W.* VI, 13–23.

—— "Das Problem des Leidens" (Speech at the Russian Academy in Berlin, March 18, 1923) *Germania*, LIII (March 20, 1923). *G.W.* VI, 36–72.

—— "Ernst Troeltsch als Soziologe," *Kölner Vierteljahrsheft für Soziologie und Sozialwissenschaften*, III (March, 1923), 7–21. *G.W.* VI, 377–390.

—— "Jugendbewegung," *Berliner Tageblatt*, No. 154 (April 1, 1923). *G.W.* VI, 391–399.

—— "Probleme einer Soziologie des Wissens," in *Versuche zu einer Soziologie des Wissens*, ed. Max Scheler. (Schriften des Forschungsinstitutes für Sozialwissenschaften in Köln, Vol. II.) Munich, Duncker and Humbolt, 1924. *G.W.* VIII.

—— "Wissenschaft und Sozialstruktur," in *Verhandlungen des vierten deutschen Soziologentages* (September, 1924) Tübingen, J. C. B. Mohr, 1925, 118–180.

—— "Mensch und Geschichte," *Die Neue Rundschau*, XXXVII (November, 1926), 449–476. Reprinted in *Philosophische Weltanschauung*. 2nd ed. Bern, Francke, 1954.

—— "Spinoza," (Speech commemorating the 250th anniversary of Spinoza's death, delivered in Amsterdam, February, 1927.) *Kölner Zeitung, Literatur und Unterhaltungsblatt*, Nos. 134 and 138 (March, 1927). Reprinted in *Philosophische Weltanschauung*. 2nd ed. Bern, Francke, 1954.

—— "Die Sonderstellung des Menschen," *Der Leuchter: Jahrbuch der Schule der Weisheit*, VII (Darmstadt, 1927), 161–254. Reprinted as *Die Stellung des Menschen im Kosmos*. Darmstadt, Reichl, 1928. 6th ed. Bern, Francke, 1962.

—— "Idealismus – Realismus," *Philosophische Anzeiger*, II (1927), 255–324.

—— "Philosophische Weltanschauung," *Münchener Neuste Nachrichten* (May 5, 1928). Reprinted in *Philosophische Weltanschauung*. 2nd ed. Bern, Francke, 1954.

Selected Posthumously Published Works

—— *Der Mensch im Weltalter des Ausgleichs*. Berlin, Rothschild, 1929.

—— *Philosophische Weltanschauung*. Bonn, Cohen, 1929. 2nd ed. Bern, Francke, 1954.

—— *Die Idee des Friedens und der Pazifismus*. Berlin, Der Neue Geist Verlag, 1931.

—— *Schriften aus dem Nachlass, Band I: Zur Ethik und Erkennt-nislehre*, ed. Maria Scheler, Berlin, Der Neue Geist Verlag, G.W. X.

—— "Metaphysik und Kunst," *Deutsche Beiträge*, I (1947), 103–120.

—— *Liebe und Erkenntnis*. Bern, Francke, 1955.

English Translations of Scheler's Works

SCHELER, MAX. *Man's Place in Nature*, tr. with introduction by Hans Meyerhoff, Boston, Beacon Press, 1961.

—— *The Nature of Sympathy*, tr. Peter Heath with introduction by Werner Stark, London, Routledge and Kegan Paul, 1958.

—— *On the Eternal in Man*, tr. Bernard Noble, London, Student Christian Movement Press, 1960.

—— *Philosophical Perspectives*, tr. Oscar A. Haac, Boston, Beacon Press, 1958.

—— *Ressentiment*, tr. William W. Holdheim, and ed. with introduction by Lewis A. Coser, New York, Free Press of Glencoe, 1961.

Selected Works on Various Aspects of Max Scheler's Life and Thought

ANON. *Der Fall Scheler* (Munich, 1910).

ANON. "Wann sagt man 'Voilà un homme'?" *Die Neue Zeitung*, CXV (May 18, 1953).

BAHR, HERMAN. "Max Scheler," *Hochland*, XIV: 2 (1916), 35–48.

BECKER, HOWARD. "Befuddled Germany: A Glimpse of Max Scheler," *American Sociological Review*, VIII (April, 1943), 207–211.

—— and Dahlke, Otto. "Max Scheler's Sociology of Knowledge," *Philosophy and Phenomenological Research, II* (March, 1942), 310–322.

—— "Some Forms of Sympathy: A Phenomenological Analysis," *Journal of Social and Abnormal Psychology*, XXVI (1931), 56–68.

BLESSING, EUGEN. *Das Ewige im Menschen: Die Grundkonzeption der Religionsphilosophie Max Schelers*, Stuttgart, Schwaben-verlag, 1954.

BUBER, MARTIN. "The Philosophical Anthropology of Max Scheler," *Philosophy and Phenomenological Research*, VI (1946), 307–321.

BUSSE-WILSON, ELIZABETH. "Max Scheler und der Homo Capital-isticus," *Die Tat*, (April, 1922), 179–186.

CASSIRER, ERNST. " 'Mind' and 'Life' in Contemporary Philosophy," in *The Philosophy of Ernst Cassirer*, ed. Paul A. Schilpp, New York, Tudor Publishing Co., 1949, 855–880. (Contains a penetrating critique of Scheler's theory of the impotence of mind and a balanced appraisal of his philosophical anthropology.)

COLLINS, JAMES. "Catholic Estimates of Sheler's Catholic Period," *Thought*, XIX (1944), 671–704.

—— "Scheler's Transition from Catholicism to Pantheism," in *Philosophical Studies in Honor of the Very Reverend Ignatius Smith, O.P.*, ed. John K. Ryan, Westminster, Maryland, Newman Press, 1952, 179–207.

DUPUY, MAURICE. *La philosophie de Max Scheler. Son évolution et son unité*, 2 vols., Paris, Presses Universitaires de France, 1959. (To date, the most exhaustive study of Scheler's intellectual development.)

—— *La Philosophie de la religion chez Max Scheler*. Paris, Presses Universitaires de France, 1959.

EINHELLINGER, ERICH. *Mensch und Bildung bei Max Scheler. Eine erziehungs-philosophische Untersuchung über Schelers Anthropologie und Wissenssoziologie*. Unpublished Dissertation, Munich, 1952.

FARBER, MARVIN. "Max Scheler on the Place of Man in the Cosmos," *Philosophy and Phenomenological Research*, XIV (1954), 393–400.

FECHNER, ERICH. "Der Begriff des kapitalistischen Geistes und das Schelersche Gesetz vom Zusammenhang der historischen Wertfaktoren," *Archiv für Sozialwissenschaft und Sozialpolitik*, LXIII (May, 1930), 93–120.

FINKE, HEINRICH, ed. "Zwei Briefe von Max Scheler" in *Internationale Wissenschaftsbeziehungen der Görresgesellschaft*. Cologne, Bachem, 1932, 48–51.

FRIES, HEINRICH. *Die katholische Religionsphilosophie der Gegenwart. Der Einfluss Max Schelers auf ihre Formen und Gestalten*. Heidelberg, F. H. Kerle, 1949.

GEBENN, HEINRICH. "Um die Religionsphilosophie Max Schelers," *Hochland*, XXI: 1 (1923), 583–597.

GEIGER, MORITZ. "Zu Max Schelers Tod," *Vossische Zeitung*, No. 126 (June 1, 1928).

GETZENY, HEINRICH. "Max Scheler," *Die Tat*, XII (1920), 181–195.

—— "Um die Religionsphilosophie Max Schelers," *Hochland*, XXI: 1 (1923–1924), 583–594.

GURIAN, WALDEMAR. "Josef Wittig und Max Scheler," *Germania*, LIV (November 13, 1924).

GURVITCH, GEORGES. "L'intuitionisme émotionel de Max Scheler," in his book *Les Tendences actuelles de la philosophie allemande*. Paris, J. Vrin, 1930.

GUTHRIE, HUNTER. "Max Scheler's Epistemology of the Emotions," *The Modern Schoolman*, XVI (1939), 51–54.

HAECKER, THEODOR. "Geist und Leben. Zum Problem Max Schelers," *Hochland*, XXIII: 2 (1926), 129–155. Reprinted in *Essays*, 2nd ed., Munich, Kösel, 1961.

—— "Der Krieg und die Führer des Geistes," in *Satire und Polemik*. 2nd ed., Munich, Lösel, 1961.

HAFKESBRINK, HANNA. "The Meaning of Objectivism and Realism in Max Scheler's Philosophy of Religion: A Contribution to the Understanding of Max Scheler's Catholic Period," *Philosophy and Phenomenological Research*, II (1942), 292–309.

HARTMANN, NICOLAI. "Max Scheler," *Kantstudien*, XXXIII (1926), ix–xvi. Reprinted in his *Kleinere Schriften*, Vol. 2, Berlin, de Gruyter, 1958, 350–357.

HEIDEMANN, INGEBORG. *Untersuchungen zur Kantkritik Max Schelers*. Dissertation, Frankfurt am Main, 1948.

HESSE, HERMANN. "Apologie des Krieges," *März*, IX (May, 1915), 167–168.

HESSEN, JOHANNES. *Max Scheler. Eine kritische Einführung in seine Philosophie. Aus Anlass des 20 Jahrestages seines Todes.* Essen, H. V. Chamier, 1946.

HILDEBRAND, DIETRICH VON. *Die Menschheit am Scheidewege. Gesammelte Abhandlungen und Vorträge*, ed. Karla Mertens, Regensburg, Habbel, 1954. (Contains several essays on various aspects of Max Scheler's life and thought.)

—— "Uber Max Schelers Abhandlungen und Aufsätze," *Hochland*, XIII: 1 (1916), 474–478.

HILLER, KURT. "Scheler spukt," *Die Weltbuhne*, XXVII (1931).

HINTZE, OTTO. "Max Schelers Ansichten über Geist und Gesellschaft" (1926). Reprinted in his *Soziologie und Geschichte: Gesammelte Abhandlungen zur Soziologie, Politik, und Theorie der Geschichte*, ed. Gerhard Oestreich (2nd rev. ed. Göttingen, Vandenhoeck and Ruprecht, 1964).

HOFFSCHULTE, HEINZ. *Der Solidaritätsgedanke in der Philosophie und Soziologie Max Schelers*. Unpublished Dissertation, Münster, 1923.

HONIGSHEIM, PAUL. "Max Scheler als Sozialphilosoph," *Kölner Vierteljahrsheft für Soziologie und Sozialwissenschaften*, VIII, No. 3 (1929), 94–108. (A superb analysis of Scheler's social and political ideas.)

—— "Max Weber und Max Scheler, Heidelberg und Köln in Memoiren und Briefen," *Kölner Zeitschrift für Soziologie,* Neue Folge, V (1952), 106–108.

HÜGELMANN, HILDEGARD. *Max Schelers Persönlichkeitsidee unter Berücksichtigung der Gemeinschaftsprobleme.* Leipzig, Helm & Torton, 1927.

JANKÉLÉVITCH, VLADIMIR. "La connaissance de soi-même selon Max Scheler," *La psychologie et la vie,* I)December, 1927), 42–55.

JERUSALEM, WILHELM. "Soziologie des Erkennens. (Bemerkungen zu Max Schelers Aufsatz 'Die positivistische Geschichtsphilosophie des Wissens und die Aufgabe einer Soziologie der Erkenntnis')," *Kölner Vierteljahrsheft für Soziologie und Sozialwissenschaften,* I, No. 3 (1921), 28–34.

KAMINTZER, ERNST. "Erinnerung an Max Scheler." Unpublished memoir quoted in John M. Oesterreicher's *Walls are Crumbling: Seven Jewish Philosophers Discover Christ* (New York, Devin-Adair, 1952).

KANTHACK, KATHARINA. *Max Scheler: zur Krisis der Ehrfurcht.* Berlin, Minerva Verlag, 1948. (The best German monograph on Scheler's social thought.)

KOLNAI, AUREL. "Max Schelers Kritik und Würdigung der Freudschen Libidolehre," *Imago,* I, No. 11 (1925), 135–146.

KOSTER, HANS DIETER. *Max Schelers Beitrag zur Rechts-und Staatsphilosophie.* Unpublished Dissertation, Hamburg, 1950.

KOYRE, ALEXANDER. "Max Scheler," *Revue d'Allemagne,* X (August, 1928), 97–109.

KRAFT, JULIUS. *Von Husserl zu Heidegger, Kritik der phänomenologischen Philosophie.* Leipzig, Buske, 1932.

KRANZLIN, GERHARDT. *Max Schelers phänomenologische Systematik* (*Studien und Bibliographien zur Gegenwartsphilosophie,* III). Leipzig, Hirzel, 1934.

KRACAUER, SIEGFRIED. "Max Scheler," *Frankfurter Zeitung* (May 22, 1928).

KUHN, HELMUTH. "Max Scheler in Rückblick," *Hochland,* LI (1959), 324–338.

LANDSBERG, PAUL. "L'acte philosophique de Max Scheler," *Recherches philosophiques,* VI (September 6, 1936), 299–312.

—— "Zum Gedächtnis Max Schelers," *Rhein-Mainsche Volkszeitung,* No. 12 (May 25, 1928).

LAUER, QUENTIN, S. J. *The Triumph of Subjectivity.* New York, Fordham University Press, 1958. (Contains a chapter on Scheler's phenomenology.)

LEHNEN, MARIA. "Max Schelers Wandlung," *Das Neue Reich*, X (1927), 441–443.

LENK, KURT. "Die Mikrokosmos-Vorstellung in der philosophischen Anthropologie Max Schelers," *Zeitschrift für philosophische Forschung*, XII (1958), 408–415.

—— "Schopenhauer und Scheler," *Schopenhauer Jahrbuch*, XXXVII (1956), 55–66.

—— *Von der Ohnmacht des Geistes, kritische Darstellung der Spätphilosophie Max Schelers*. Tübingen, Hopfer, 1959. (A brilliant left-Hegelian critique of Scheler's sociology of knowledge.)

LENZ-MEDOC, PAUL. "Max Scheler und die französische Philosophie," *Philosophisches Jahrbuch der Görresgesellschaft*, LXI (1951), 297–303.

LIEBER, HANS JOACHIM. "Zur Problematik der Wissenssoziologie bei Max Scheler," *Philosophische Studien*, I (1949), 62–90.

LILGE, FRIEDRICH. *The Abuse of Learning: The Failure of the German University*. New York, Macmillan, 1948. (The last chapter discusses Scheler's philosophy of education.)

LÖWITH, KARL. "Max Scheler und das Problem einer philosophischen Anthropologie," *Theologische Rundschau*, Neue Folge, VII, No. 6 (1935), 349–372.

LUTZ, HEINRICH. *Demokratie in Zwielicht*. Munich, Kösel, 1964.

LUTZLER, HEINRICH. *Der Philosoph Max Scheler*. Bonn, Bouvier, 1947.

—— "Zu Max Schelers Persönlichkeit," *Hochland*, XXVI: 1 (1928), 413–418.

MCGILL, V. J. "Scheler's Theory of Sympathy and Love," *Philosophy and Phenomenological Research*, II (March, 1942), 273–291. (Highly critical of Scheler's anti-rationalism.)

MERLAU-PONTY, MAURICE. "Christianisme et ressentiment," *La vie intellectuelle*, VII (June, 1935), 278–306.

MEINECKE, FRIEDRICH. "Die Ursachen des Deutschenhasses," *Die Neue Rundschau*, XXIX (January, 1919), 13–23.

MOLITOR, JACOB. *Max Schelers Kritik am Pragmatismus*. Unpublished Dissertation, Frankfurt am Main, 1961.

MÜLLER-FRIENFELS, RICHARD. "Die Wissensformen und die Gesellschaft," *Kölner Vierteljahrsheft für Soziologie und Sozialwissenschaften*, VI (1925), 190–194.

MULLER, PHILLIPE. *De la psychologie à l'anthropologie. À travers l'oeuvre de Max Scheler*. Neuchâtel, Ed. de la Baconnière, 1946.

OESTERREICHER, JOHN M. *Walls Are Crumbling: Seven Jewish Philosophers Discover Christ.* New York, Devin-Adair, 1952. (Contains a brief account of Scheler's life.)

ORTEGA Y GASSET, JOSÉ. "Max Scheler," *Neue Schweizer Rundschau,* XXXIV (October, 1928), 725–729.

PAPE, INGETRUD. "Das Indivuum in der Geschichte, Untersuchung zur Geschichtsphilosophie von Nicolai Hartmann und Max Scheler," in *Nicolai Hartmann, Der Denker und sein Werk: Fünfzehn Abhandlungen mit einer Bibliographie,* ed. Heinz Heimsoeth and Robert Heiss, Göttingen, Vandenhoeck and Ruprecht, 1952. (Contains some quotations from Scheler's unpublished *Geschichtsphilosophie.* Mrs. Pape worked as Frau Maria Scheler's assistant for several years.)

PLESSNER, HELMUTH. "Max Scheler," in the *Handwörterbuch der Sozialwissenschaften,* Vol. 9, 2nd ed., Stuttgart, Fischer, 1956, 115–117.

PRZYWARA, ERICH. *Religionsbegründung: Max Scheler—J. H. Newman.* Freiburg am Breisgau, Herder, 1923. (A most perceptive analysis of Scheler's philosophy of religion.)

—— "Zu Max Schelers Religionsauffassung," *Zeitschrift für katholische Theologie,* XLVII (1923), 24–49.

ROTHACKER, ERICH. *Max Schelers Durchbruch in die Wirklichkeit.* Bonn, Bouvier, 1949.

RÜSSEL, HERBERT. "Max Scheler und der europäische Gedanke," *Abendland,* V (1930), 27–32.

—— "Max Scheler und die Probleme der deutschen Politik," *Hochland,* XXVII: 2 (1930), 518–529.

RYCHNER, MAX. "German Chronicle" [Max Scheler †] tr. Marjorie Gabain, *The Monthly Criterion,* VIII (1928), 298–304.

SCHELER, MARIA. "Bericht über die Arbeit am philosophischen Nachlass Max Schelers," *Zeitschrift für philosophische Forschung,* II, No. 4 (1947), 597–602.

SCHLIPP, PAUL A. "The Doctrine of Illusion and Error in Scheler's Phenomenology," *Journal of Philosophy,* XXIV (1927), 624–633.

—— "Formal Problems of Scheler's Sociology of Knowledge," *Philosophical Review,* XXXVI (1927), 101–120.

—— "Max Scheler 1874–1928," *Philosophical Review,* XXXVIII (1929), 574–588.

SCHMIDT, CARL. "Die Ursachen des Deutschenhasses," *Das literarische Echo,* XXII (1920), 1528–1530.

SIGMAR, J. "Max Scheler als Erzieher," *Katechetische Blätter*, Neue Folge XXIX (1928), 465–482.

SCHUTZ, ALFRED. "Max Scheler" in *Les Philosophes célèbres*, ed. Maurice Merleau-Ponty, Paris, Lucien Mazenod, 1956, 330–335.

—— "Max Scheler's Epistemology and Ethics," *Review of Metaphysics*, XI (1957), 304–314 and 486–501. Reprinted in Schutz's *Collected Papers*, III, *Studies in Phenomenological Philosophy*, ed. Ilse Schutz, The Hague, Martinus Nijhoff, 1966, 145–178. (The best brief discussion of Scheler's phenomenology.)

—— "Scheler's Theory of Intersubjectivity and the General Thesis of the Alter-Ego," *Philosophy and Phenomenological Research*, II (1942), 323–347. Reprinted in Schutz's *Collected Papers*, I, *The Problem of Social Reality*, ed. Maurice Natanson, The Hague, Martinus Nijhoff, 1962, 150–180.

SCHUSTER, GEORGE N. "Introductory Statement to a Symposium on the Significance of Max Scheler for Philosophy and Social Science," *Philosophy and Phenomenological Research*, II (1942), 269–272.

STARK, WERNER. Introduction to *The Nature of Sympathy*, tr. Peter Heath, London, Routledge and Kegan Paul, 1954.

VIERKANDT, ALFRED. "Besprechung zu Max Schelers *Versuche einer Soziologie des Wissens*," *Historische Zeitschrift*, CXXXV (1925), 290–291.

WEIGER, JOSEPH. "Neue Menschen und katholisches Erbe," *Die Tat*, XIV (April, 1922), 57–68. (Discusses Scheler's influence on the Catholic youth movement in Weimar Germany.)

WILLIAMS, RICHARD HAYS. "Scheler's Contributions to the Sociology of Affective Action with Special Attention to the Problem of Shame," *Philosophy and Phenomenological Research*, II (1942), 348–358.

WUST, PETER. "Max Schelers Lehre vom Menschen," *Das Neue Reich*, XI (1928), 102–140.

—— "Zum Tode Max Schelers," *Kölnische Volkszeitung* (May 23, 1928). Reprinted in *Wege einer Freundschaft. Peter Wust-Marianne Weber, Briefwechsel 1927–1939*, ed. Walter Theodor Cleve, Heidelberg, 1951, 129–133.

ZUCKER, WOLF. "Max Scheler in Berlin," *Die Weltbühne*, XXIII, No. 7 (February 15, 1927), 276–278.

—— "Max Scheler," *Die Weltbühne*, XXIV (1928), 843–844.

Selected Works on European Philosophy,
Politics, and Intellectual History

ADORNO, THEODORE W. *Metakritik der Erkenntnistheorie.* Stuttgart,
Kohlhammer, 1956.

ALLEN, J. W. *Germany and Europe,* London, Bell, 1914.

ANDERSON, PAULINE. *The Background of Anti-English Feeling in
Germany, 1890–1902.* Washington, D.C., American University Press, 1939.

ANTONI, CARLOS. *From History to Sociology, The Transition in German Historical Thinking,* tr. Hayden V. White, Detroit, Wayne
State University Press, 1959.

BARNES, HARRY ELMER *and* HOWARD BECKER, eds. *Contemporary Social Theory.* New York, Appleton-Century, 1940.

BARTH, HANS. *Wahrheit und Ideologie,* 2nd ed. Zürich and Stuttgart,
Eugen Rentsch, 1961.

BECKER, ERNEST. *Beyond Alienation. A Philosophy of Education for
the Crisis of Democracy.* New York, George Braziller, 1967.

BECKER, HOWARD. *German Youth, Bond or Free.* New York, Oxford
University Press, 1946.

—— *Kant und die Bildungskrise der Gegenwart.* Leipzig, Dunker
und Humboldt, 1924.

BENEDICT, RUTH. *Patterns of Culture,* 8th ed. New York, New American Library, 1958.

BENDIX, REINHARD. *Max Weber, An Intellectual Portrait.* New York,
Doubleday, 1962.

BERGER, PETER *and* THOMAS LUCKMANN. *The Social Construction of
Reality, A Treatise in the Sociology of Knowldege.* New
York, Doubleday, 1966.

BERGSON, HENRI. "Introduction to Metaphysics" in *The Creative
Mind,* tr. Mabelle Adison. New York, Philosophical Library,
1946.

VON BERNHARDI, FRIEDRICH. *Deutschland und der nächste Krieg,* 5th
ed., Stuttgart and Berlin, Cotta, 1913.

BONN, MORITZ JULIUS. *The Crisis of European Democracy.* New
Haven, Yale University Press, 1925.

BOUTROUX, EMIL. "La conception francaise de la nationalité," *Bibliotheque Universelle et Revue Suisse,* LXXX, No. 38 (1915).

BRACHER, KARL DIETRICH. *Die Auflösung der Weimarer Republik:
Eine Studie zum Problem des Machtverfalls in der Demokratie* (Schriften des Instituts für politische Wissenschaft, Vol.
IV). 3rd ed., Stuttgart, Ring Verlag, 1957.

BRINKMANN, CARL. *Wirtschafts- und Sozialgeschichte.* Berlin and
Munich, Oldenbourg, 1927.

BROD, MAX. *Streitbares Leben: Autobiographie.* Munich, Kindler, 1960.

BRUFORD, W. H. *Culture and Society in Classical Weimar, 1776–1806.* London, Cambridge, University Press, 1962.

BUNTZ, GEORGE G. *Allied Propaganda and the Collapse of the German Empire in 1918.* Stanford, Hoover War Library Publication No. 13, 1938.

BUSSMAN, W. "Politische Ideologien zwischen Monarchie und Republik," *Historische Zeitschrift,* XCX (1960), 12–24.

CASSIRER, ERNST. *An Essay on Man, An Introduction to a Philosophy of Human Culture.* New York, Doubleday, 1953.

CHAMBERS, FRANK P. *The War Behind the War, 1914–1918: A History of the Political and Civilian Fronts.* New York, Harcourt Brace, 1939.

CONZE, WERNER. "Deutschlands politische Sonderstellung in den zwanziger Jahren, in *Die Zeit ohne Eigenschaften, Eine Bilanz der zwanziger Jahre,* ed. Leonhard Reinisch, Stuttgart, Kohlhammer, 1961, 32–49.

—— "Nationalstaat oder Mitteleuropa: Die Deutschen des Reiches und die Nationalitätsfragen Ostmitteleuropas im ersten Weltkrieg," in *Deutschland und Europa: Historische Studien zur Völker und Staatenordung des Abendlandes,* ed. Werner Conze, Düsseldorf, Dröste, 1951.

CRAMB, J. A. *Germany and England.* London, Bradley, 1914.

CURTIUS, ERNST RORERT. *Französischer Geist im neuen Europa.* Berlin and Stuttgart, Deutsche Verlag-Anstalt, 1925.

CURTIUS, LUDWIG. *Deutsche und antike Welt. Lebenserinnerungen.* Stuttgart, Deutsche Verlags-Anstalt, 1950.

DAHRENDORF, RALF. "The New Germanies: Restoration, Revolution, Reconstruction," *Encounter,* XXII, No. 4 (April, 1964).

DEHIO, LUDWIG. *Germany and World Politics in the Twentieth Century,* tr. Dieter Pevsner. London, Chatto and Windus, 1959.

DEMOF, ALOIS. *Theoretische Anthropologie.* Bern, Francke, 1950.

DILTHEY, WILHELM. *Weltanschauung und Analyse des Menschen seit Renaissance und Reformation,* Gesammelte Schriften, II. 6th ed. Göttingen, Vandenhoeck and Ruprecht, 1960.

DIWALD, HELMUTH. *Wilhelm Dilthey, Erkenntnistheorie und Philosophie der Geschichte.* Berlin, Musterschmidt, 1963.

DORPALEN, ANDREAS. "Wilhelmian Germany, a House Divided Against Itself," *Journal of Central European Affairs,* XI (1951), 240–247.

DRIESCH, HANS. *Lebenserinnerungen. Aufzeichnungen eines Forschers und Denkers in entscheidender Zeit.* Basel, Reinhardt, 1951.

DURKHEIM, ÉMILE. *The Elementary Forms of the Religious Life.* Glencoe, Ill., Free Press, 1947.

ECKERT, WILLEHAD PAUL. *Kleine Geschichte der Universität Köln.* Cologne, Bachem, 1961.

EPSTEIN, KLAUS. *Matthias Erzberger and the Dilemma of German Democracy.* Princeton, Princeton University Press, 1959.

EUCKEN, RUDOLF. *Der Kampf um einen geistigen Lebensinhalt.* 2nd ed., Berlin and Leipzig, de Gruyter, 1925.

—— *Lebenserinnerungen: ein Stück deutschen Lebens.* Leipzig, Koehler, 1921.

—— *Life's Basis and Life's Ideal, The Fundamentals of a New Philosophy of Life,* tr. Alban A. Widgery, 2nd ed. London, Black, 1912.

—— *The Meaning and Value of Life,* tr. Lucy Judge Gibson and W. R. Boyce Gibson. London, Black, 1909.

—— *The Problem of Human Life as Viewed by the Greatest Thinkers from Plato to the Present Time,* tr. Williston S. Hough and W. R. Boyce Gibson, 2nd ed. New York, Scribner's, 1912.

FISCHER, FRITZ. *Griff nach der Weltmacht.* Düsseldorf, Dröste, 1961.

FREUD, SIGMUND. *The Future of an Illusion,* tr. W. D. Robinson-Scott. London, Hogarth Press, 1949.

GATZKE, HANS. *Germany's Drive to the West: A Study of Western War Aims During the First World War.* Baltimore, Johns Hopkins Press, 1950.

GESCLER, OTTO. *Reichswehr-Politik in der Weimarer Zeit,* ed. Kurt Sendtner, Stuttgart, Deutsche Verlags-Anstalt, 1959.

GROSCHE, ROBERT. "Der geschichtliche Weg des deutschen Katholizismus aus dem Ghetto" in his book *Der Weg aus dem Ghetto.* Cologne, Bachem, 1955.

GRÜNWALD, ERNST. *Das Problem der Soziologie des Wissens.* Vienna and Leipzig, Wilhelm Braumüller, 1934.

GOLL, CLAIRE. *Der gestohlene Himmel.* Munich, List. 1962.

VON GRONICKA, ANDRÉ. "Thomas Mann and Russia" in *The Stature of Thomas Mann,* ed. Charles Nieder, New York, New Directions, 1947.

HAECKEL, ERNST. *The Riddle of the Universe,* tr. Joseph McCabe. New York and London, Harper and Brothers, 1900.

HARTMANN, NICOLAI. *Die Philosophie des deutschen Idealismus,* 2 vols. Berlin and Leipzig, de Gruyter and Co., 1923–1929.

HEIDEGGER, MARTIN. *Being and Time,* tr. John Macquarrie and Edward Robinson. London, SCM Press, 1962.

—— *Kant and the Problem of Metaphysics*, translated by James S. Churchill. Bloomington, Indiana University Press, 1962.

HEINEMANN, FRITZ. *Neue Wege der Philosophie*. Leipzig, Quelle and Meyer, 1929.

HELLER, ERICH. *The Disinherited Mind*. New York, Farrar, Strauss, and Cudahy, 1957.

HEUSSI, KARL. *Die Krisis des Historismus*. Tübingen, J. C. B. Mohr, 1932.

HODGES, H. A. *The Philosophy of Wilhelm Dilthey*. London, Routledge and Kegan Paul, 1952.

HÖLZLE, ERWIN. *Der Osten im ersten Weltkriege*. Leipzig, Koehler and Amerland, 1944.

HOFMANN, WERNER. *Gesellschaftslehre als Ordnungsmacht*. Berlin Dunker and Humbolt, 1961.

HONIGSHEIM, PAUL. "The Time and the Thought of the Young Simmel" in *Georg Simmel: A Collection of Essays with Translations and a Bibliography*, ed. Kurt Wolff, Columbus, Ohio, Ohio State University Press, 1959, 167–174.

HORKHEIMER, MAX. "Bemerkungen zur philosophischen Anthropologie," *Zeitschrift für Sozialforschung*, IV, No. 1 (1935).

HUGHES, H. STUART. *Consciousness and Society, The Reorientation of European Social Thought 1890–1930*. New York, Knopf, 1958.

—— *Oswald Spengler, A Critical Estimate*. New York, Scribner, 1962.

HUSSERL, EDMUND. *Logische Untersuchungen*, 2 vols. Halle, Niemeyer, 1900–1901.

JÄCKH, ERNST. *Weltstaat, Erlebtes und Erstrebtes*. Stuttgart, Deutsche Verlags-Anstalt, 1960.

JÄCKH, ERNST and OTTO SUHR. *Geschichte der deutschen Hochschule für Politik* (Schriftenreihe der deutschen Hochschule für Politik). Berlin, Weiss, 1952.

JASPERS, KARL. *Psychologie der Weltanschauungen*. Berlin, Springer, 1919.

JOST, DOMINICK. *Stefan George und seine Elite, Studien zur Geschichte der Eliten*. Zurich, Speer-Verlag, 1949.

VON KAHLER, ERICH. *Der Beruf der Wissenschaft*. Berlin, Bondi, 1920.

KAUFMANN, FRITZ. *Geschichtsphilosophie der Gegenwart*. Berlin, Junker and Dunnhaupt, 1931.

KAUFMANN, WALTER. *Nietzsche: Philosopher, Psychologist, Anti-Christ*, 2nd ed. New York, Meridian Books, 1958.

KESSLER, GRAF HARRY KLEMENS ULRICH. *Walther Rathenau, His Life and Work*, tr. W. D. Robinson-Scott and Lawrence Hyde. New York, Harcourt Brace, 1930.

KEYSERLING, COUNT HERMAN. *The World in the Making*. New York, Harcourt Brace, 1927.

KLEMPERER, KLEMENS VON. *Germany's New Conservatism: Its History and Dilemma in the Twentieth Century*. Princeton, Princeton University Press, 1957.

KONIG, RENÉ. "Die Begriffe 'Gemeinschaft' und 'Gesellschaft' bei Ferdinand Tönnies," *Kölner Zeitschrift für Soziologie und Sozialpsychologie*, Neue Folge, VII (April, 1955), 348–420.

—— "Zur Soziologie der zwanziger Jahre" in *Die Zeit ohne Eigenschaften: Eine Bilanz der zwanziger Jahre*, ed. Leonhard Reinisch, Stuttgart, Kohlhammer, 1961.

KOHN, HANS. *The Mind of Modern Germany*. New York, Scribner, 1960.

—— "Political Theory and the History of Ideas," *Journal of the History of Ideas*, XXV, No. 2 (1964), 303–307.

KOHN-BRAMSTADT, ERNST. *Aristocracy and the Middle-Classes in Germany: Social Types in German Literature 1830–1900*, 2nd rev. ed., Chicago, 1964.

KOTSCHNIG, WALTER M. *Unemployment in the Learned Professions*. London, Oxford University Press, 1937.

KROCKOW, CHRISTIAN GRAF VON. *Die Entscheidung: Eine Untersuchung über Ernst Jünger, Carl Schmitt, Martin Heidegger*. Stuttgart, Enke, 1958.

KU, HUNG-MING. *Der Geist des chinesischen Volkes und der Ausweg aus dem Krieg*, Jena, Diedrichs, 1915; tr. in English as *The Spirit of China*, Peking, Peking Daily News, 1915.

KUHN, HELMUT. "Das geistige Gesicht der Weimarer Zeit," *Zeitschrift für Politik*, Neue Folge, VIII (1961), 1–10.

LABEDEZ, LEOPOLD, ed. *Revisionism: Essays on the History of Marxist Ideas*. New York, Praeger, 1962.

LANDAUER, CARL. *European Socialism: A History of Ideas and Movements*, 2 vols. Berkeley and Los Angeles, University of California Press, 1959.

LANDSBERG, PAUL LUDWIG. *Einführung in die philosophische Anthropologie*. Frankfurt am Main, Klostermann, 1960.

LAQUEUR, WALTER Z. *Young Germany*. New York, Basic Books, 1962.

LENK, KURT. *Ideologie: Ideologiekritik und Wissenssoziologie*. Neuwied, Luchterhand, 1961.

—— "Soziologie und Ideologienlehre," *Kölner Zeitschrift für Soziologie und Sozialpsychologie,* XIII (1961), 227–238.

—— "Das tragische Bewusstsein in der deutschen Soziologie der zwanziger Jahre," *Frankfurter Hefte,* XVIII (May, 1963), 313–320.

LERSCH, PHILIPP. *Lebensphilosophie der Gegenwart* (Philosophische Forschungsberichte No. 4). Berlin, Junker and Dunnhaupt, 1932.

LESSING, THEODOR. *Einmal und Nie Wieder, Lebenserinnerungen.* Leipzig, Quelle and Meyer, 1936.

LIEBER, HANS JOACHIM. *Philosophie, Soziologie, Gesellschaft: Gesammelte Studien zum Ideologieproblem.* Berlin, de Gruyter, 1965.

—— *Wissen und Gesellschaft, Die Probleme der Wissenssoziologie.* Tübingen, Max Niemeyer, 1952.

LICHTHEIM, GEORGE. "The Concept of Ideology" in *History and Theory,* IV, No. 2 (1965), 164–195.

LÖWITH, KARL. *Gesammelte Abhandlungen. Zur Kritik der geschichtlichen Existenz.* Stuttgart, Kohlhammer, 1960.

—— *Von Hegel zu Nietzsche.* Zurich, Europa-Verlag, 1940.

LOTZE, HERMANN. *Microcosmos,* tr. Elizabeth Hamilton and E. Constance Jones, Edinburgh, Clark, 1885.

LOVEJOY, ARTHUR O. *The Great Chain of Being, A Study in the History of an Idea.* Cambridge, Mass., Harvard University Press, 1936.

LÖWENTHAL, LEO. "Die Auffassung Dostojewskis im Vorkriegsdeutschland," *Zeitschrift für Sozialforschung,* III (1934), 344–381.

DE LUBAC, HENRI. *The Drama of Atheist Humanism.* New York, Sheed and Ward, 1950.

LUBBE, HERMAN. *Politische Philosophie in Deutschland, Studien zu ihrer Geschichte.* Basel and Stuttgart, Schwabe, 1963.

LUKÁCS, GEORG. *Geschichte und Klassenbewusstsein.* Berlin, Der Malik-Verlag, 1923.

—— *Die Zerstörung der Vernunft.* Berlin, Aufbau-Verlag, 1954.

MANDELBAUM, MAURICE. *The Problem of Historical Knowledge.* New York, Liveright, 1938.

MANN, THOMAS. *Betrachtungen eines Unpolitischen.* Berlin, Fisher, 1922.

MANNHEIM, KARL. *Essays on the Sociology of Knowledge,* ed. Paul Keckskemeti, London, Routledge and Kegan Paul, 1952.

—— *Ideology and Utopia, An Introduction to the Sociology of Knowledge.* New York, Harcourt Brace, 1936.

—— *Man and Society in the Age of Social Reconstruction,* tr. Edward Shils. London, Kegan Paul, Trench and Trubner, 1944.

MARCEL, GABRIEL. *Être et Avoir.* Paris, Aubier, 1936.

MARCUSE, HERBERT. *Eros and Civilization: A Philosophical Inquiry into Freud.* Boston, Beacon Press, 1955.

—— *Reason and Revolution: Hegel and the Rise of Social Theory,* 2nd ed. New York, Humanities Press, 1954.

MARITAIN, JACQUES. *De Bergson à Saint Thomas d'Aquin, essais de metaphysique et de morale.* Paris, Hartmann, 1947.

MARTIN, ALFRED VON. *Ordnung und Freiheit.* Frankfurt am Main, Josef Knecht, 1956.

—— *The Sociology of the Renaissance,* tr. W. L. Luetkens. London, Kegan Paul, Trench and Trubner, 1945.

MARX, KARL and FRIEDRICH ENGELS. *Marx and Engels' Basic Writings on Politics and Philosophy,* ed. Lewis Feuer, Garden City, New York, Doubleday, 1959.

MAUSS, HEINZ. "Bemerkungen zu Comte," in *Kölner Zeitschrift für Soziologie,* Neue Folge, V (1953), 513–527.

MEINECKE, FRIEDRICH. *Die deutsche Erhebung von 1914: Vorträge und Aufsätze.* Stuttgart and Berlin, Botta, 1914.

—— *Probleme des Weltkrieges: Aufsätze.* Munich and Berlin, Oldenbourg, 1917.

MERTON, ROBERT K. *Social Theory and Social Structure.* Glencoe, Ill., Free Press, 1949.

MEYER, HENRY CORD. *Mitteleuropa in German Thought and Action, 1815–1945.* The Hague, Martinus Nijhoff, 1955.

MICHELS, ROBERT. *Political Parties: A Sociological Study of the Oligarchical Tendencies of Modern Democracy,* tr. Eden and Cedar Paul. New York, Dover, 1959.

MÖHLER, JOHANN ADAM VON. *Patrologie.* Regensburg, Manz, 1840.

—— *Symbolism.* New York, Dunigan, 1844.

MOSSE, GEORGE L. *The Crisis of German Ideology.* New York, Grosset and Dunlap, 1964.

MÜLLER, KARL ALEXANDER VON. *Aus Gärten der Vergangenheit,* 2nd ed., Stuttgart, Deutsche Verlag Anstalt, 1958.

MUIR, RAMSEY. *Britain's Case Against Germany.* Manchester, The University Press, 1914.

MUNCY, LYSBETH WALKER. *The Junker in the Prussian Administration Under William II, 1888–1914.* Providence, R.I., Brown University, 1944.

MUTH, CARL. "Begegnungen: Hinterlassene Notizen," *Hochland,* XLVI, October, 1953.

NIETZSCHE, FRIEDRICH. *The Portable Nietzsche*, Walter Kaufman, ed., 2nd ed. New York, Viking Press, 1963.
—— *The Genealogy of Morals*, tr. Francis Golfing. New York, Doubleday, 1956.
—— *The Use and Abuse of History*, tr. Adrian Collins, The Library of Liberal Arts, 2nd rev. ed. Indianapolis and New York, Bobbs-Merrill, 1957.
NISBET, ROBERT A. *Community and Power.* New York, Oxford University Press, 1963.
—— *The Sociological Tradition.* New York, Basic Books, 1966.
NOLTE, ERNST. *Three Faces of Fascism.* New York, Holt, Rinehart and Winston, 1966.
PARSONS, TALCOTT. *The Structure of Social Action*, 2nd ed. Glencoe, Ill., Free Press, 1949.
PESCH, HEINRICH. *Liberalismus, Sozialismus und christliche Gesellschaftslehre.* Freiberg at Breisgau, Herder, 1901.
PINSON, KOPPEL. *Modern Germany, Its History and Civilization.* New York, Macmillan, 1954.
PLENGE, JOHANN. "Christentum und Sozialismus" in *Zur Vertiefung des Sozialismus.* Leipzig, Der Neue Geist Verlag, 1919, 218–254.
—— *Der Krieg und die Volkswirtschaft.* Münster, Borgmeyer, 1915.
PLESSNER, HELMUTH. "Die Aufgabe der philosophischen Anthropologie" in *Zwischen Philosophie und Gesellschaft.* Bern, Francke, 1953.
—— *Die verspätete Nation. Über die politische Verführbarkeit bürgerlichen Geistes.* Stuttgart, Kohlhammer, 1959.
—— *Zwischen Philosophie und Gesellschaft.* Bern, Francke, 1953.
PROESLER, HANS. "Zur Genesis der wissenssoziologischen Problemstellung," *Kölner Zeitschrift für Soziologie und Sozialpsychologie*, Neue Folge, XII, No. 1 (1960), 41–52.
RADBRUCH, GUSTAV. *Rechtsphilosophie.* Leipzig, Quelle and Meyer, 1932.
ROGGER, HANS and EUGEN WEBER, eds., *The European Right: A Historical Profile.* Berkeley, University of California Press, 1965.
ROHAN, KARL ANTON. *Heimat Europa. Erinnerungen und Erfahrungen* Cologne and Düsseldorf, Diederich, 1954.
ROSENBERG, ARTHUR. *The Birth of the German Republic, 1871–1918*, tr. Ian F. D. Murrow. New York and London, Oxford University Press, 1931.
ROTHACKER, ERICH. *Heitere Erinnerungen.* Frankfurt am Main and Bonn, Athenäum Verlag, 1963.

ROYCE, JOSIAH. *Lectures on Modern Idealism.* New Haven, Yale University Press, 1919.

SCHAAF, JULIUS. *Grundprinzipien der Wissenssoziologie.* Hamburg, Meinger, 1956.

SCHELTING, ALEXANDER VON. *Max Webers Wissenschaftslehre.* Tübingen, J. C. B. Mohr, 1934.

SCHILPP, PAUL A., ed. *The Philosophy of Ernst Cassirer.* Evanston, Ill., Library of Living Philosophers, 1949.

SCHORSKE, CARL. *German Social Democracy 1905–1917. The Development of the Great Schism.* Cambridge, Harvard University Press, 1955.

SETON-WATSON, R. W., JOHN DOVER WILSON, ALFRED E. ZIMMERN and ARTHUR GREENWOOD. *The War and Democracy.* London, Macmillan, 1914.

SHLOMO, AVINERI. "The Problem of War in Hegel's Thought," *Journal of the History of Ideas,* XXII, No. 4 (1961), 463–474.

SIMMEL, GEORG. *Philosophie des Geldes.* Leipzig, Duncker and Humbolt, 1900.

SOMBART, WERNER. *Händler und Helden: Patriotische Besinnungen.* Leipzig and Munich, Duncker and Humbolt, 1915.

SPENGLER, OSWALD. *The Decline of the West,* tr. Charles Francis Attkinson, 2 vols. New York, Knopf, 1932.

SPIELBERG, HERBERT. *The Phenomenological Movement, A Historical Introduction,* 2 vols. The Hague, Martinus Nijhoff, 1960.

SPRANGER, EDWARD. *Das humanistische und das politische Bildungsideal im heutigen Deutschland.* Berlin, Mittler, 1916.

STARK, WERNER. *The Sociology of Knowledge, An Essay in Aid of a Deeper Understanding of the History of Ideas.* Glencoe, Ill., The Free Press, 1958.

STEINHAUSEN, GEORG. *Deutsche Geistesgeschichte von 1870 bis zur Gegenwart.* Halle [Saale], Niemeyer, 1931.

STERLING, RICHARD W. *Ethics in a World of Power: The Political Ideas of Friedrich Meinecke.* Princeton, N.J., Princeton University Press, 1958.

STERN, FRITZ. *The Politics of Cultural Despair, A Study in the Rise of the Germanic Ideology.* Berkeley, University of California Press, 1961.

STERN, WILHELM. "Antobiographical Sketch," in *The History of Psychology in Autobiography,* ed. Charles Murchison, New York, Russell and Russell, 1961.

THIMME, HANS. *Weltkrieg Ohne Waffen, Die Propaganda der Westmächte gegen Deutschland, ihre Wirkung und ihre Abwehr.* Stuttgart and Berlin, Cotta, 1932.

TÖNNIES, FERDINAND. *Die Entwicklung der sozialen Frage bis zum ersten Weltkriege.* Berlin, de Gruyter, 1926.
—— *Gemeinschaft und Gesellschaft.* Berlin, Curtius, 1882.
TROELTSCH, ERNST. *Aufsätze zur Geistesgeschichte und Religionssoziologie, Gesammelte Schriften,* Vol. IV, ed. Hans Baron, Tübingen, J. C. B. Mohr, 1925.
—— *Christian Thought, Its History and Application,* ed. Baron von Hügel, New York, Meridian Books, 1957.
—— *Deutscher Geist und Westeuropa,* ed. Hans Baron, Tübingen, J. C. B. Mohr, 1925.
—— *Der Historismus und seine Probleme, Gesammelte Werke,* Vol. III. Tübingen, J. C. B. Mohr, 1922.
—— *The Social Teachings of the Christian Churches,* tr. Olive Wyon, 2 vols. 3rd ed. New York, Harper, 1960.
—— *Spektator-Briefe, Aufsätze über die deutsche Revolution und die Weltpolitik 1918–1922,* ed. Hans Baron, Tübingen, J. C. B. Mohr, 1924
TYMIENIECKA, ANNA-TERESA. *Phenomenology and Science in Contemporary European Thought.* New York, Farrar, Strauss and Cudahy, 1962.
WACH, JOACHIM. *The Comparative Study of Religions,* ed. Joseph Kitagawa, New York, Columbia University Press, 1958.
WATNIK, MAURICE. "Relativism and Class Consciousness: Georg Lukacs" in *Revisionism, Essays on the History of Marxist Ideas,* ed. Leopold Labedez, London, 1962, New York, Praeger, 1962.
WEBER, ALFRED. *Gedanken zur deutschen Sendung.* Berlin, Fischer, 1915.
WEBER, MAX. *Gesammelte Aufsätze zur Religionssoziologie,* 3 vols. Tübingen, J. C. B. Mohr, 1920–1923.
—— *Gesammelte Aufsätze zur Wissensschaftslehre.* Tübingen, J. C. B. Mohr, 1922.
—— *The Methodology of the Social Sciences,* tr. Edward A. Shils and Henry A. Finch. Glencoe, Ill., Free Press, 1949.
—— "Politics as a Vocation" in *From Max Weber: Essays in Sociology,* ed. Hans Gerth and C. Wright Mills, New York, Oxford University Press, 1946.
—— *Politische Schriften,* ed. Johannes Winckelmann, Munich, Drei Masken Verlag, 1921.
—— *The Protestant Ethic and the Spirit of Capitalism,* tr. Talcott Parsons. New York, Scribner's, 1958.
—— "The Vocation of Science" in *From Max Weber: Essays in Sociology,* ed. C. Wright Mills and Hans Gerth, New York, Oxford University Press, 1962.

WEINGARTNER, RUDOLPH. *Experience and Culture: The Philosophy of Georg Simmel.* Middletown, Conn., Wesleyan University Press, 1962.

VON WIESER, FRIEDRICH FRIEHERR. *Recht und Macht.* Leipzig, Duncker and Humbolt, 1910.

WOLFF, THEODOR. *The Eve of 1914,* tr. E. W. Dicker. New York, Knopf, 1936.

WUST, PETER. *Dialektik des Geistes.* Augsberg, Filser Verlag, 1928.

ZILSEL, EDGAR. "The Sociological Roots of Modern Science," *American Journal of Sociology,* XLVII (January, 1942), 544–560.

ZIMMERMAN, LUDWIG. *Deutsche Aussenpolitik in der Ära der Weimarer Republik.* Göttingen, Musterschmidt, 1958.

ZITTA, VICTOR. *Georg Lukács Marxism: Alienation, Dialectics, Revolution: A Study in Utopia and Ideology.* New York, Humanities Press, 1964.

ZWEIG, STEFAN. *The World of Yesterday: An Autobiography.* New York, The Viking Press, 1943.

Index

Index

Printed in the United States
By Bookmasters